The Industrial Revolution

Other books in the Turning Points series:

Turning | Points
IN WORLD HISTORY

DISCARD

The Industrial Revolution

Brenda Stalcup, *Book Editor*

Daniel Leone, *President*
Bonnie Szumski, *Publisher*
Scott Barbour, *Managing Editor*

GREENHAVEN PRESS
SAN DIEGO, CALIFORNIA

THOMSON

GALE

Detroit • New York • San Diego • San Francisco
Boston • New Haven, Conn. • Waterville, Maine
London • Munich

Every effort has been made to trace the owners of copyrighted material. The articles in this volume may have been edited for content, length, and/or reading level. The titles have been changed to enhance the editorial purpose.

Library of Congress Cataloging-in-Publication Data
The industrial revolution / Brenda Stalcup, book editor.
    p. cm. — (Turning points in world history)
    Includes bibliographical references and index.
    ISBN 0-7377-0926-X (pbk. : alk. paper) —
ISBN 0-7377-0927-8 (hardback : alk. paper)
    1. Economic history—1750–1918. 2. Industrial revolution.
3. Inventors—Europe—History. 4. Industrialists—Europe—
History. 5. Working class—Europe—History. 6. Europe—
Economic conditions—1789–1900. 7. Technological innovations—
Europe—History. I. Stalcup, Brenda. II. Turning points in world
history (Greenhaven Press)

HC52.5 .I53 2002
330.9'034—dc21   2001008418

Cover photo: © Austrian Archives/CORBIS
Dover Publications, 47
Library of Congress, 17, 70, 126, 156, 164, 177, 191, 203
North Wind Picture Archives, 93

Printed in the U.S.A.

Contents

Chapter 2: The Great Innovators of the Industrial Revolution

Foreword

Certain past events stand out as pivotal, as having effects and outcomes that change the course of history. These events are often referred to as turning points. Historian Louis L. Snyder provides this useful definition:

> A turning point in history is an event, happening, or stage which thrusts the course of historical development into a different direction. By definition a turning point is a great event, but it is even more—a great event with the explosive impact of altering the trend of man's life on the planet.

History's turning points have taken many forms. Some were single, brief, and shattering events with immediate and obvious impact. The invasion of Britain by William the Conqueror in 1066, for example, swiftly transformed that land's political and social institutions and paved the way for the rise of the modern English nation. By contrast, other single events were deemed of minor significance when they occurred, only later recognized as turning points. The assassination of a little-known European nobleman, Archduke Franz Ferdinand, on June 28, 1914, in the Bosnian town of Sarajevo was such an event; only after it touched off a chain reaction of political-military crises that escalated into the global conflict known as World War I did the murder's true significance become evident.

Other crucial turning points occurred not in terms of a few hours, days, months, or even years, but instead as evolutionary developments spanning decades or even centuries. One of the most pivotal turning points in human history, for instance—the development of agriculture, which replaced nomadic hunter-gatherer societies with more permanent settlements—occurred over the course of many generations. Still other great turning points were neither events nor developments, but rather revolutionary new inventions and innovations that significantly altered social customs and ideas, military tactics, home life, the spread of knowledge, and the human condition in general. The developments of writing, gunpowder, the printing press, antibiotics, the electric light, atomic energy, television, and the computer, the last two of which have recently ushered in the world-altering information age, represent only some of these innovative turning points.

Each anthology in the Greenhaven Turning Points in World History series presents a group of essays chosen for their accessibility. The anthology's structure also enhances this accessibility. First, an introductory essay provides a general overview of the principal events and figures involved, placing the topic in its historical context. The essays that follow explore various aspects in more detail, some targeting political trends and consequences, others social, literary, cultural, and/or technological ramifications, and still others pivotal leaders and other influential figures. To aid the reader in choosing the material of immediate interest or need, each essay is introduced by a concise summary of the contributing writer's main themes and insights.

In addition, each volume contains extensive research tools, including a collection of excerpts from primary source documents pertaining to the historical events and figures under discussion. In the anthology on the French Revolution, for example, readers can examine the works of Rousseau, Voltaire, and other writers and thinkers whose championing of human rights helped fuel the French people's growing desire for liberty; the French *Declaration of the Rights of Man and Citizen*, presented to King Louis XVI by the French National Assembly on October 2, 1789; and eyewitness accounts of the attack on the royal palace and the horrors of the Reign of Terror. To guide students interested in pursuing further research on the subject, each volume features an extensive bibliography, which for easy access has been divided into separate sections by topic. Finally, a comprehensive index allows readers to scan and locate content efficiently. Each of the anthologies in the Greenhaven Turning Points in World History series provides students with a complete, detailed, and enlightening examination of a crucial historical watershed.

Introduction

In its most basic terms, the Industrial Revolution refers to the changes that take place when a primarily agricultural economy begins to shift to the mechanized manufacturing of goods on a large scale. The use of the term "revolution" is somewhat a misnomer, since industrial development occurs over a long period of time. But when considered in the entire course of human civilization, the Industrial Revolution affected the population of the world as have few other events in history.

The sweeping changes brought about by industrialization altered the entire nature of work: the way in which it is performed, the role of human labor vis-á-vis machines, the reliance on the time clock and the division of time into small increments, and the organizational levels necessary for coordinating specialized labor. Industrialization transformed a largely rural population into an urban one, accompanied by both the positive and negative effects of rapid urbanization. Concurrently, it impacted the natural environment and our relationship to it. New inventions and means of transportation radically changed the way we communicate, travel, work, and play. The Industrial Revolution also modified the general standard of living, the structure of the social classes, and the international balance of political and military might. As historians Peter N. Stearns and John H. Hinshaw write, "These changes inevitably have ramifications reaching into almost every aspect of human experience—into the habits of thought and the relations between men and women as well as into systems of production and exchange."

The articles contained in *Turning Points in World History: The Industrial Revolution* examine the causes of the Industrial Revolution, its spread throughout the Western world, the invention of new technology, and the long-term impact of industrialization. Authors debate the merits and drawbacks of the Industrial Revolution, especially in respect to

11

the lives of workers. Every essay in this volume has been chosen for its accessibility and is accompanied by aids for understanding. The introduction of each essay concisely summarizes the main thesis and provides biographical information about the contributing writer. Occasional inserts serve to underscore or elaborate upon an important point made in the readings.

These articles are supplemented by an appendix of primary source documents, presenting the varying opinions of the entrepreneurs, factory workers, union organizers, and ordinary citizens whose lives were affected by the Industrial Revolution. Other useful features include the historical overview that begins this volume and the detailed chronology, both of which place in context the events discussed in the essays and the primary source documents. In addition, the comprehensive bibliography provides excellent resources for further research into the topic of the Industrial Revolution.

According to many historians and economists, the Industrial Revolution is still in progress; recent advancements in computer technology are part of an ongoing trend toward further industrialization, they maintain. This fact makes it all the more important for young people to study the changes already caused by industrialization and to carefully consider the path to be taken in future developments. The selections included in this volume offer a comprehensive starting point for investigating the Industrial Revolution and its myriad effects on the world.

A Brief History of the Industrial Revolution

Envision a British industrial town of the early nineteenth century. Near the river, a brick factory building stands seven stories high, its chimneys expelling huge clouds of smoke produced by the mighty steam engines. Inside, hundreds of mechanical looms thrum in constant motion: shuttles flying, wheels whirling, pistons churning. Each worker operates two or more looms simultaneously. Young children scurry up and down the rows of massive machines, mending broken threads or replacing empty bobbins with new ones. The entire building buzzes with energy and productive activity.

The factory owner surveys the scene, pleased with what he sees. Through the use of these machines, his workers are able to manufacture three times the amount of cloth that could be woven by hand, and with much greater consistency in the quality of the product. Not only has this textile mill made him a rich man, but it has also brought new prosperity to the town. His employees enjoy the security of steady jobs, as opposed to the seasonal fluctuation of agricultural work. The child workers are all from impoverished families; by providing these youngsters with paying jobs, he has saved them from the poorhouse or the streets. His workers spend their wages at local merchants' shops, thus enabling the rapid growth of the town's middle class. In fact, this factory and thousands of others have propelled Britain's emergence as an economic powerhouse the like of which has never before been seen in the world.

Now travel to the edge of town, to a small and dilapidated hovel where a middle-aged man sits with his head bowed in despair. For generations, the men of his family have been weavers, working at small looms set up inside their cottages. Like his father and grandfather before him, he learned the craft of weaving with the expectation of being able to support his family well. But he cannot begin to make cloth as quickly or as cheaply as the mechanical looms. Ever since the textile factory started operations, he has had fewer and fewer orders to fill. The weaver has repeatedly applied to the factory for work, but the owner prefers to hire women and children because he can pay them less.

So every morning at five o'clock, the weaver awakens his wife and children and sees them off to their jobs in the textile mill. They will not come home until seven in the evening at the earliest, often not until nine. Many times his wife returns with the smallest boy sleeping in her arms, too tired to wake up long enough to eat his supper. Occasionally one of the children arrives bearing bruises, having been struck by the overseer for working too slowly or falling asleep on the job. It breaks the weaver's heart to see his children suffer, but the family desperately needs the money to survive. The only skilled trade he knows is now useless, and no matter how hard he looks, he cannot find a decent-paying job.

These conflicting images of prosperity and destitution, of optimism and hopelessness, epitomize the two sides of the Industrial Revolution, a world-altering event that changed life both for the better and for the worse.

Life Before the Industrial Revolution

The word "revolution" is most commonly used to describe a major political upheaval, especially one that involves the violent overthrow of a leader or government. In its more general sense, however, the word can refer to any dramatic and fundamental change in society. According to historians, there have been two great revolutions that transformed the entire framework of human existence. The first was the Agricultural Revolution, which began around seven thousand years ago. Before this time, early humans survived primarily through hunting and gathering; they lived in small nomadic bands, following the migration of the herds each year. As humans started to develop agricultural methods, they found that they could grow food more easily and in greater quantities than had been possible through hunting and gathering. The shift to agricultural production allowed them to live in permanent settlements, eventually establishing towns and cities. The excess food provided through agriculture enabled some people to specialize in other types of work, such as pottery or weaving. Ultimately, the Agricultural Revolution spurred the rise of complex cultures, the development of trade, sweeping advances in technology and the arts, and many new religions and political systems. However, the Agricultural Revolution did not take place simultaneously throughout the world; instead, a few groups of people independently developed agricultural techniques at various times, and their knowledge gradually spread to other regions. Even in the present day, a small percentage of the world's population continues to live primarily as hunter-gatherers.

The second radical shift in human history was the Industrial Revolution. As with the Agricultural Revolution, the Industrial Revolution did not happen everywhere at the same time. In fact, many countries are currently in the process of industrializing or have yet to make the transition to industrialization. For these reasons, some historians and economists speak of multiple industrial revolutions. Nevertheless, it is generally accepted that the Industrial Revolution originated in Great Britain during the eighteenth century.

Prior to the 1700s, the nations of the world were predominantly agrarian. Compared to the earliest agricultural civilizations, these societies had made considerable advancements in science and technology, but their economies were still primarily based on agricultural production. The manufacture of goods such as cloth took place on a relatively small scale, and the tools employed in the production of these goods were typically powered by human or animal labor. The main exception was the waterwheel, which was used almost exclusively in mills to grind grain into flour. Even in the most technologically advanced countries, the majority of the population lived on farms in rural areas. Farm families generally lived near subsistence level, producing just enough food to support themselves and perhaps a small amount to sell or trade. They also made most of their own cloth, furniture, tools, and other necessities.

Some people did specialize in the manufacture of certain goods, such as shoes, clothes, or glassware. They set up their workshops in their own homes, making their products by hand, determining their own hours and pace. Often the entire family was involved in these cottage industries, as English author Andrew Ure depicted in his 1836 book *The Cotton Manufacture of Great Britain*:

> The workshop of the weaver was a rural cottage, from which when he was tired of sedentary labour he could sally forth into his little garden, and with the spade or the hoe tend its culinary productions. The cotton wool which was to form his weft was picked clean by the fingers of his younger children, and was carded and spun by the older girls assisted by his wife, and the yarn was woven by himself assisted by his sons.

It was not unusual for the family's small children to help with the work, just as on the farm young children were assigned their daily chores. Like farmers, those who specialized in crafts tended to work from sunrise to sunset, but their long hours were punctuated by frequent rest spells. They could start and stop working whenever they desired; if their interest in one task began to lag, they could switch to another.

Although most of these workers centered their operations around their own household, sometimes a very successful craftsperson would take on apprentices or hire neighbors in order to meet the demands for his or her product. These small workshops were not mechanized, but they are considered by many historians to be the forerunners of the factories in that they introduced the concept of gathering together a larger number of specialized workers in a single workspace for the purpose of improving production.

Early Innovations

The first industry to be affected by the Industrial Revolution was cloth manufacturing, especially the production of cotton fabrics. Imported cotton cloth from India was very popular in Great Britain during the eighteenth century. British entrepreneurs sought to profit from this trend, importing raw cotton from India or the American colonies and producing cotton cloth locally. However, they discovered that they were unable to make the cloth fast enough to satisfy the growing demand for it. They began to search for ways to accelerate the processes of spinning the raw cotton into thread and weaving the cloth.

Whether in homes or in factories, it was not unusual for children to work. Families depended upon all members to help with the workload.

In 1733, John Kay improved the shuttle, a device used by weavers to pass horizontal threads through the vertical threads strung on a loom. His invention, called the flying shuttle, let weavers send the shuttle rapidly across the loom simply by pulling on a string. Although the flying shuttle was essentially hand-powered, it sparked a cycle that ultimately led to the industrialization of textile production. Weavers using the flying shuttle were able to produce far more cloth in a shorter period of time than before. However, their increased productivity created a shortage of cotton thread—the weavers now needed more cotton thread than the spinners could supply.

Seeking to remedy this problem, James Hargreaves invented the spinning jenny, a hand-driven mechanism that could spin multiple spindles of thread simultaneously. Around the same time, Richard Arkwright invented the spinning frame, which used rollers to spin the thread. Arkwright's device was also dubbed the water frame, in reference to the waterwheel that provided the power to operate it. The spinning frame was too bulky to be placed inside a cottage, and it required a source of running water in order to function. So Arkwright housed his machines in large buildings similar to the water mills where grain was ground; therefore, these early factories were often called mills. Arkwright's textile mills were the first true factories, where workers congregated outside their homes to tend machines powered by a continuous and untiring source of energy.

The adoption of Hargreaves's and Arkwright's new spinning machines rapidly closed the gap between thread production and the weavers' demands. Then in 1779, Samuel Crompton invented the spinning mule, which combined the best features of the water frame and the spinning jenny and further accelerated the manufacture of cotton thread. Eventually, the efficiency of these three machines resulted in a surplus of thread; the spinners were now making thread faster than the weavers in the cottage industries could use it. In 1785, Edmund Cartwright devised a solution: the first water-powered loom. Like the water frame and the spinning mule, Cartwright's mechanized loom was too large to fit into private homes, and the process of weaving was transferred to the factories.

Another important innovation was the development of the steam engine. Because the early factories relied on running water for their power source, they had to be built next to rivers. A winter freeze or a summer drought could seriously affect operations, perhaps even bringing the factory to a standstill for several weeks. These limitations spurred inventors to create a more reliable energy source: the steam engine, which burns coal to heat water to the point where it produces steam powerful enough to run the immense machines. The first practical steam engine was invented by Thomas Newcomen in 1712, but it was not until James Watt made improvements to Newcomen's engine in the 1760s that it started to come into common use. Watt's steam engine was more versatile than the original version, capable of being joined to a power loom or spinning jenny. Its introduction to the textile industry made cloth production even more efficient.

The Spread of the Factory System

This new industrial system was highly successful, resulting in a tremendous increase in the number of goods one individual worker could produce. Between 1770 and 1790, the production of cotton yarn in Great Britain increased tenfold. By 1800, the manufacture of cotton cloth had become the nation's single most important industry.

Taking note of this impressive accomplishment, craft workers in other fields began looking for ways to industrialize their own trades. Inventors and entrepreneurs also searched for new and profitable ways to use mechanized equipment. In the flurry of invention that followed, steam power emerged as the dominant source of energy fueling the machines of the Industrial Revolution. According to science writer Isaac Asimov,

> The steam engine, bringing the use of energy to all mechanical devices in far greater quantity than anything else had offered in the past was the key to all that followed . . . when the face of the world was changed as drastically (and far more rapidly) than at any time since the invention of agriculture, nearly ten thousand years before.

As more and more industries arose, Britain's economy took off like a shot. "By 1800," historian W.O. Henderson writes,

> various regions [of Great Britain] were already specializing in the manufacture of particular products. Cotton yarn and piece-goods were made in Lancashire, woollens in the West Riding, hosiery in Nottinghamshire, steel and cutlery in Sheffield, iron and steel in southern Wales, metal goods and hardware in Birmingham and the Black Country and pottery in Staffordshire. Already Britain was indisputably 'the workshop of the world'.

Many of the products made by these factories were exported to other countries. By the start of the nineteenth century, Britain was flooding the European and American markets with its inexpensive manufactured goods.

European and American entrepreneurs quickly realized that if they were to compete with Britain economically, they would also have to industrialize. However, British companies tried to keep their techniques secret so that they could continue to dominate the markets. The British government encouraged this tactic by passing several laws that banned the exportation of industrial know-how and forbade the emigration of skilled artisans. Some Europeans and Americans resorted to industrial espionage, sneaking into Britain under false identities to spy on the new machinery. They also attempted to lure away factory workers who knew how to construct and operate the machines.

One British worker did not need to be enticed by others to leave: In 1789, a young man named Samuel Slater came to that decision on his own. Apprenticed for several years to a man who constructed machinery for textile mills, Slater had learned a great deal about building and operating industrial equipment. He recognized that his technical knowledge would be more valuable in the United States, where it was rare, than in his homeland. Disguising himself as a farmer, Slater sailed from London to New York, where he soon formed a partnership with two American investors. In 1790, working entirely from memory, Slater designed the machines to be used in his water-powered cotton mill, the first factory to be established in the United States.

Although the United States did copy a substantial amount of Britain's technological innovations during its early industrial period, Americans were already making independent contributions to the Industrial Revolution. For example, Eli Whitney invented the cotton gin in 1793; this device greatly accelerated the speed at which seeds could be removed from raw cotton, making the fiber ready for spinners to use. A few years later, while working on the manufacture of firearms, Whitney came up with the idea of producing interchangeable parts, making it simpler and cheaper to build the guns. This concept quickly spread to Britain and Europe, where it was called "the American system" of manufacturing. Whitney also instituted the first assembly line, a technique that would gain in importance over the next century.

America's Rise to Dominance

The United States continued to industrialize rapidly throughout the 1800s, challenging Britain's lead and ultimately surpassing it to become the world's top industrial manufacturer by the beginning of the twentieth century. American inventors introduced many new technological marvels, including the steamboat, the tractor, the mechanical reaper, the sewing machine, the typewriter, and the phonograph.

Perhaps the most significant breakthrough was the harnessing of electricity as a source of power. More versatile and flexible than steam power, electricity could be used to run a wide variety of devices, many small enough to operate in homes as well as in factories. Electricity was crucial to the development of new communication tools, including the telegraph and the telephone. Thomas Edison not only invented the incandescent lightbulb but also formulated an entire system of electrical generation that enabled individual homes and businesses to easily use electric-powered lights and machines. As authors Gary Cross and Rick Szostak explain,

> With electric lighting in the forefront, electricity was steadily applied to areas well beyond lighting. In the late 1880s, 180 cities introduced electric streetcars. With the development of an efficient electric motor came a stream of machines for home, office, and factory. . . . Electricity, from the 1880s, was also applied directly in the production of chemicals and steel.

Electricity would eventually be utilized in machines as diverse as the computer, the dishwasher, and the motion picture projector.

Along with electricity, the gasoline-fueled internal combustion engine gradually replaced steam as a source of power in factories and transportation. While the engine was perfected by the German inventor Gottlieb Wilhelm Daimler, it was popularized in America, especially through the work of Henry Ford. His inexpensive and reliable automobile, the Model T, made personal transportation available to the general public for the first time. Ford was able to offer the Model T at a low price through his cost-saving adaptation of Whitney's assembly

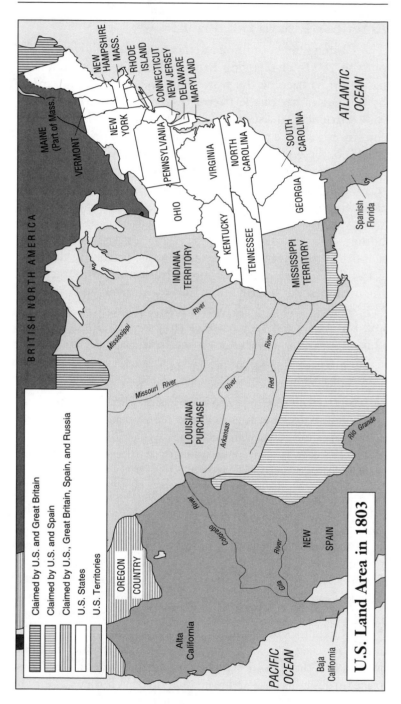

U.S. Land Area in 1803

Claimed by U.S. and Great Britain
Claimed by U.S. and Spain
Claimed by U.S., Great Britain, Spain, and Russia
U.S. States
U.S. Territories

line. He created the first moving assembly line, which used conveyor belts to transport the unfinished automobiles from one specialized worker to the next. This idea would be adopted by factory owners in many different industries.

America's industrial expansion was based on yet another source of power: human muscle. The steady stream of immigrants to the United States provided an enormous labor base for the factories, unequaled by any European country. In fact, the majority of the immigrants employed in U.S. factories were originally from Europe, usually from impoverished backgrounds. Hoping for a better life in America, these immigrants congregated in the industrial cities, where they could easily find jobs in the factories even with limited knowledge of English. Since these immigrants were generally willing to work for less money than native-born Americans, factory owners were eager to hire them. Unfortunately, many employers also exploited the immigrants, who were reluctant to complain in fear of losing their jobs.

The Price of Progress

Such ill treatment was not unusual during the course of the Industrial Revolution. From its earliest days, industrialization took its toll on the common workers and laborers. The switch from cottage-based handicrafts to factory work was a difficult adjustment to make. The cottage laborers realized that the introduction of the machines would drastically alter their way of life, and some opposed these changes outright. Frequently, they focused their anger and frustration on the machines themselves, which the skilled workers saw as taking away their jobs. Mobs of workers would break into the mills and smash the new machinery, sometimes burning down the factories as well.

These riots occurred more often in Great Britain and Europe than in the United States. They reached their zenith with the Luddite movement of the early nineteenth century, which began in Nottingham, England, in November 1811. The Luddites derived their name from a mythological character, similar to Robin Hood, known as Ned Ludd or King Ludd. Whereas the earlier machine-breaking riots had been more or less spontaneous, the Luddite rebellion was organized, militaristic, and clandestine. After each raid, letters signed by "Ned Ludd" would appear, taking credit for the destruction and warning of further violence to come. According to author Kirkpatrick Sale,

> At least a hundred [knitting] frames were attacked in the last week of November [1811], another hundred fifty or more in December, over an area of nearly thirty square miles . . . affecting a swath of nearly fifty thousand people. At the same time Luddites were reported to be going around the countryside soliciting—or, as the authorities would have it, extorting—contributions from fellow knitters and nonknitters alike.

The Luddite movement quickly spread to other regions, but it was met by a strong response from law-enforcement authorities. Those found guilty of machine-breaking or arson were summarily executed. The movement fizzled out almost as rapidly as it had arisen.

However, the problems that sparked the Luddite movement did not fade away. The new machines *did* throw skilled artisans out of work. Many of the machines were simple enough to be operated by children. The owners tried to keep costs down as much as possible, which meant that they preferred to pay their employees very low wages. Children and women typically expected less pay than grown men, so most factory owners preferred to hire them over the older artisans. And because factory owners could undersell cottage artisans, the market for handmade goods dried up.

The factory system also imposed a new type of work environment on the laborers, one in which they no longer had any control over their daily lives. Instead of setting their own hours, factory operatives awoke to bells summoning them to the mill, where they put in ten to sixteen hours of labor. Only a few short breaks for meals were allowed, and even then, the workers were often expected to continue tending the machines while eating. Foremen kept constant watch over the workers, noting if anyone moved too slowly; punishments ranged from docked wages to physical blows. Factory work was unrelenting: The machines never rested, and an operative who let his or her attention be distracted for just a second risked being mangled in the gears.

This hectic and stressful environment was a far cry from the old cottage workshop. As Sale relates, the laborers knew

> what they would have to give up if they were to accept such a technology: the camaraderie of the [small] shop, with its loose hours and ale breaks and regular conversation and pride of workmanship, traded for the servility of the factory, with its discipline and hierarchy and control and skillessness.

Artisans who had been accustomed to autonomy did not willingly trade their old way of life for the factory system. According to historian Harold Perkin the fact,

> that so many handloom weavers and framework knitters in the 1830s and 1840s preferred to starve rather than accept the discipline of the factory shows that many who did accept felt themselves to be driven there as a last resort.

Ultimately, though, the revolutionary change in work patterns brought about by industrialization left these workers with no choice but to enter the factories.

The Luddite movement was superseded by cooperative associations of workers who banded together in order to improve the conditions of factory employment. First known as combinations, these organizations eventually were called trade unions or labor unions. The unions operated on the basis of collective bargaining and utilized tactics such as work slowdowns and strikes. Their demands included better wages, safer working conditions, the reduction of the workday to eight hours, and the elimination of child labor. The United States, Canada, Great Britain, and most European nations ultimately passed laws that codified the reforms desired by the labor movement. The worst abuses of the factory system were thus made illegal.

The Benefits of Industrialization

However, the Industrial Revolution did not only bring about negative changes; it also had many positive effects. Most historians and economists agree that after a period of readjustment to the new factory system, industrialization actually created a rise in the standard of living for workers in every class of society. The sudden increase in production and trade enabled industrialized nations to better provide for their growing populations.

Women especially benefited, since prior to industrialization few jobs outside the home had been available to them. Numerous young women chose to work in the mills to earn money before marrying. In fact, so many young women took to the factories that housewives began to have trouble finding any girls willing to work as domestic servants. Lucy Larcom, who was employed in the textile factories of Lowell, Massachusetts, during the 1830s and 1840s, explained in her 1890 reminiscences *A New England Girlhood:*

> We used to see it claimed, in public prints, that it would be better for all of us mill-girls to be working in families, at domestic service, than to be where we were. Perhaps the difficulties of modern housekeepers did begin with the opening of the Lowell factories. Country girls were naturally independent, and the feeling that at this new work the few hours they had of every-day leisure were entirely their own was a satisfaction to them. They preferred it to going out as "hired help."

The factory day might be long, but at least when it was over, the young women were on their own time, not subject to the beck and call of the mistress of the household into the wee hours of the night.

The process of mass production made factory goods widely affordable and available to the general public. Many products that before the Industrial Revolution were too expensive for any but the upper classes now fell within the means of the working classes. For example, prior to industrialization, cotton cloth was a luxury item for the rich. Most people's clothes were made of wool, which was difficult to wash. Once cotton manufacturing became industrialized, the price of cotton clothing dropped. More people began to buy and wear cotton clothes, which they cleaned more frequently than their old wool clothing, leading to an increase in hygiene and good health.

Likewise, the new technology that was developed during the Industrial Revolution benefited the general populace. Improvements in transportation—such as railroads and airplanes—made travel safer and easier, enabled fresh produce to be brought from the farms into the cities, and promoted the shipment of consumer goods to rural communities. The telegraph and the telephone allowed for long-distance communication. Entertainment was forever changed by devices like the record player, the radio, the movie camera, and the television.

Housekeeping was radically changed through the development of new household implements made possible by the technology invented during the Industrial Revolution. The sewing machine, the electric iron, and the vacuum cleaner are some of the myriad appliances that simplified housekeeping. Many of these inventions also improved hygiene and promoted better health: For instance, the washing machine made it possible to wash the laundry more often, while the refrigerator increased the amount of time food could be kept before spoiling. These and many other devices brought about by industrialization are still in use at the present time, contributing to our high standard of living today.

A Continuing Process

Placing an end point on the Industrial Revolution is difficult. A number of historians and other commentators believe that it has yet to conclude; they argue that the so-called computer revolution is just another facet of the ongoing Industrial Revolution. And as noted above, the Industrial Revolution did not affect all parts of the world at the same time. Many nations are only beginning to industrialize, and they are currently experiencing most of the same changes and problems that Great Britain, America, and other Western nations went through in the early days of the Industrial Revolution. Humanity is also still coping with industrialization's detrimental effects on the environment, including the possibility of global warming. Overall, the ultimate impact of the Industrial Revolution on humankind and the earth has yet to be determined, and will only become clear with the passage of time.

Chapter 1

The Start of the Industrial Revolution

Turning Points
IN WORLD HISTORY

The Causes of the Industrial Revolution in Britain

Eric Pawson

Eric Pawson is the head of the geography department at the University of Canterbury in Christchurch, New Zealand, where he specializes in historical and cultural geography. His books include *Transport and Economy: The Turnpike Roads of Eighteenth Century Britain* and *The Early Industrial Revolution: Britain in the Eighteenth Century*, from which the following selection is excerpted. According to Pawson, the birth of the Industrial Revolution in Britain in the eighteenth century was caused by numerous factors that created a unique climate for the rapid growth of technology and the economy. This relatively sudden shift from an agricultural economy to an industrialized one radically altered the social order, he maintains, affecting almost every aspect of daily life.

Historians have long recognised many apparent breaks in the continuity of history. The Fall of Rome, the Norman Conquest, the Renaissance, the Reformation, the French Revolution: all conspicuously claim attention as symbolic turning points. Yet none has had such far-reaching effects on the pattern of human existence as the Industrial Revolution that began in Europe in the eighteenth and nineteenth centuries. It is this great economic discontinuity, rather than the political and cultural upheavals littering history, that holds the key to the understanding of progress, to the increase in the wealth of nations.

The undisputed leader in this transition from a traditional rural to an urban-industrial society was Britain, in the late seventeenth century of no great importance. But it was Britain (rather than England alone, for Wales and Scotland contributed fully) that of all the countries of Europe, became the first industrial state: a place that she held unchallenged until the rise of America as a great economic power in the last quarter of the nineteenth century.

The Industrial Revolution in Britain was, however, rather more than just the rise of industry. It was a whole transformation from the relative economic and social stability of preceding centuries into a new experience of sustained economic growth and social change. Population and towns grew, production and trade grew, incomes grew. There was expansion within all the economic sectors, agriculture, industry and the services, bringing not only a rise in output, but with the increasingly efficient use of resources, rising per capita output as well. Accompanying this expansion was a relative shift of importance between sectors. Out of an agricultural economy, with small-scale craft industries and few basic services, emerged a new structure dominated by mass-industry and overseas trade, with a wide range of service functions and a flourishing stratum of professional activities. Alongside these shifts in economic structure came important social changes. A rural society gave way to an urban one, and with this, the age-old division between the landed and the landless was replaced by the now familiar consciousness of the urban middle and working classes. These four basic trends: per capita economic expansion, structural change, the transition from rural to urban, and the emergence of a new social order, are the essential facets of the period labelled the Industrial Revolution. They brought fundamental alterations in the way of life, as well as a long-term rise in the standard of living that has been continuous and pervasive. The Industrial Revolution had many casualties, far too many to be dismissed so callously, but as a process of *sustained economic growth*, it generated increasing wealth and opportunity for more and more people, to the eventual immense benefit of all.

The problem of dating the Industrial Revolution has most frequently been analysed in terms of its starting point. There are two common, but essentially complementary interpretations of this. The 1780s have traditionally been regarded as the key decade of economic acceleration, a point of view associated particularly with the economic historian T.S. Ashton, and sealed in the famous take-off theory of W.W. Rostow. This is however an oversimplification of the evidence, although it is undeniable that the 1780s and 1790s were the period of most rapid change in the eighteenth century. Phyllis Deane and W.A. Cole, the most assiduous collectors of quantitative information relating to Britain's industrialisation, have shown very clearly that the upturn is earlier, with sustained growth beginning in the 1740s, slowing in the 1770s with financial crisis and the American War, then being re-invigorated in the 1780s. The best available estimates of agricultural and industrial output, and graphs of population, foreign trade and urban growth support this two-phase pattern. Some important elements of change, in particular the introduction of certain agricultural and transport innovations, the seeds of scientific advance, the expansion of trading links and the growth of London, can be traced further back still, into the seventeenth century. There was no simple or stark take-off, but a long period of gradual preparation, that was translated in the 1740s into sustained growth, with a notable acceleration in the years after 1780.

But if the Industrial Revolution has its origins in the eighteenth century, and its roots even earlier, the period of most rapid change is nevertheless the nineteenth century. Britain in 1800 was certainly different to Britain in 1700. Industrial activity in a whole range of spheres had begun to grow rapidly. The spatial pattern of industry had shifted: away from the south to the Midlands and north of England, and into south Wales and central Scotland. A significant number of provincial towns had expanded to a considerable size. Yet two-thirds of the population still lived in the countryside in 1800, and agriculture remained the most important economic sector. In the nineteenth century however, the mechanisms of change moved altogether into a higher gear. Britain in 1900 was not just different, but vastly different to Britain in 1800. . . .

Two important points follow from this brief discussion. Firstly, the extent of change in the eighteenth century must

The Role of Education

As a young man, M.W. Flinn worked as a clerk in the cotton industry of Manchester, England. He later became a professor of social history at the University of Edinburgh in Scotland and wrote extensively on the economic and social history of England in the eighteenth and nineteenth centuries. In the following excerpt from his book The Origins of the Industrial Revolution, *Flinn examines the expansion of education in Britain and its relationship to the birth of the Industrial Revolution.*

A prerequisite for major economic expansion was the provision of an educational system suitable for the new orientation of society. This involved the replacement of what was virtually a single scheme involving a traditional curriculum for a small aristocratic and middle-class elite by a dual provision which offered, on the one hand, a new curriculum far more relevant to commerce and industry for a new, broader, middle-class elite; and, on the other hand, an elementary education catering for the needs of a fairly substantial section of the working class. Both of these new forms of education appeared in Britain during the century before the Industrial Revolution. In England the academies, and in Scotland the universities, began to offer the middle classes, for the first time, an education more directly orientated to the needs of commerce and industry. At the same time the educational needs of the growing artisan class were met by the creation of the parish schools in Scotland after 1696, and the charity schools in England from the beginning of the eighteenth century.

M.W. Flinn, *The Origins of the Industrial Revolution*, 1966.

be kept within the perspective of the massive transformation in the nineteenth. Problems studied in isolation invariably assume an exaggerated importance, which is why it is necessary to set them in context, and consider their general interrelationships with adjacent problems or periods. But, secondly, the eighteenth century nonetheless is of considerable interest per se. It well repays close study. It is the period of transition from the relative stability of pre-industrial life to a growing, industrialising economy, the century when the essential nature and direction of change were worked out. The eighteenth century in Britain can realistically be labelled the Early Industrial Revolution.

Causes

There has been considerable variation in emphasis on the possible causes of the Industrial Revolution. A whole range of factors from fortunate resource endowments to scientific advance and the growth of foreign trade, as well as less concrete qualities such as 'inventive genius' and 'the will to industrialise' have been singled out as prerequisites or even prime-movers. Another drawback of the take-off theory is that it also unduly emphasises one factor—a rise in the rate of capital investment. Yet it can be said with certainty of the process of growth that it is highly complex and any single or simple prescription (as the experience of many Third World countries has shown) is false. Growth is multi-causal, depending on change and interaction between all factors on both the demand and supply side of the economic equation.

Rising demand was, of itself, of considerable importance. It was not, however, simply a matter of growing numbers. Rapid population growth has certainly not brought industrialisation of its own accord in the Third World today, but this is because so much of the population is self-subsistent, divorced from the wage-economy and market. This was not true of the state of England in 1700, and it became steadily less true of Scotland and Wales as the eighteenth century progressed. Britain's relatively undeveloped pre-industrial economy was nonetheless characterised by short (and some long) distance exchange within agriculture, craft industry and the urban service sectors. Because of this, the rising demand of a growing population was widely felt throughout the economy, and likewise the benefits of this rising demand, in terms of increasing returns, were equally widely felt. There was a slow but general rise in the level of real wages, the evidence of this being the increasing and widespread consumption of a growing range of foodstuffs (both home-produced and imported), simple industrial goods (such as cotton textiles and small items of metalware), as well as basic and professional services. It was the middle-income groups (in particular the farmers, traders, merchants and members of the professions) which led the way, but rising demand in the early Industrial Revolution was very broadly based.

Rising demand on its own, however, was insufficient to generate economic growth. To bring benefits, it had to be met by responsiveness from supply inputs. Had the economy not attained a sufficient degree of advancement in the eighteenth century to produce this responsiveness, then Britain might well have entered a Malthusian trap (if population had continued to grow quickly), or become heavily reliant on the products of overseas trade to satisfy the demands of middle and higher income groups. But neither happened. Britain possessed both a plentiful supply of resources and the means to exploit them with increasing efficiency, so as to produce a gradual rise in output per capita over time.

The Efficient Exploitation of Resources

The country was well endowed with natural resources, such as good farming land, minerals, waterways and harbours. The effective supply of these could be boosted by bringing into production those unused or under-used. The area of cultivated land expanded considerably in the eighteenth century, for example. Some basic materials of industrialisation had to be imported—cotton being the obvious case—but these were earnt by trade. The country was not short of labour, and its supply increased as population grew. There was also sufficient capital available to sustain the economy, deriving essentially from agriculture, trade and the profits of new enterprise, i.e. the pooled savings of an economy operating above subsistence level. Yet an expanding supply of these resources, with a growing population, need have done no more than merely sustain production per head. Economic growth, or development, meant a rise in per capita production, which only came about by increasing efficiency in the use of the resources, or supply inputs, available. This was achieved in three ways: by innovation, by improving organisation and by the conquest of space.

Eighteenth century Britain was extremely innovative, both in respect of the classic series of technical changes traditionally associated with the Industrial Revolution and of the less obvious innovations in commerce (such as the wider use of the mortgage and other instruments of credit), education and administration. Innovations enabled a higher scale of production to be achieved by increasing the efficiency of men themselves, or the equipment with which they worked, and permitted an increasing division of labour. The innovations underlying the change from organic to inorganic sources of raw material (such as the introduction of coke-smelting in the iron industry and coal-generated steam as a means of power) removed low ceilings to production, thus greatly raising its potential. Innovations in agriculture which were both technical (new crops and better rotations, for example) and structural (enclosure) underlay a rise in food production that not only fed the growing population, but enabled it to be fed better. The series of technical changes in the textiles industries so cheapened the final product, by expanding supply to ever increasing levels, that cheap quality cloth was available to nearly all the population by 1800.

The exact source of this upsurge of innovation is impossible to pinpoint, however. It was obviously encouraged by the general economic climate; by experimentation, argument, discussion in the firms and towns of the day; by education, and not least, by Britain's overseas links, which provided ideas and skills as well as goods and markets. It was associated with rising capital accumulation, although the economy's requirements were modest and per capita investment levels did not rise dramatically in the eighteenth century. As a means of increasing efficiency in the use of resources, this particular concept—rising per capita investment—is more applicable to the nineteenth century.

Collective Efforts

The organisation of enterprise, or entrepreneurship, is one of the least understood aspects of the development process. To a certain extent, all producers can be regarded as entrepreneurs, but the early Industrial Revolution was certainly characterised by the emergence of a type of bold, successful organisers, particularly in industry and trade. These entrepreneurs played a critical role, harnessing the other factors of production and directing their collective efforts towards the exploitation of markets, thereby bringing supply and demand forces together. Again, the exact reasons for this emergence are obscure: it is difficult to be any more specific than for the sources of innovativeness. But the role of Protestantism, proposed by R.H. Tawney in a famous work *Religion and the Rise of Capitalism*, was of less direct significance than once thought, although it is undoubtedly true that some groups, bound by ties of kinship and belief, did produce clusters of successful businessmen. The Quakers are the best example.

The conquest of space was the third source of increasing efficiency. Improving transport and communications (an important aspect of capital accumulation) permitted an increasing amount of exchange within the economy. It allowed entrepreneurs to assemble raw materials from a wide area, and enabled them to break out of local markets, so encouraging specialisation in agriculture, industry and the services: rational specialisation being one of the most potent forces of economic advance. Better transport cut real costs of movement, whilst better communications, channelling flows of information, were fundamental to the extension of markets, to the organisation of large scale enterprises, and to services such as banking and insurance. The conquest of space thus not only improved the efficiency of supply factors, but was another necessary link between them and rising demand.

It is apparent, therefore, that a whole range of factors must be considered as causes of the Industrial Revolution. Individually, many of these factors were necessary, but none were sufficient. Assessing the relative importance of each is difficult, if not impossible, which is why as often as not they are listed in seemingly random and unconnected order in the texts, if they are explicitly identified at all. It is however, possible to group these causes into three broad, and interrelated, categories: firstly, rising demand; secondly, an increasing supply of resources, or factors of production; and thirdly, increasing efficiency in the use of those resources.

The Spread of the Industrial Revolution to Europe

W.O. Henderson

Although the Industrial Revolution began in Great Britain, other nations soon realized the benefits of the new technologies and attempted to import or copy them, W.O. Henderson explains in the following selection from his book *Britain and Industrial Europe, 1750–1870: Studies in British Influence on the Industrial Revolution in Western Europe.* Since the British zealously guarded their new machines, he writes, Europeans sometimes resorted to illegal means to obtain the secrets of industrialization. Henderson also explores the various reasons why the Industrial Revolution first occurred in Britain rather than in one of the nations on the European continent. A former professor of international economic history at the University of Manchester in Great Britain, Henderson is the author of *The Genesis of the Common Market* and *The Industrial Revolution in Europe, 1815–1914.*

It is well known that the development of modern large-scale industrial capitalism took place in Britain at an earlier period than on the Continent. A number of factors contributed to the rapid expansion of British manufactures in the second half of the eighteenth century. For the development of the machine age adequate supplies of capital, raw materials and labour as well as access to suitable home and overseas markets were necessary. In Britain wealth was accumulating in the eighteenth century. Overseas trade, particularly with the colonies, was profitable and there were great landlords whose incomes from rents were sufficient to enable them to

Excerpted from *Britain and Industrial Europe, 1750–1870: Studies in British Influence on the Industrial Revolution in Western Europe,* by W.O. Henderson (Liverpool, UK: University Press of Liverpool, 1954). Copyright © 1954 by the University Press of Liverpool. Reprinted with permission.

invest money in mining and manufactures. The Bank of England, the London financial houses, the country banks and the various exchanges provided the necessary financial framework within which new industrial enterprises could expand. If the typical business was still the family concern or the partnership there were also important joint stock companies operating on a large scale. As far as raw materials were concerned Britain had adequate supplies of coal and iron-ore which were conveniently situated near good ports. Important industries, such as the manufacture of woollen and leather goods, had ample supplies of raw materials which were produced on farms at home. The growing population provided both the labour force for the new factories and an expanding home demand for manufacturers. The growth and importance of London was also a factor of some significance. G.D.H. Cole pointed out in *Periods and Persons* that in the 1720s Daniel Defoe "never wearied of recording how much London's greatness contributed to the prosperity of the whole country." The expansion of British agriculture provided additional supplies of raw materials to certain industries as well as the extra food needed to feed a growing population. High wages in the towns led to an exodus from the countryside to the towns which helped to increase the labour force available in the new factories and workshops. Britain's favourable geographical location on world trade routes and her efficient mercantile marine gave the country relatively easy access to foreign markets. . . .

Problems on the Continent

At first sight it might appear surprising that the Continent did not become industrialised at about the same time as Britain. The Continent too, had great resources of coal, iron-ore, timber, wool and other valuable raw materials. In some respects technical knowledge on the Continent—as in mining and metallurgy—was still in advance of Britain in the middle of the eighteenth century. There was no lack of inventive genius on the European mainland. Some epoch-making machines, such as the Jacquard loom, the Seguin multitubular locomotive boiler and the Heilmann comb, were invented on the Continent. In the eighteenth century the banks of Holland and Switzerland were as important as those in Britain. And in the same period on the Continent the State itself owned industrial establishments and public utilities and gave valuable financial and other assistance to private enterprise in a way that was less customary in Britain. In France, for example, under the ancien régime, there were both nationalised factories and private establishments controlled and subsidised by the Crown. Moreover the Continental System shielded much of the European mainland from British competition at a critical period. Nevertheless it was some time after the Napoleonic Wars before Continental countries began to overtake the lead which Britain had secured in the industrial field.

Explanations for the relatively slow progress of industrialisation on the Continent are not far to seek. Wars and civil disturbances inevitably delayed progress. In many parts of the Continent there was a serious shortage of capital and not even the assistance offered by governments could bridge the gap between the capital needed to start new enterprises and the money available from private sources. In the eighteenth century Continental trade was hampered both by poor communications and by a fantastic multiplicity of customs duties, excises and tolls of various kinds. Gild restrictions, too, sometimes hindered the expansion of manufactures. Before 1789 there were on the Continent few changes in the agrarian economy comparable with what was occurring in Britain. Peasants on the European mainland were sometimes prepared to undertake industrial work in the towns for part of the year but they were reluctant to break all ties with the countryside by becoming full-time factory workers. Restrictive commercial policies encouraged local and regional monopolies and the absence of competition not infrequently removed an important incentive to industrial progress.

Generalisations of this kind are, however, of only limited value since conditions varied considerably in different parts of the Continent. It is necessary to examine separately the situation in individual countries in order to discover reasons for the relatively slow progress that was made in industrialisation in the second half of the eighteenth century. In Germany, for example, the existence of a large number of virtually sovereign states retarded manufacturing progress. Each of some 300 independent territories had its own system of customs and excises, currency, weights and measures. The great coalfields of the Ruhr and Upper Silesia were too far from the sea and from the main centres of population to be adequately exploited in the eighteenth century. It was not until the establishment of the Zollverein [the German customs union] and the construction of a network of railways that these difficulties could be overcome. And a comparison between the fortunes of Hamburg and Liverpool in the eighteenth century would show how the Hansa port suffered from the absence of an economically unified hinterland and the lack of both a German navy and of German overseas territories.

France, on the other hand, suffered from a shortage of coal and other important raw materials. The rigid bureaucracy of the ancien régime, the privileges of the gilds, the burden of taxation and the restrictive system of commerce and navigation (inherited from the seventeenth-century statesman and financier Jean-Baptiste Colbert) were inimicable to industrial progress in the new age of machinery, steam power and factories. Undue concentration upon luxury industries—such as silk—was another unfavourable factor in the situation. Industrial expansion was delayed in the Belgian provinces by the closing of the Scheldt River and by foreign rule and in Switzerland by lack of coal and by remoteness from populous markets.

The great expansion of British industries in the reign of George III naturally excited much interest in neighbouring countries. On the Continent both Governments and far-seeing industrialists soon realised that by developing her industries in a new way Britain was becoming both wealthy and powerful. It was clear that a significant shift in the European economic balance of power was taking place. From the European mainland envious glances were cast across the Channel and energetic efforts were soon made to wrest from Britain the secrets of industrial progress.

Technical knowledge spread from Britain to the Continent

in various ways. Much information published in England was available to readers on the other side of the Channel. The *Journal of the Society of Arts*, the transactions of the Royal Society and the proceedings of the professional bodies—such as the Institution of Civil Engineers—contained details of inventions and new industrial processes. Some of this information was reprinted in technical journals on the Continent. An examination of the files of the *Annales des Mines* for example shows how assiduously foreign observers studied English periodicals which described the advances that were being made in the production of new machines.

Industrial Spies

Many foreigners visited Britain in the hope of acquiring sufficient information about recent inventions and technical processes to enable them to introduce this new technical knowledge into their own countries. Sometimes these "industrial spies" had a legitimate excuse for seeking permission to enter British factories and workshops. If they were agents of foreign customers who were buying machines they might not unreasonably ask to be shown how the machinery should be handled. Other visitors however had no intention of buying machinery and they came to this country in the hope of learning some of the secrets of the new machine age. Some foreigners secured employment in British factories with the object of learning enough about the machines they handled to be able to build similar machines for themselves when they returned home. The reception accorded by British industrialists to foreign visitors varied considerably. When Barthélemy Faujas de Saint-Fond came to Manchester at the end of the eighteenth century he could not secure admission to a single cotton mill while at Carron he was allowed to see only the ironworks and not the cannon foundry. On the other hand many foreigners such as Gabriel Jars (1764), Marchant de la Houlière (1775), J.C. Fischer (1814–51) and Frédéric le Play (1842) appear to have had little or no difficulty in inspecting the industrial establishments in which they were interested.

Some foreigners tried to export blueprints, models and

machine-parts out of England. This was not necessarily illegal. The export of some machinery was permitted and there were occasions on which the authorities issued licenses for the export of "prohibited" machines. But many models and machines were smuggled out of the country in defiance of the law. When offenders were caught they were fined or imprisoned but there can be little doubt that much smuggling escaped detection. Similarly a number of skilled artisans were enticed abroad although this was illegal until 1825. The severe punishments inflicted upon labour recruiting agents did not deter either Englishmen or foreigners from smuggling operatives and mechanics out of the country.

British industrialists in the eighteenth century made strenuous efforts to secure the enforcement of laws prohibiting the export of machinery and the emigration of skilled workers. . . .

Heavy penalties were imposed upon those who defied these laws. In 1785 a German named Baden was fined £500 at Lancaster and in 1792 a native of Alsace named Charles Albert was sent to prison and fined £500. Shortly afterwards an Englishman named Paul Harding, who was acting as labour recruiting agent for Lièven Bauwens, of Ghent, was fined and imprisoned. When James Cockerill landed in Hull in September 1802 to buy textile machinery and to engage operatives he was promptly arrested and lodged in York Castle. He succeeded in escaping however and he reached the Continent in safety.

But the authorities let many labour recruiting agents and smugglers of machinery and blueprints slip through their fingers. When one considers the numbers of British workers employed by John Holker at Rouen, by Lièven Bauwens at Ghent, by John Cockerill at Seraing, by Scipion Périer and Humphrey Edwards at Chaillot, by Nicholas Schlumberger at Guebwiller and by Friedrich Harkort at the Wetter—to mention only a few—it is clear that the British laws prohibiting the emigration of skilled men were often successfully evaded. These establishments, and many others, contained machinery which had either been smuggled from Britain or had been constructed from British blueprints or models.

The Lifting of the Bans

After the Napoleonic Wars there was some controversy in Britain concerning the desirability of maintaining the laws restricting the export of machinery and the emigration of skilled workers. The parliamentary enquiries of 1824–5 and 1841 showed how difficult it was in practice to enforce these regulations. While many textile manufacturers and ironmasters still felt that it was in the best interests of the country to do everything possible to stop foreigners from acquiring or copying new British machines and industrial processes the representatives of the machine-building industry complained that this policy deprived them of their export markets and threatened the prosperity of a growing branch of manufacture. They argued that if foreigners could not get machinery from Britain they would get it elsewhere or invent machines of their own. Eventually both the emigration of skilled workers (1825) and the export of machinery (1842) was freed from all restrictions.

Englishmen played a significant part in the industrialisation of western Europe in three ways. First, British skilled workers installed new machinery and then instructed foreign workers how to use it. Thus in the second half of the eighteenth century British textile workers were teaching Frenchmen how to use the fly-shuttle, the waterframe and the mule-jenny, while British engineers installed steam pumps on the Continent. In the second quarter of the nineteenth century groups of English puddlers moved from one ironworks to another in Belgium and Germany instructing foreigners in their craft. A little later the English driver on the footplate of a locomotive was as familiar a figure on the Continent as the marine engineer on a river steamboat or the foreman in a cotton mill.

Secondly, there are several examples of Britons who were important as entrepreneurs and managers. In the middle years of the eighteenth century John Holker not only successfully managed a "royal manufactory" at Rouen but he supervised a group of model textile mills in Normandy and helped to modernise the cotton industry of a whole province. In the 1830s Thomas Ainsworth exercised a similar influence in the Twente textile region in Holland. His contemporary Aaron Manby had an influence over the French engineering industry which extended far beyond the great ironworks and machine-building plants of Charenton and Le Creusot. In the middle of the nineteenth century Thomas Brassey not only built the Paris-Rouen railway and many other lines on the Continent but he showed foreigners how the complex business of constructing a railway could be efficiently organised. At the same time W.T. Mulvany not only founded the Hibernia and Shamrock coalmines in the Ruhr but he played a leading part in bringing the Ruhr coalowners and industrialists together to discuss common problems.

Thirdly, for fifty years or so after the Napoleonic Wars, British investors found some of the money necessary to start important industrial enterprises on the Continent. Railway companies, river navigation companies, gasworks, waterworks, cotton and other textile mills, and engineering establishments were set up with the aid of British capital. Manby's engineering workshops at Charenton and Le Creusot, Mulvany's coalmines in the Ruhr, the Lister-Holden woolcombing establishments in France, John Douglas's cotton mill in the Vorarlberg—these and a host of other factories were started with British money. It would be rash even to guess at the actual amount of British capital involved but the significance of this aspect of Britain's contribution to the industrialisation of the European mainland was undoubtedly of some importance.

Americans Debate the Merits of Industrialization

George Soule

After winning independence from Great Britain, the new nation of the United States faced many decisions concerning its future, including whether to follow Britain's lead in industrialization or to remain an agricultural nation. This question was hotly contested: While many Americans felt that industrialization was crucial to the country's economic future, others feared that the negative social effects of the Industrial Revolution would prove deadly to America's fledgling democracy.

In the following piece from his book *Economic Forces in American History*, economist and labor authority George Soule describes the opinions on both sides of this controversy, especially as epitomized by the debate between the famous statesmen Thomas Jefferson and Alexander Hamilton. A former professor of economics at Bennington College in Vermont, Soule wrote over twenty-five books, including *Ideas of the Great Economists*, *What Automation Does to Human Beings*, and *Men, Wages, and Employment in the Modern U.S. Economy*.

It is interesting that while the new nation was still primarily agricultural the two greatest statesmen of the time—Thomas Jefferson and Alexander Hamilton—debated whether machine manufacture should deliberately be introduced. Both assumed that this development would not automatically and inevitably occur; both believed that it was not likely to take place in the United States without an effort to encourage it by government and the leaders of the community. Jefferson opposed this effort and Hamilton favored it; Hamilton won the argument.

Neither, of course, could look back from some future time to see what a completed industrial revolution had meant; even in Britain, where the process started, it was then still in its early stages. And neither had heard the term "industrial revolution," which was of much later coinage. It is doubtful whether either Jefferson with his fears or Hamilton with his hopes understood fully the immensely dynamic but disruptive force that modern scientific technology was about to release.

Like a basic theme running all through the highly varied orchestration of American life, the steadily increasing output of goods per man-hour, together with means necessary to achieve that end, changed and disturbed the national culture. Through railroads it pulled the continent together, while through occupational and regional specialization it tore the social fabric apart. It furnished the means to support a rapidly enlarging population at a rising material level of life, yet in doing so it multiplied the problems of control of civilization for humane ends.

Without the invention of the cotton gin and the growth of the cotton textile industry, slavery might have waned in the South; without the industrialization of the North and the extreme rapidity of Westward extension the slavery issue might have been settled without war. After industrialism had won, the nation devoted most of its working energies to building and elaborating the industrial principalities and the industrial empire. Political controversy revolved mainly about the power exercised by the industrial princes and their financial allies.

Yet back of all the technologist and the manager steadily wove their increasingly complex web, created the material means for a rich civilization, changed the nature of production and consumption. Neither Jefferson, Andrew Jackson, nor any succeeding great democrat could stay this mighty force.

The Industrial Status of Early America

Though one of the grievances of the American colonists against the English government had been the restrictions on manufacture, factory industry did not spring to life as soon as the barriers were removed. During the War of Independence the people in regions not controlled by the Redcoats suffered severely for lack of customary imports of manufactured goods. Prices were high and rising, and anyone who could have produced merchandise in large quantities quickly and cheaply could have made ample profit. But the colonists possessed little of the necessary equipment, skilled labor or managerial experience. Home spinning and weaving on hand looms was called upon to supply textiles, and other handicrafts flourished.

Before the industrial age arrived in America, skilled workers produced textiles by spinning and weaving on hand looms.

The art of smelting iron in small charcoal furnaces had long been practiced in the colonies wherever the raw materials were locally available. The demands of the army stimulated erection of such scattered furnaces and kept busy the hand forges which fashioned the refined iron into useful shapes. Iron chains were laid across the Hudson River to prevent the penetration of British vessels above West Point. Locksmiths turned to the making of firearms. Gun factories received bounties from various states; the Continental Congress established the Springfield arsenal in Massachusetts to cast cannon. Powder still had to be imported, though small amounts were made in the colonies. Governmental initiative stimulated attempts to provide other metal necessities; in Connecticut, Nathaniel Niles of Norwich was granted a subsidy of £300 for four years in return for making the wire used for the teeth of wool-cards, and Massachusetts offered a bounty of £100 for the first thousand pounds of card wire made from domestically mined iron.

The only available power aside from that exerted by the muscles of men and animals was obtained from water falling on millwheels in streams; this had long been used for grist mills and sawmills—processing industries involving the earliest application of power machinery in the form of gears, millwheels and saws. Paper-making was still a handicraft, as was the tanning of leather and the fulling of wool, but these occupations were largely commercialized and were carried on in small establishments that might be called factories, since in many cases they used hired labor. Shipbuilding was a familiar and successful colonial industry. Indeed, the word manufacturing in its literal sense—making by hand—arose to describe just such establishments, and only later was applied to industrial units using mechanical power to drive labor-saving machinery.

The Rift of Opinion on Manufactures

After the Revolution, there arose a difference of opinion among statesmen about the desirability of encouraging in the United States large industrial establishments employing labor, such as were already flourishing in England, as a result of the invention of power-driven spinning and weaving machinery. Thomas Jefferson entertained a well-founded dislike of the poverty and exploitation which had accompanied the beginning of the industrial revolution in England, as well as of the overcrowded and unhealthy cities in which industrial workers lived. These workers then had no vote and few political rights. How could a propertyless class of wage earners, uneducated, herded in crowded hovels and dingy factories, possibly form a basis for a democratic, egalitarian society? Jefferson favored a nation of landowners, principally engaged in farming. Many Federalists, however, disagreed. Chief of these was Alexander Hamilton, Secretary of the Treasury under George Washington.

Hamilton was a convinced and active economic planner. Here was a new country to be developed; its potentialities seemed almost unlimited, though after the Revolution it had to struggle with problems that seemed almost too great for its strength. Prices were high, the public debt was in default, there was a general shortage of consumer goods, and transportation, except by water, was deplorable. These troubles, Hamilton believed, would not remedy themselves. Firm and intelligent action by the central government was required. In a series of remarkable recommendations and reports he laid down a comprehensive program for governmental economic policy. Under the authority of the new Constitution he planned the national currency and established a mint. He obtained from Congress federal assumption of the debts of the states and the funding of the national debt. He pleaded for and won a governmentally sanctioned central bank, the Bank of the United States. Finally, he argued for governmental action to encourage an as yet non-existent factory industry.

Hamilton has often been regarded as a partisan of the rich and the powerful, an opposite number to Jefferson, the apostle of democracy, liberty and equality. It is true that Hamilton's plans involved, as a necessary instrument, nourishing a class of investors and facilitating the use of private capital in development of the country. It is true also that he himself participated in banking and other pursuits out of which money capital was accumulated. But partiality to private wealth was not the essence of the difference between him and the Jeffersonians. Jefferson and his friends were also rich and powerful; they had no objection to personal gain from plantation agriculture or land speculation. This was not a conflict between capitalism and socialism. Nobody proposed that the government own and manage all productive wealth; the state of the economy was not yet ripe for the promulgation or acceptance of such a doctrine by anybody, though both parties were willing for governments (state or federal) to do many things which today are often called socialistic. Nor was Hamilton alone in his vision of the possible benefits of science and technology. Jefferson was a confirmed student of the sciences; he introduced many improvements in agriculture, and his house, Monticello, is full of ingenious gadgets.

The Real Basis of the Disagreement

The difference must be understood on grounds more germane to the ideas of the time. Jefferson was a protagonist of agrarian interests against the merchants, bankers and manufacturers of the towns. He liked to live on his estate, he liked to plan and manage it himself without outside interference. He loved the smell of the soil and the trees. The independence of the individual landed proprietor seemed to him the basis of human dignity and culture. The nation had thrown off the yoke of distant English misrule; he did not want any new centralized power substituted for it, either public or private.

Government was a necessity, but Jefferson thought it should be strictly curbed and as decentralized as possible. The national government should step in only to supplement the action of sovereign states. This, to him, was the intention of the Constitution, and that document ought to be strictly construed. When one remembers the vast extent and thin population of the nation, at the time without railroads, steam power, modern machinery, or the widespread markets which were at once the result and the necessary accompaniment of these developments, Jefferson's position on government seems a natural one. One of the ironies of history is that a century later this position had been appropriated by the very industrial forces which Jefferson abhorred.

Hamilton was essentially a city man, interested in management and promotion of the national economy as a whole. He sensed in part the tremendous implications of the industrial revolution, though it was still in its infancy, and he wanted this country to adopt and encourage it. He was no lobbyist for an existing powerful factory interest, for there was yet no such interest. His argument was, rather, that the nation would benefit from factory production. Nor was he a lobbyist for capitalists who wanted to invest in factories; most persons with money to spare then preferred to use it in shipping, trade, or land speculation. Scarcity of capital was, indeed, a major obstacle to the growth of manufacture, as Hamilton pointed out. He favored stimulation of capital accumulation as an instrument of national development. If all this should interfere with the safeguarding of democracy as understood by Jefferson, Hamilton did not care; he was impressed by the disorderliness and tendency to disunion evinced by the decentralized democracy which existed. This decentralization was a major cause of the problems which concerned him; without a wider vision and a firmer hand at the center, the problems of the national community, which adversely affected all the citizens, could not be solved.

The Planning of Manufactures

Hamilton's "Report on the Subject of Manufactures," issued in 1791, argued for factory industry as a substitute for handicrafts, on the familiar ground that division and specialization of labor was a more efficient method of production. Though he did not explicitly answer the contention that factory-made products might just as well be bought abroad as produced in this country, several of his other points bore on that theory. Manufacture would increase employment by drawing into factories people not otherwise "engaged in business." (He did not here refer to unemployed wage earners, of whom there were few, but to others who might be brought into the labor force, especially women.) Manufacture would attract immigration—one of the major needs of a developing country. It would offer more opportunity to differing talents than an almost exclusively agricultural economy. And finally, the growth of an industrial population would enlarge the market for agricultural products. Every one of these predictions was proved true when, after much trial and error, manufacturing did take root and spread in the United States.

The obstacles to manufacture, as outlined by Hamilton, were typical of those found today in many "underdeveloped" nations. One was the general prejudice in favor of agriculture, a prejudice which was one of the main reasons for his report. Perhaps more serious was the scarcity of skilled labor and of capital willing to take a chance on untried enterprises of this sort, as well as the disadvantage which businessmen without experience would encounter in competing with established and successful concerns. Hamilton lived long before the phrase "know-how" was coined, but if he had used it, he obviously would have spoken of the lack of American "know-how" as compared with that of the English.

Hamilton did not expect many American males to work in the mills; the chances of farming and the ease of getting land were too great. Moreover, there were few with the necessary training in operation of machinery. Skilled workers were to be induced to immigrate by the fact that jobs were open. The less skilled work was to be done by women and children—as in fact most of it was in England. Capital also might be imported; but Hamilton hoped to build up native savings by funding the national debt, thus establishing a safe reservoir for investment, and by the growth of banking. Development of roads and canals would broaden the market for goods produced by quantity methods, as, Hamilton correctly observed, it had done in England. He did not foresee how long the lag of good transportation would hamper manufacturing in this country. Lack of business experience and the risks inherent in new enterprises might be overcome by governmental bounties and import duties.

Early Manufacturing Difficulties

The accuracy of Hamilton's forebodings about difficulties confronting American industrial pioneers was soon demonstrated by an ambitious enterprise of which he was one of the sponsors. This was the Society for Establishing Useful Manufactures—known as S.U.M. This corporation, chartered by the New Jersey State legislature two weeks before the Report on Manufactures was sent to Congress, was authorized to sell shares with a par value of $1 million, and announced that it would make a large variety of articles ranging from wire to women's shoes.

The idea was not original with Hamilton. Benjamin Franklin had a similar plan to encourage industry in Pennsylvania. An article in a Philadelphia periodical, *American Museum* (April, 1791) suggested a society to develop a carefully selected area, build a town and raise public subscriptions for machine manufacture. Tench Coxe talked to Jefferson about it, who then was Secretary of State, but of course Jefferson was not interested. Coxe later became Assistant Secretary of the Treasury and enlisted Hamilton's favor. The corporation started with important tangible as well as intangible public support. The charter exempted the society from state taxation for ten years, and from local taxation in perpetuity. The state invested $10,000 in its stock. The corporation was granted a large tract of land including the Great Falls of the Passaic River in the neighborhood of what is now—and was then named by the society—Paterson. Major Pierre-Charles L'Enfant, the planner of Washington, D.C., was engaged to lay out the town and factories. The original stockholders included many public officials. More than $100,000 was almost immediately subscribed, and in a few months the stock had trebled in price.

But none of the incorporators possessed manufacturing experience. Most of the money was spent on expensive construction, and the few products (mostly coarse textiles) could not be sold in competition with English merchandise. The manufacturing operation failed within five years. Thereafter the society survived, and eventually made money for those who succeeded in gaining control of it, by selling land for mill sites and by its monopoly of valuable water. Its strange and checquered history did not end until 1945 when, after a political and legal battle with the city of Paterson concerning the tax exemption granted it 150 years before, it sold out to the city.

Tariff duties passed by Congress before 1816 were mainly for revenue, and tariffs did not produce infant industries with long life-expectancy for many years. During the Napoleonic Wars native manufacture was encouraged, as during the Revolution, by the almost complete cessation of imports, but such factories as were established suffered again from English competition when peace came in 1815. Protection won in 1816, but the advance of industry in a nation without much good transportation, skilled labor or engineering training was still slow. The building, first of canals and then of railroads, was required before many kinds of manufacture really could begin to flower.

The United States Imports the Industrial Revolution

Carroll Pursell

Carroll Pursell is the Adeline Barry Davee Distinguished Professor of History at Case Western Reserve University in Cleveland, Ohio, and the president of the International Committee for the History of Technology. He is the author of *White Heat: People and Technology* and *Early Stationary Steam Engines in America: A Study of the Migration of a Technology.* In the following excerpt from his book *The Machine in America: A Social History of Technology,* Pursell examines the Americans' decision to commit to expansion through industrialization and their subsequent efforts to import the technological know-how of the Industrial Revolution from Great Britain.

The most important fact about the history of early American technology—and perhaps about our entire early history—is that the American Revolution and the Industrial Revolution happened at the same time. In those years of political turmoil between 1763 (when the French and Indian Wars ended) and 1787 (when the Constitution was adopted), James Watt improved the steam engine; James Hargreaves, Richard Arkwright, Edmund Cartwright, Samuel Crompton, and others mechanized the textile industry; the first canal was built in England; the first steamboats were constructed; and the iron industry was revolutionized by the introduction of fossil coal, the puddling process, and rolling mills.

It was during these same years that the American colonies carried out their political revolution against the British Empire and set out to erect an empire of their own. By the

1770s the original colonies had begun to experience tremendous growth both in population and in economic potential. Their premier cities were second only to the imperial seat of London, and already their iron industry was larger than that of England. The population growth, largely the result of natural increase, but of immigration as well, created a tempting market for businesspeople. The attempts of the British Crown to regulate and change the direction of this activity led some bold thinkers to dream of an American empire, free to grow at its own pace and to appropriate its resources for its own benefit.

Once free of the British throne, most of the leaders of the new United States believed that growth—primarily economic growth—was essential to the survival of the nation, which was then still a thin strip of land along the Atlantic Coast. The increase in demand was partly the result of a growing population but also of growing expectations. People were confident that the United States would settle the West, create its own literature, preserve its liberty, increase its foreign trade, encourage a flowering of science, and support a rising standard of living for its citizens. . . .

The Transit of Technology

The problem of stimulating a growing economy with a continuing shortage of labor was solved by the contemporaneous Industrial Revolution in England. The American Revolution safely won, American leaders looked across the Atlantic with shock to discover the changes that had been wrought there in so short a time. When Thomas Jefferson was sent as U.S. minister to France he stopped over in England and got his first glimpse of the technological changes then taking place. "Strange as it may appear," he reported, they "card, spin, and even weave, it is said, by water in the European manufactories." He also saw his first Watt steam engine. He had studied the older engine of Thomas Newcomen in books while a student at William and Mary College, but this was different.

Here was the technological solution to the nation's economic problem: hands could be replaced by machines. Machines were especially effective in industry, and manufactures could therefore be encouraged. To the objection that there were no such machines in America, Alexander Hamilton, in his 1791 *Report on Manufactures*, replied: "To procure all such machines as are known in any part of Europe can only require a proper provision and due pains. The knowledge of several of the most important of them is already possessed. The preparation of them here is, in most cases, practicable on nearly equal terms."

Thus Hamilton advocated, and James Madison heartily seconded, what was much later termed the "Transit of Technology." When the American colonies were first settled, the immigrants had brought with them the essentially medieval technology they had known at home. In their absence, a new, industrial technology had been born. It was now necessary to import that as well. The transformation was not easy, but it was done largely through the expatriation of British mechanics, the very route that the Crown had feared and hoped to guard against. The process was most encouraged, and is best studied, in the textile industry.

As late as 1750, the production of textiles was still an ancient art. The process consisted of four basic steps developed at different times: the fiber was prepared by hand carding; the spinning was done on the familiar spinning wheel, which had reached its near-final form in the fifteenth century; the weaving was done on looms not much changed from pre-Christian times; and the fulling mill, introduced by A.D. 1000, was the only mechanical aid to finishing (fulling, dyeing, trimming). Between 1750 and 1800 all of these basic steps were greatly improved and aided by mechanical power. Furthermore, partly in response to the introduction of power machinery, the textile industry, both in England and later in America, was reorganized during these same years from the predominant cottage or household system to the new factory system.

The improvement of the spinning process began in England in the 1730s when John Wyatt and Lewis Paul developed a hand-powered spinning machine, patented in 1738. The first mill using their machinery was placed in operation in 1740. Until about this time, cotton was not a particularly popular fabric. Imported mainly from India, cotton was exotic and ranked well below wool and linen as common cloths. Then, about midcentury, cotton cloth became something of a fad, which, along with calico printing, helped establish a new cotton textile industry in the Lancashire district of England. The resulting increase in demand for cotton yarn was too great for the Wyatt and Paul mechanism to handle. Then came that astonishing series of inventions so closely identified with the Industrial Revolution. James Hargreaves is said to have invented his spinning jenny in 1764, but little is known about it before 1767, and it was not patented until 1770. Operated by a large hand crank, this device pulled rovings (long rolls of cotton) into thread and twisted it as it was taken up on a roller.

In 1769 Richard Arkwright patented his water frame, a device not unlike the jenny but operated by waterpower. In 1775 he also patented a carding engine (to replace the hand cards) and the use of rolls in preparing the rovings. With the water frame, four pairs of rollers pulled threads out of the rovings and fed them onto bobbins, giving them a twist for strength. In about 1774 Samuel Crompton began work on his mule, so named because it was a hybrid of the jenny and the water frame. . . .

Weaving was mechanized somewhat later than spinning. The first major improvement of the eighteenth century was John Kay's flying shuttle of 1733. It is often said that this development made such an improvement in weaving that a shortage of yarn developed, which led to improvements in spinning and again put pressure on weaving until the introduction of the power loom. . . .

The Reverend Edmund Cartwright patented a power loom in 1785, and two years later a small factory with twenty of his looms was established. The type of loom that eventually became dominant in England was developed by others between 1813 and 1821. Then between 1822 and 1830 Richard Roberts, an English machinemaker, brought the power loom to something like its ultimate dimensions and workings. Between 1813 and 1833 the number of power looms in England jumped from 2,400 to 85,000. Although in 1830 there was still a great deal of room for improvement in all the cotton textile machines and the mechanization of wool production was not yet as perfect as that of cotton, it is safe to say that the industry as a whole had become mechanized.

Smuggling Machines and Workers

Needless to say, all of this development was British rather than American. As Hamilton and others pointed out, the American problem was how to get a hold of these devices rather than how to invent them. A jenny was exhibited in Philadelphia on the eve of the Revolution, but that long and difficult war isolated Americans from British improvements for a decade. At the end of the war, American textile manufacturers were totally hand powered and discontinuous. Then within the next twenty-five years they became mechanically powered and continuous.

As late as 1790 the only yarn spun anywhere in the world by waterpower was manufactured in England on Arkwright machines. Then, during the winter of 1790–91, a cotton spinning mill using Arkwright machinery began production in Pawtucket, Rhode Island. This machinery was the handiwork of Samuel Slater, a young spinner from England familiar with the industry there and the first to escape England and use his knowledge to set up a mill in America. He was shortly followed by a number of others.

During the eighteenth century (as before and after) many nations engaged in a great game of "beggar-your-neighbor." England was one of the most successful, having attracted a steady flow over the years of German miners, Italian silkmakers, and Flemish and French craftspeople of various kinds, who plied their old trades in this new setting, very much to the benefit of the British economy. Perhaps because they were themselves so successful, the British were exceedingly jealous of their own capabilities. In 1750 Parliament passed an act that forbade the exportation of silk- or wool-making machinery and the expatriation of workers in those trades. In 1774, in recognition of the recent explosion of the cotton industry, Parliament passed an act prohibiting the export of tools or utensils used in the manufacture of cotton and linen-cotton textiles. Loopholes in previous legislation were plugged in 1781 by a law that attempted to prevent the escape of sketches, plans, models, and other methods of reporting information about the construction of textile machines.

Despite fines of £500 and twelve months of imprisonment for transgressing these laws, Americans interested in manufactures busily scoured the British countryside for workers willing to go to America. Machines, too, were sought [and smuggled across the ocean]. . . .

The Growth of the U.S. Textile Industry

American manufacturers pressed ahead to establish the industry. In 1792 the *Gazette of the United States* reported that "an association in Virginia, another in the territory south of the Ohio, and a company in the western district of South-Carolina, have provided themselves with carding and spinning machinery on the British plan, to manufacture their *native* cotton." Tenche Coxe asserted that "a large proportion of the most successful manufacturers in the United States are persons, who were journeymen, and in a few instances were foremen in the work-shops and manufactories of Europe, who have been skillful, sober and frugal, and having thus saved a little money, have set up for themselves with great advantage in America."

Out of such beginnings an American textile industry began to develop. Through an uncoordinated system of bounties, patents, investment of public funds, industrial espionage, encouragements to emigration, permission to incorporate, and a large amount of self-education from practice, reading technical descriptions, and talking with others, Americans gained sufficient knowledge to construct and sustain a textile industry on modern principles.

Furthermore, the contemporary turmoils of the French Revolution and Napoleonic wars served as a twofold boon to manufacturers: it tended to cut Americans off from foreign sources, thus producing a kind of protected market for home manufactures; and it influenced a large but unknown number of British artisans to seek the peace and patronage of the

United States. By 1813, in the midst of the War of 1812, when foreign cloth was completely cut off, *Niles' Weekly Register* reported that there were seventy-six cotton mills within a 30-mile radius of Providence, Rhode Island, operating a total of 51,454 spindles.

At the end of the War of 1812, large quantities of British textiles were dumped on the American market, especially in New York, a practice that caused great distress in the industry. Many mills, overcapitalized in the beginning, went bankrupt and were then reopened under new owners with a lower capitalization and better chance of economic success. By the fall of 1816 E.I. Du Pont's woolen mill in Delaware was in operation, and he found it necessary to advertise in the Philadelphia newspapers for "any person lately arrived from Europe, and well acquainted with some branch in the finishing department of a CLOTH FACTORY." The "late" arrival of such a person would, he hoped, ensure that they were knowledgeable about the latest technological improvements in England. He also wanted "as apprentices, two lads of good disposition, and respectable connections." This, too, was significant, because the shift from using apprentices who had to be taught the entire business and "hands" who could be exploited for their labor alone was already under way. . . .

The eventual future of the American textile industry lay with the new "factories" of New England. Partly the result of the introduction of power looms, but more the result of a combination of machines and new organization, the first true factory was probably the one established by the Boston Manufacturing Company at Waltham, Massachusetts, in 1813. It was the earliest textile mill in the country in which all the processes, including weaving, were power operated. Here, and at Lowell, large factories drew power from specially dug waterpower canals and recruited young women (the so-called Lowell Girls) from nearby farms to live in supervised dormitories. . . .

Meanwhile improvements continued to be made in England, and each, in turn, was imported. The mule was made self-acting about 1830 by Richard Roberts of Manchester, but because the export of textile machinery was still forbidden by British law, it, too, had to be brought over discreetly. . . .

By this time, the country's textile industry was already quite large, ranking as a major industry along with flour grinding, sawmilling, and iron production. By 1840 the cotton industry alone operated 2¼ million spindles. Until the mid-twentieth century, it proved to be a hearty transplant. Furthermore, it became the nursery of two other important developments. One was the rise of the machine-tool industry, which received a strong impetus in the shops maintained or patronized by the textile mills. The other was the knowledge of waterpower and its use that grew out of such careful studies as those of James B. Francis, undertaken at the Lowell mills in the 1840s and 1850s.

The American Iron Industry

Like the textile industry, the manufacture of iron in England, which had changed little since the Middle Ages, began experiencing a series of changes after 1750 that both precipitated and also exemplified the Industrial Revolution. During the next half century (1) mineral coal replaced charcoal as the principal fuel, (2) blast furnaces became larger and more efficient, (3) tilt hammers and forges were replaced by rolling mills for the production of wrought iron, (4) steam replaced water as the source of power for both furnaces and forges, and (5) the puddling furnace replaced the forge fire in the refining of pig iron. As with the new developments in the textile industry, new processes and devices in the British iron industry eventually arrived in America and transformed the iron industry on this side of the Atlantic as well. . . .

Between 1750 and 1830 American ironworks were generally scattered in area, small in size, and conservative in technique. The pressures of fuel exhaustion and the demands of war that were forcing English ironmasters to use steam engines, rolling mills, puddling furnaces, and mineral coal were not operating to the same degree in America.

After 1830, however, dramatic changes took place in the American industry as well. Shortages of labor and of fuel made improvements necessary, first in the secondary (forges) and then in the primary (furnaces) manufactories. The country's population was growing, manufacturers and builders (especially builders of steam engines) were demanding more iron, public works were multiplying, and railroads were beginning to fan out across the nation, gathering the reaches of a continental empire.

By the time of the Civil War, America's iron production was second in value only to that of flour milling and, like the latter, was moving its center westward from the scene of its colonial beginnings. . . .

The Key to Economic Growth

The founding generation of the Republic had committed itself to the creation of a new American empire through economic growth. From Alexander Hamilton's *Report on Manufactures* to Thomas Jefferson's grudging realization that industry would have to join agriculture and commerce to safeguard the nation's liberty and prosperity, technology was seen as the key to growth. Many Americans enthusiastically joined in the general effort to invent a new technology for the nation, but it was universally acknowledged that the hardware and know-how of the British Industrial Revolution would also have to be imported, by fair means or foul. In this they were successful.

The Birth of the Factory

Gary Cross and Rick Szostak

Gary Cross is a professor of modern European history at Pennsylvania State University. His books include *Immigrant Workers in Industrial France: The Making of a New Laboring Class* and *A Quest for Time: The Reduction of Work in Britain and France, 1840–1940*. Rick Szostak, a professor of economics at the University of Alberta in Edmonton, Canada, is the author of *The Role of Transportation in the Industrial Revolution: A Comparison of England and France*. In the following selection, taken from their book *Technology and American Society: A History*, Cross and Szostak trace the origins of the factory system in both Britain and the United States. The Industrial Revolution spurred the development of factories in a variety of ways, they note, while the factory system encouraged further innovations in machinery that promoted industrial growth.

The modern factory is a recent phenomenon in human history. Until the late eighteenth century there were no buildings housing lines of machines churning out thousands of identical products with the aid of human attendants. The factory's origins can be most readily traced in textile manufacture, although factories emerged simultaneously in other industries. Factories might seem to emerge naturally from new technology. But centralized workplaces had other origins. The textile factory symbolized a new age to many Europeans and Americans. It promised limitless economic growth but also threatened to undermine the dignity of work and the cohesiveness of family life based on shared labors. But even if these early mills were islands of mechanization in seas of agrarian and craft society, they were

Excerpted from *Technology and American Society: A History*, by Gary Cross and Rick Szostak (Englewood Cliffs, NJ: Prentice-Hall, 1995). Copyright © 1995 by Prentice-Hall, a division of Simon and Schuster. Reprinted with permission.

linked to the traditional world of work and family. These factories originated in Britain, but they were adopted quickly by Americans—although with distinct features peculiar to the early United States. . . .

From Cottage to Factory in Britain

It would be only natural to suspect that the technology developed during the early Industrial Revolution provided the inducement for the emergence of the factory. As machinery became larger and more complex, and came to be powered by waterwheels or steam engines rather than by hand, we might expect that it would come to be located in centralized workplaces. Cottages would have neither the room nor the access to power; workers would have to follow the machines to the factory. Certainly, as the Industrial Revolution progressed, technological developments would greatly encourage factory production. It is clear, though, that in the all-important early days of the Industrial Revolution, the first factories used technology that was similar to that used in cottages. This not only indicates that some other forces must have been at work to bring about the factory, but also suggests that technological innovation may have been more a result than a cause of factories. Once factories existed, innovators naturally turned their attention to larger more powerful machines that would not have been feasible in the cottage setting. A great deal of technical advance resulted from simple attempts to hook machines together and attach them to external power sources.

Before 1750, one can, to be sure, find some examples of production occurring in a centralized manner. Ship making and sugar refining had never been performed in the home for obvious technical reasons (or not so obvious, given that many ironworking tasks, such as nail making, were performed in the home). Governments had occasionally sponsored workshops that produced high-quality luxury goods (such as Gobelins tapestries in France) or military goods. But such enterprises depended for their success on government support rather than productive efficiency. Before 1750 there were virtually no large-scale industrial works set up by entrepreneurs without government support and based on a decision that factories could produce cheaper or better goods than those produced in the home.

After 1750, in Britain, we see a number of entrepreneurs gathering workers together, not just in cotton but in metal work, pottery, and wool as well. These factories dotted the English countryside decades before James Hargreaves developed the spinning jenny, James Watt the separate condenser steam engine, or Henry Cort the puddling and rolling method of iron manufacture.

Why did entrepreneurs move toward factory production after 1750 and only in Britain? One common explanation is that factories were chosen because they allowed employers to better exploit workers. In the factory setting workers could be forced to work long hours for low wages, while in their own homes they were masters of their own time. To be sure, workers were hesitant to give up their freedom and many stayed in their cottages for decades even as piece rates fell. It was their children who would take up factory employment. Still, we must be careful not to idealize the life of the cottage worker. We do not know how many hours workers had previously worked at home, but there is reason to believe that total hours worked were not much different in home or factory. We must also ask how the earliest entrepreneurs were able to lure any workers into this exploitative relationship. Once factories came to dominate industrial production, workers may have faced little choice; but this would seem not to have been the case at the very beginning.

A more benign argument is that factories were simply a more efficient form of organization. Entrepreneurs who employed workers in their own homes in the putting out system suffered in many ways: They incurred transport costs in moving raw materials to homes and furnished goods back; workers often embezzled their materials; dispersed workers could not produce a standardized product; and it was impossible to respond quickly to changes in fashion in the putting out system. Employers, then, preferred factories not because of a desire to exploit workers, but largely so that they could exercise more control over the productive process. Yet cottage production also had its advantages: It was more flexible, so that if demand dropped production could be cut back readily (there was little capital invested and workers could seek temporary employment in other sectors); and employers were spared the necessity of supervising and feeding their employees.

Neither the exploitation nor efficiency arguments address the question of timing. If the factory had always been advantageous, we would have to wonder why cottage production had survived for centuries. It was certainly not because nobody had thought of the idea of the factory, for, as we have seen, there were many examples of factories before 1750. The fact that entrepreneurs had not previously copied the government-sponsored works must lead us to suspect that factories were not advantageous before 1750. Something must have changed to make them so.

The Role of Improved Transportation

Dramatic changes occurred in the British transport system over the course of the eighteenth century. If we imagine a "typical" entrepreneur trying to decide between factory and cottage production, there are a number of ways in which transport improvements would tip the balance toward the factory (only a few of which we discuss here). In some industries, access to wider markets would be an important consideration. As transport costs fell, a greater variety of raw materials could be used: Buckle makers, for example, who had previously used just iron and tin, came to use copper, brass, zinc, glass, and alloys imitating gold and silver. This increased the difficulties of carrying materials to workers and severely exacerbated the problem of embezzlement. As transport costs fell, industries became concentrated in particular regions as low-cost producers there were able to invade the markets of inefficient local producers elsewhere. One natural result was a division of labor: Workers came to specialize in one operation rather than performing a number of distinct tasks. Entrepreneurs now were forced to arrange for the movement of semiprocessed goods between houses. Although it might seem that falling transport costs should have eased the problem of transporting goods to workers, they served in important ways to worsen this problem. We noted earlier that cottage production was inherently more flexible. A factory manager would have to worry about keeping his capital stock and regular working force steadily employed. But as speed and reliability of transport were improved, the size of raw material inventories necessary for this purpose declined. On the output side, entrepreneurs were able to take advantage of a nationwide system of professional carriers that emerged as the roads were made capable of supporting year-round wagon movement. Whereas entrepreneurs had previously spent months on the road leading packhorse trains to fairs and markets, around 1750 they began to send out catalogues or salesmen with samples, receive orders by mail, and distribute goods by carrier. This had two effects: First, it freed entrepreneurial time for the supervisory tasks that the factory entailed; second, it forced entrepreneurs to produce the standardized output expected by distant customers—cottage workers simply could not do this.

These trends encouraged early entrepreneurs to set up centralized workplaces that employed exactly the same technology used in the home. Once factories were in place, though, innovators often turned their minds toward technology suited to the new setting. Once a number of looms were gathered together in one building, inevitably they were joined together and attached to an external power source such as a waterwheel or later a steam engine. It is not surprising that innovators had not previously developed technology totally unsuited to cottage production. Instead, once the factory was in place for other reasons, the technological potential of this new setting was gradually explored. As large externally powered machinery grew in importance, factories became even more advantageous.

The centralized workplace did not at first emerge in the large cities. Industry had for centuries been located in the country, and both waterpower and cheap unskilled labor could readily be found there. Only after factories came to require an extensive pool of both skilled and unskilled labor, as well as access to repair facilities and other services, did factories begin to concentrate in new industrial centers. Even more important, the shift from rural waterwheels to steam engines as an industrial power source facilitated the emergence of industrial cities such as Manchester and Birmingham. Ramshackle worker housing surrounded these factories. Those countries, including the United States, that strove to catch up to Britain technologically in the nineteenth century also strove to avoid these unsightly slums.

Transforming Labor

The factories changed the meaning of labor. Even if hours worked were roughly the same in factory and home, wage earners lost control over the pace and methods of their work. Home workers were legendary for extending their weekend drinking into "Saint Monday" and then madly trying to make up for lost time later in the week. Constant supervision was also a novel experience, at least for the head of household. Even though families often worked together in the first factories, something was nevertheless lost in terms of family togetherness. It is clear that a wage premium had to be paid in factories to entice workers into that setting. Even with that, most cottage workers (especially hand loom weavers, who were the most studied of these) chose to stay in their homes. Men especially largely avoided factory work in the early nineteenth century. As factory production grew, such home workers saw their earnings shrink. The next generation would find its choice tipped much more heavily toward factories.

British factories themselves were dark, dusty, and poorly ventilated. The cities in which they came to concentrate were overcrowded and polluted, and thus natural breeding grounds for communicable diseases. Although one should not romanticize the rural huts of poor cottage workers, it is clear that cities had always been unhealthy and became more so during the Industrial Revolution. Most workers who abandoned rural labor for life in the factory lowered their life expectancy and that of their family.

The increased innovation and emergence of factories, which together comprise the Industrial Revolution, would cause British per capita incomes to rise at unprecedented rates after 1820. Yet while it was happening, that revolution made much of the British working class worse off. Real wages stagnated while workers sacrificed freedom, health, and family.

Such a transformation naturally had an impact in the political arena. Workers in their rural cottages had been a weak political force. Gathered in factories and concentrated in cities, they could not be so easily ignored. They soon gained a collective identity, and an interest in improving their collective lot. Worker agitation was a major force behind a number of reforms in the nineteenth century: These included extension of the right to vote to working-class males; legalization of unions, strikes, and collective bargaining; and industrial safety and child labor laws. Many of these initiatives spread to other countries along with the technology of the Industrial Revolution and helped these countries evade some of the excesses of English industrialization—Continental political leaders of various ideological stripes would gloat that they had nothing like the slums of Manchester. This hostility to the English pattern also made it somewhat more difficult for other countries to catch up to England to the extent that their workers and farmers agitated against further changes in technology or organization.

Americans Learn to Compete

Soon after independence from Britain, American merchants dreamed of manufacturing textiles. The financial rewards of the transatlantic trade were dwindling. With nationhood, American exporters faced import duties on most products sent to England; and Yankee shippers lost their old privileged status in the British Empire. Americans had little difficulty in "borrowing" English textile technology. The machines were simple, requiring little more than the woodworking skills that abounded in the United States. As early as 1774, a decade after Hargreaves's invention, an English immigrant made two spinning jennies in Philadelphia. Thomas Digges, a disgraced son of a wealthy Maryland family who had a background of double espionage during the Revolution,

Living in company-run boardinghouses, young single women contributed significantly to the textile industry, often working long hours for low wages.

turned his penchant for intrigue to the art of smuggling; he brought about 20 English textile machine makers to the United States. Several went to work for Alexander Hamilton.

But a shift to manufacturing posed distinct disadvantages to Americans: In 1790, there were only 2,000 spindles in the

United States compared to the 2.41 million in Britain. Americans had yet to adopt sophisticated water frame or mule technology. Because English textiles were light in weight in relation to their value, transportation charges for export to the United States were not so burdensome as to make them uncompetitive. Thus few American manufacturers were successful in challenging the glut of English exports that flooded the United States between 1793 and 1807.

An exception, however, was Samuel Slater (1768–1835). Born in the English textiles district of rural Derbyshire, the young Slater was apprenticed to a local manufacturer to learn how to manage a mill. After six years of training, he immigrated in 1789 and was hired by a New York workshop to construct spinning jennies. Soon thereafter, he read an advertisement from two merchants, William Almy and Moses Brown of Providence, Rhode Island. These investors were seeking a mechanic capable of running some old spinning equipment to supply yarn to local weavers. Slater demanded and won a partnership with Almy and Brown. In 1793, he built water frames and carding machines from memory. In an old clothier's shop in Pawtucket, his spinning mill employed 9 children between the ages of 7 and 12. These young workers labored 12 hours daily in winter and 14 to 16 hours in summer. This use of juvenile workers was not unusual. Few families believed that they could survive or prosper without the labor of their children.

Slater carefully followed traditional hiring practices. Because fathers resisted work in the mills (considering it humiliating), Slater offered them employment as watchmen and construction workers, jobs deemed appropriate for men used to the freedom of outside labor. Only then did these men allow their children to work in the mills. . . . Married women remained at home. . . . Until the 1820s, Slater built a business empire around a number of cotton and woolen spinning mills, which he placed on streams near local rural labor supplies. He supplied his workers with cottages and household needs, deducting rent and purchases from weekly pay. Slater built churches in the hope of instilling habits of temperance and duty to work; punctuality was taught in Sunday schools. In many ways this paternalism eased the transition from the rural to the factory work and way of life. . . .

The "Lowell System"

A second stage of American textile industrialization took place in Massachusetts in the 1810s. Its pioneer was Francis Cabot Lowell. Unlike Slater, whose life was the factory, Lowell began his career in the transatlantic trade and as a speculator in land and bulk commodities. On a trip to England, he observed an improved "Scotch loom" and related machines, probably making detailed notes of what he saw. Upon his return to Boston, he had a local mechanic build an imitation. In 1813, Lowell formed the Boston Manufacturing Company (BMC) with 11 other investors. In 1814, Lowell and his engineer Paul Moody constructed an improved, but still very simple, power loom that efficiently produced a coarse, but cheap cloth that appealed to the American frontier market. . . .

The BMC's factory at Waltham, Massachusetts, combined spinning and weaving (these tasks remained separate in Britain). This innovation required the invention of machines that linked these two processes. The BMC soon operated a factory that employed 10 times the number of workers at the Slater mills. Each process from cleaning, carding, and spinning to weaving was carried out by machines in the same building and under the close supervision of overseers. These Massachusetts innovators abandoned Slater's child (and family) workforce for young farm women. Faster machines and the desire to eliminate the informal influence of the parents of mill children may account for the switch to an older, more homogeneous workforce. Unlike the British, who continued to use mule spinning machines (which required heavy pulling and pushing by adult men), the American water frame machinery allowed for a labor force consisting mostly of young females. It was probably the first such workforce in the United States to be totally isolated from seasonal weather fluctuations. By 1835, 6,000 people were employed in the mills of the Boston manufacturers.

The pace and methods of work were dictated by the machine—and the market. As important, these machines were centralized in a factory. This forced weavers into accepting employers' schedules and abandoning farm and other work that interfered with steady hours of weaving. Twelve-hour workdays for 309 days a year were common. Factories often had a central bell and clock tower above a gate that strictly controlled access to the mill. The clock was symbolic of the new emphasis on punctuality and time discipline. Work was simple and repetitive: Mill hands pieced together broken yarns on the spinning machines; weavers did the same and replaced bobbins when they ran out.

However, American textile mills in the 1830s and 1840s were probably more traditional than were the British factories that slowly were adopting the steam engine and becoming urbanized. Most American mills continued to be located on streams and rivers in rural villages into the 1840s. . . .

Women and Immigrants in American Mills

From the 1820s through the 1840s, the Massachusetts textile mill symbolized the American factory. The "Lowell System" was in some ways unique for it created a disciplined but respectable workforce. In one mill, the female workforce comprised 85 percent of the total; 80 percent of them were between 15 and 30 years old. Most of them were daughters of relatively modest, but respectable, farmers and were hardly the downtrodden. Few of their families seemed to rely on their daughters' earnings for survival. In many cases, their savings became "dowries"—income that attracted ambitious prospective husbands. When they worked in the mills, these young women were merely adapting the old custom of single women taking jobs as domestic servants or farm hands in order to save for marriage. In this case, the mill's wages were an especially lucrative option. Many of these Lowell women moved from farm backgrounds to urban trades upon leaving the mill and marrying. Still most were not individualists— they came and worked with other relatives in the mills.

European visitors regularly stopped to admire the cleanliness and civility of the unmarried female workforce and their company-run boarding houses. This boarding arrangement was essential because of the distance of the factories from populated areas. Moreover, parents of these young women insisted that the company provide a protected environment for their children. The matrons who controlled the boarding houses of the "factory girls" encouraged punctuality and hard work and discouraged drinking and rough language. Weekly church attendance was expected. Freed from the obligations of family, these young women could be trained to work by the clock. But the dormitory-style living arrangements encouraged social and cultural contact among women—even if they worked 73 hours per week. In 1842, Charles Dickens wrote in glowing terms of their libraries, the poetry in their own magazine, *The Lowell Offering*, and their piano recitals. He compared these happy conditions with the English mills where children continued to be exploited (even though similar conditions prevailed in American mills in Pennsylvania and elsewhere).

But, already in the 1830s, as the BMC's patent protection ended, increased competition and sharply declining prices for manufactured cloth led employers to cut wages. Textile workers, facing increased workloads and lower wages in the 1840s, joined a movement for a 10-hour workday. This led to the unexpected—a series of strikes led by young women workers. Female strikers justified this "unladylike" behavior by evoking the memory of their ancestors, the farmers who fought the Revolutionary War against aristocratic despotism. They did not see themselves as oppressed proletarians but as defenders of "republican liberty."

In response to labor unrest (and increased demand for coarse cotton cloth), the New England textile industry expanded its mills and sought new sources of labor. Finding native-born women both too demanding and insufficient in numbers, employers sought immigrant workers from Ireland and French Canada. The percentage of immigrants in one company rose from 8 percent in 1845 to 60 percent in 1860. The old paternalism of the boarding house matron declined and eventually disappeared. Whole families worked for low wages and lived in rented tenements. Immigrants were often placed in poorly paid jobs in carding and spinning, leaving more lucrative posts in weaving to Yankees.

Young people were expected to contribute their wages to their parents for the survival of their families. By the 1860s, about 65 percent of the immigrant family's income came from children. The fact that daughters often contributed 10 years of wage labor to their families was the source of much family conflict: The young sometimes ran away or fought over spending money with parents. These changes dramatically altered the meaning of work in the American factory. Factory jobs may have been better than what immigrants were used to. But, by the 1860s, the American mill became more like the English factory decried by Dickens than the enlightened model factory of the 1820s.

The Rise of the Company Town

Daniel Nelson

The institution of the company town arose as a solution to the problem of housing laborers in remote or rural factory sites, Daniel Nelson relates in the following excerpt from his book *Managers and Workers: Origins of the Twentieth-Century Factory System in the United States, 1880–1920.* The factory owners who built these towns exercised a great deal of control over the inhabitants' personal lives and community affairs, he explains. According to Nelson, many manufacturers provided beneficial services in their company towns, such as schools, libraries, and hospitals. However, he points out, company towns were also notorious for exploiting the workers who lived there, especially through the elevated prices of the company store. Professor emeritus of history at the University of Akron in Ohio, Nelson is the author of *Shifting Fortunes: The Rise and Decline of American Labor from the 1820s to the Present* and *Farm and Factory: Workers in the Midwest, 1880–1990.*

Whether manufacturers built factories in rural areas to gain access to raw materials, water power, or cheap land, to avoid city taxes or labor unions, or to pay lower wages, they often found that a company town was an essential part of their investment. To attract a labor force they had to build houses, schools, churches, and stores; provide water, sanitation, and, later, lighting for their employees' homes; and employ clergymen, doctors, teachers, and other public servants. A minority sought to institute a program of social reform; the majority merely bowed to necessity. In either case they soon learned, as Holland Thompson wrote in the 1906 book *From the Cotton Field to the Cotton Mill,* that the

Excerpted from *Managers and Workers: Origins of the Twentieth-Century Factory System in the United States, 1880–1920,* by Daniel Nelson (Madison: University of Wisconsin Press, 1995). Copyright © 1995 by the University of Wisconsin Press. Reprinted with permission.

"best operatives will not go where the tenements are bad."

Late-nineteenth-century company towns—communities owned or dominated by a single firm—reflected this pragmatic approach. They dated from no particular era, social movement, or school of managerial thought. Some—like Whitinsville, Massachusetts; Millville, New Jersey; Manchester, New Hampshire; and Johnstown, Pennsylvania—were as old as the factory system. Others were lineal descendants of earlier types of communities. The steel towns of the Birmingham district of Alabama often bore a remarkable resemblance to the iron "plantations" of the eighteenth and early nineteenth centuries. The textile towns of the southern Piedmont likewise recalled the early days of Lowell and Lawrence in Massachusetts. The village of the Joseph Bancroft & Sons Company, near Wilmington, Delaware, was a tangible symbol of this tie. Erected between the 1830s and the Civil War, the period of New England "paternalism," the Bancroft community remained a small, isolated, family-owned industrial site long after the best-known of the New England textile towns had evolved into cities. . . . Finally, there were new company towns—such as Pullman, Illinois; Tacony, Pennsylvania; and Gary, Indiana—that were products of the nineteenth-century revolutions in transportation, building materials, and plant layout.

The Factory and the Community

The hallmark of the company town was the clarity of the relationship between the factory and the surrounding community. In most cases the manufacturer viewed the company town as little more than an extension of the plant. The principles of utility and economy prevailed in both cases. In practice this meant that the village or at least the workers' houses were clustered around the plant to minimize travel time and tardiness. Few employees objected. At South Manchester, for example, the Cheney Company workers informally divided the company houses into "aristocratic" and "plebian" groups, depending on their distance from the plant. In many company towns it was a mark of status to live in the shadow of the factory walls.

The manufacturer's businesslike approach also accounted for the drabness of most company towns. At Schoolfield, Virginia, supposedly a "model" southern village, "the monotony of row upon row of houses, essentially the same in design, materials, and color was accentuated by standard outhouses, fifty paces removed from each back door," according to Robert Sidney Smith's book *Mill on the Dan*. Even the idyllic New England towns seldom deviated from the standard. Yet there was at least one compensating feature. Most company towns were located in rural or suburban areas and had ample space for streets, lawns, and gardens. Residents raised vegetables or flowers. In the South, pigs, chickens, and cows were familiar sights as well. In that region, at least, farm and factory life were not mutually exclusive.

Although most manufacturers usually went no further than these elementary measures, they had to make two additional decisions that often had a greater impact on the social life of the community than the location or arrangement of housing. The first was whether to sell property or houses to the employees or to other private interests. Home ownership, or at least the prospect of home ownership, supposedly engendered thrift, sobriety, and loyalty to the firm. On the other hand, such sales inevitably weakened the company's hold on the town. In most cases the possible benefits outweighed the costs, and manufacturers initiated a policy of sales to skilled workers. The major exceptions were the southern textile manufacturers, who took their paternal responsibilities seriously, and the northern "model" town owners. The Ludlow Manufacturing Associates of Ludlow, Massachusetts, for example, at first sold company houses to employees but reversed this policy and even bought back the homes when they discovered that their workers, as private homeowners, could not be forced to maintain the company's high standards.

A related problem appeared when the town expanded into areas not owned by the company. In these situations private builders and real estate speculators often usurped the manufacturer's role as town planner. In Gary, perhaps the best example, they were able to alter drastically the company's "plan" for the city despite the managers' strenuous objections. The ethnic neighborhoods where unskilled immigrants often found their homes were usually the products of "private" enterprise.

The second decision manufacturers had to make was whether to enforce ethnic or racial segregation. In the southern mill towns they seldom hesitated: whites and blacks were customarily located in separate areas or districts, the former often enjoying somewhat better accommodations. In the North, particularly in larger towns, the companies often confined their building programs to substantial, well-built structures designed for skilled workers. Only the working-class elite could afford most company housing in Manchester and Johnstown.

In both regions company housing was generally superior to the available "private" housing. Only in New Jersey glass towns were company houses reported to be markedly inferior to housing in neighboring non-company areas. Millville's "Grumble Alley," for example, resembled the "private" slums of other industrial towns. But most managers viewed housing as a means to an end, not an end in itself. If a modest increase in housing expenditures resulted in a substantial decrease in labor turnover, the company benefitted. Most "private" owners, on the other hand, could not afford the luxury of a long-term viewpoint. They sought to recoup their investment from their rental incomes—and quickly.

Paternalism and Exploitation

In small company towns the management provided not only basic public services but schools, churches, and libraries. Often, however, there was a difference in the manner of presentation: the company supplied gas, water, and electricity for a fee, albeit a nominal one; the mill manager or owner provided schools, churches, and other public buildings as "gifts" to the operatives. Even in the larger towns where schools were tax-supported, company officials often built public auditoriums, gymnasiums, libraries, or trade schools. In many cases the owner or manager and his wife were active community leaders, serving as the honorary or real heads of the church, school, fire department, library association, hospital, and other company-sanctioned organizations. In the 1880s the general manager of the Cambria Iron Company even taught geology in the company's evening school, the Cambria Scientific Institute. His classes were unusually well attended.

Company involvement in community affairs seldom was confined to the erection of buildings or the participation of high officials. Mill managers also used their influence to guide the residents' behavior in "constructive" ways. Perhaps the best example was their approach to the liquor issue. To mill officials the saloon was a source of absenteeism, crime, and domestic strife. They often used their authority to abolish the saloon and to educate the operatives to the evils of drink. Saloons were prohibited, company stores and hotels refused to sell liquor, and social events sanctioned by the management were "dry.". . .

The extent of the manufacturer's power and the temptations that it created are most apparent in the company store issue. The New Jersey glass companies were particularly notorious: their policy, as tersely stated by one operative, was "trade or no work." Southern manufacturers, on the other hand, used the store as a crude device for reducing labor turnover. According to the U.S. Immigration Commission, Birmingham steel makers, for example,

> stated that negroes were preferred because their improvident habits prevented them from being able to live on cash incomes paid monthly, and thus forced them to draw their wages weekly, and even daily, in the form of commissary checks or store credits. . . . As a result, the negroes are always a little in debt to the commissaries; they are rarely the possessor of any currency, and stay in the employ of one company as long as their employers will allow them.

In either case company store abuses, perhaps more than any other flaw in the operation of the company town, resulted in attacks on the manufacturers and their power. In New Jersey the glass workers' unions waged a relentless war against the company store. When they struck to abolish stores "the sympathies of the people in the localities affected were entirely with the strikers," according to the 1899 report of New Jersey's Department of Statistics of Labor and Industry. By the turn of the century most northern legislatures had already taken steps to curb or abolish the stores and prohibit payment in kind, long intervals between paydays, and other related evils.

It would be misleading, however, to assume that the workers' actions ever meaningfully limited the employers' authority. In the first place most manufacturers took their paternal responsibilities seriously; they did not attempt to cheat or exploit their employees, at least in a financial sense. In the second, they had good reasons for treating the workers in a reasonable, even benevolent way. The purpose of the company town, after all, was to attract and maintain an adequate labor force. Policies that led to unrest, antagonism, or turnover were, from the company's viewpoint, irrational. When coupled with a paternalistic social outlook, this fact usually dictated a policy of cooperation. But even when the manufacturer failed to anticipate and neutralize potential sources of discord, the relatively small size of the company town, the personal relations that existed between managers and workers, the employees' economic dependence on the company (most company housing leases provided for eviction in the event of discharge or a strike), and the virtual impossibility of holding a private meeting were major deterrents to concerted action.

Differences in the Success of Controls

If the company town succeeded in attracting workers and the informal system became operative, traditional company town controls rarely survived if the newcomers were "un-Americanized" immigrant workers. Almost without exception manufacturers were unable or unwilling to control their foreign employees. Whatever the employers' policy, the immigrants persisted in establishing their ethnic enclaves, complete with stores, churches, and social organizations, in effect forcing the company to deal with intermediaries—storekeepers, "boarding bosses," "bankers," and priests. As a result the social organization of the town changed. The managers retained their grasp on the natives and "immigrant leaders," but the foreign quarters became a community apart.

Southern workers were less fortunate. Except for some of the steel towns of the Birmingham district, southern factories relied almost entirely on native workers, with newly arrived farmers filling the positions that southern and eastern European immigrants occupied in northern factories. Moreover, managers often continued their earlier policies. To outsiders they explained that controls were necessary because of the poverty, ignorance, and irresponsibility of the operative class. To buttress their case they pointed to the workers' crudities: their insistence on sending their children to work at an early age; their custom of putting the whole family in one bedroom, perhaps in one bed; their unfamiliarity with modern sanitary facilities, even privies. . . . Yet the workers' poverty and ignorance had little to do with the growth of industrial paternalism in the South. For while southern mill employees undoubtedly lacked resources and education, they were by immigrant standards relatively well off. They understood the English language and were familiar with "American ways." In short, it was because they understood English and "American ways" and were therefore understandable to their employers that they were subjected to greater restrictions.

Chapter 2

The Great Innovators of the Industrial Revolution

Turning | Points
IN WORLD HISTORY

Eli Whitney and the Cotton Gin

Dennis Karwatka

Dennis Karwatka is a professor in the industrial education and technology department at Morehead State University in Kentucky. He has also worked as a propulsion engineer on the Saturn 5 rocket for Boeing. In the following article from his book *Technology's Past: America's Industrial Revolution and the People Who Delivered the Goods*, Karwatka provides a brief sketch of Eli Whitney, the American who revolutionized agriculture in 1793 with the invention of the cotton gin, a machine that was capable of cleaning cotton fifty times faster than the average worker could. The author also describes Whitney's other significant accomplishments, especially his introduction of the concept of manufacturing uniform and interchangeable parts for firearms.

At the beginning of the Industrial Revolution, entrepreneurs used their technical skills to establish modern production facilities. Some also called on acting and marketing ability to sell an idea. Eli Whitney was such a person. He was an inventor, an opportunist, and an expert at public relations. He persuaded the government to grant him a musket contract in 1798 because he offered the possibility of producing interchangeable parts—a goal he never achieved.

An Early Interest in Machines

Like most people in the eighteenth century, Whitney was born into a farming household. His father and mother both descended from successful agricultural families, and Whitney had a comfortable upbringing. Although he did not like farm work, it gave him the opportunity to work with simple machines. He seemed to have an almost instinctive understanding of mechanisms. Raised during the Revolutionary War, the teenaged Whitney worked at several jobs. He became a nail maker at 15 and was successful enough that he needed to hire an assistant. He switched to hat-pin making at the end of the war and was the major manufacturer in eastern Massachusetts.

Early on, Whitney showed no particular interest in school, but he changed his mind at 18 when he realized the value of an education. He worked his way through a preparatory school to gain admittance to college. He entered Yale College in New Haven, Connecticut, at the age of 23. His father helped him financially, but Whitney also worked at repairing laboratory equipment and instruments. He graduated in 1792 with a degree in law. The young man then traveled south, anticipating finding a law or teaching position. On the way to Savannah, Georgia, he met Catharine Greene, widow of General Nathanael Greene. She offered him a room in the mansion located on a plantation that her husband had received from the state of Georgia. Perhaps infatuated with the wealthy woman, Whitney accepted. He made himself useful by making and repairing items around the plantation.

Cotton was the family's main form of income. However, removing seeds by hand from ripe cotton was so tedious that one person could produce only one pound of cleaned cotton per day. Greene noticed how the tines of a comb passed through a person's hair and wondered if that process could be applied to removing cotton seeds. She discussed it with Whitney. Using his mechanical abilities, Whitney soon constructed a cotton gin based on the comb principle. After some experimentation, a machine he built in 1793 cleaned 50 pounds of cotton a day. Whitney established a partnership with Phineas Miller and returned to New Haven to work on the patent. The cotton gin was such a straightforward machine that a person seeing one could easily copy it. The new federal patent law was quite weak, and so many infringing machines were built that Whitney exhausted himself and his money while fighting them in court. By 1798, he was almost penniless and his patent, important as it was to the economy of the South, was worthless to him. Whitney turned his back on the cotton gin forever.

About that time, the new United States government was

Unexpected Repercussions

British author Ritchie Calder is considered a pioneer in the field of scientific journalism and is especially noted for his ability to communicate complex technical information in an engaging and understandable style. He also served as the Montague Burton Professor of International Relations at the University of Edinburgh in Scotland. In the following excerpt from his book The Evolution of the Machine, *Calder examines the unforeseen social effects of the creation of the cotton gin.*

The social implications of industrial machinery were greater than almost any of their inventors realized. Of the many machines of the Industrial Revolution which substituted mechanical effort for human drudgery, surely one of the most important was Eli Whitney's cotton gin. Few devices of any period have had such a dramatic impact on history. In 1793, while he was studying law in Savannah, Georgia, Whitney invented a simple and inexpensive apparatus that would remove the tough green seeds from the fibers of cotton. Until then it had been a nearly worthless crop, since to clean a single pound by hand took one man an entire day. Whitney's gin, operated by one man, could clean as much as fifty pounds a day, and because of it cotton suddenly became a cash crop. Production soared from about one hundred thousand bales per year in 1801 to more than five million bales by 1859.

The repercussions of Whitney's machine in human terms were something else again. Negro slavery, which had been slowly dying in the South since the Revolutionary War, quite rapidly became profitable for the planters. Whitney's little "laborsaving device" did as much as anything to encourage the entrenchment of a massive system of slave labor that only a long and bloody war would destroy. It would also leave on the human spirit and human society scars that are still apparent.

Ritchie Calder, *The Evolution of the Machine*, 1968.

looking for a manufacturer to provide 10,000 flintlock muskets in two years. The muskets got their name from a mechanism that locked a piece of flint in a small vise. Pulling the trigger caused the flint to strike a metal pan and create a spark. The spark ignited a small gunpowder trail that fired the main charge inside the gun barrel. Whitney had no background in making firearms, the most sophisticated product in the world. He had no factory, no raw materials, and no workers. Even well-established armories had never produced 5,000 muskets in one year. Whitney won the contract in June 1798 by offering the possibility of producing interchangeable parts. Interchangeability of parts appealed to the government because it would allow for easy manufacture and repair of the muskets.

Using money from 10 local investors, Whitney built a water-powered factory in New Haven. It did not have any particularly unique machinery, but Whitney hoped that a division of labor would improve production. Unlike his competitors, he did not have each worker make one musket from start to finish. He had his 50 workers making or assembling particular individual parts. Whitney broke the process into simple, easy-to-complete jobs. He was the first to use this method and had some problems getting it established. Although his contract eventually took 10 years to complete, Whitney completed a later one for 15,000 muskets in only two years. Stung by his experience with the cotton gin, Whitney never revealed the details of his factory. No descriptions or drawings were ever found.

Shortcomings and Successes

The first delivery of 500 muskets to the U.S. government came in 1801. To assure government officials that production was going well, Whitney conducted a well-publicized demonstration at the Capitol in January 1801. His audience included President John Adams, President-elect Thomas Jefferson, members of Congress, and other officials. In an attempt to show that he was making firearms with interchangeable parts, he fastened 10 different flintlock mechanisms to the same musket using only a screwdriver. The officials present were impressed and had no reason to believe the muskets had been specially prepared.

Whitney, however, had not disassembled the locks, mixed the parts, and then reassembled them. Jefferson said of the demonstration: "Mr. Whitney has invented molds and machines for making all the pieces of his locks so exactly equal, that take 100 locks to pieces and mingle their parts and the 100 locks may be put together as well by taking the first pieces which come to hand." In reality, no such demonstration had taken place.

The belief that Whitney had made interchangeable parts continued into the twentieth century. Then, in the 1960s, researchers noticed differences between written records and existing muskets. The physical evidence was unmistakable. Individual components had special identifying marks, something unnecessary for truly interchangeable parts. Also, Whitney muskets in collections such as those at the Smithsonian Institution do not have parts that interchange. It appears that Whitney purposely duped the government authorities.

In spite of that shortcoming, Whitney was still a technical pioneer. His division of labor was a landmark innovation. The government saved $25,000 a year after using it at two federal gun-making factories. Whitney also made the first milling machine worthy of the name. It was a tabletop device about the size of a bread box. Driven by a worm gear and screw thread, it had a multiple-edge cutting wheel and a movable work bed.

Whitney might have married Catharine Greene, if his partner Phineas Miller had not proposed to her first. Greene accepted Miller's offer. Whitney was 51 when he married Henrietta Edwards, a widow 20 years his junior. His unstable business life prevented him from marrying at an earlier age. His new wife brought her three children with her to the marriage, and Whitney finally had a normal domestic life.

Whitney suffered from an incurable abdominal ailment for many years. Before his death at 59, he made sure that his new family would control his factory. The Whitney Arms Co. remained a dominant manufacturer for 90 years, until the Winchester Repeating Arms Co. purchased it in 1888.

Robert Fulton and the Steamboat

Franklin M. Reck

Robert Fulton was not the first person to invent a working steamboat, author Franklin M. Reck admits in the following excerpt from *The Romance of American Transportation*. Rather, he explains, Fulton built upon the previous research and experiments of other inventors, identifying and correcting their mistakes in order to create the first commercially successful steamboat. According to the author, Fulton's *Clermont* was capable of maintaining an average speed of five miles an hour against the river's current, making it much faster and more reliable than previous steamboats. Reck has written widely on industry and transportation, including the books *Sand in Their Shoes: The Story of American Steel Foundries* and *The Dilworth Story: The Biography of Richard Dilworth, Pioneer Developer of the Diesel Locomotive*.

In no sense can Robert Fulton be called the inventor of the steamboat. Rather, he is the man who took the inventions and devices of others and combined them into the first commercially successful steamboat in the world.

A Series of Clues

When we read in our histories that in 1807 the *Clermont* made its maiden voyage from New York to Albany and back, we are likely to think that the builder, after a few months of secretive labor, unveiled to the world an undreamed-of miracle. This is so far from the truth that it will pay us to trace the train of events that led to the building of the *Clermont*. It is not a connected story. Rather it is like the clues picked up by a detective and put together to form a pattern.

The first clue is found in Lancaster County, Pennsylvania, where Fulton was born in 1765. A friend of Fulton's family, William Henry, had built a steamboat model and tried it out in a small stream. As a boy, Fulton had doubtless first heard the strange word "steamboat" used in connection with Henry's experiment.

But Fulton, as a young man, was not primarily interested in steamboats. He was interested in art. In 1786, when John Fitch was beginning his experiments with steam-powered boats on the Delaware River, Fulton was a miniature painter in Philadelphia, living only a few minutes' walk from the riverfront where Fitch's experimental skiff was moored. Whether Fulton showed any interest in it or not, nobody seems to know. But he must have heard it discussed.

The clues that follow are indirect. Fulton went to England in 1786 to study art under the American painter, Benjamin West, who was then living in England. But England was just swinging into the industrial age. James Watt was making steam engines, and Richard Arkwright and Samuel Crompton were operating textile factories. In this atmosphere Fulton's interest in art waned and his interest in engineering grew. Such devices as a machine for twisting hemp into rope, a machine for sawing marble, and a plan for raising and lowering canal boats over an inclined plane engaged his attention.

More important, during these years when Fulton was turning to mechanics, English inventors built and operated at least five experimental steamboats, and it is known that Fulton talked to one of them—a Lord Stanhope.

Then comes a definite clue linking Fulton to Fitch. In 1788 a Virginia man named James Rumsey came to England. Rumsey had written a pamphlet on steamboats and was conversant with all of Fitch's work. Fulton and Rumsey spent considerable time together, and it is reasonable to suppose that Fulton learned the story of Fitch's mistakes and successive attempts to correct them.

From this point on we must follow a new trail—a trail

that starts in the United States and leads to the Seine River, in Paris.

Stimulated by Fitch's heroic work, a number of Americans began experimenting with steamboats in the 1790's. The most significant one, from our standpoint, is Samuel Morey, who ran a stern-wheeler from Hartford, Connecticut, to New York, in 1794, making five miles per hour.

One of the men who inspected this boat was Robert R. Livingston, chancellor of the state of New York, the man who had administered the oath of office to George Washington in 1789. Livingston was a man of vision. He must have thought, as he rode on Morey's boat from New York to Greenwich, Connecticut, that here was an idea which would not die. Steamboats were the coming thing. And if they were the coming thing, why would it not be a good idea to obtain from New York the monopoly that had been granted to Fitch some years before?

So Livingston induced the state to revoke Fitch's monopoly and give it to him, on condition that he build a boat capable of

---

A Fast-Growing Industry

With Robert Fulton's success, steamboats quickly became a popular form of transportation, as Curtis P. Nettels describes in the following passage from The Emergence of a National Economy, 1775–1815. *Nettels taught history for many years at the University of Wisconsin and Cornell University.*

Before Robert Fulton died in 1815, he had designed twenty-one successful steamboats. He enlarged his later vessels, striving for greater capacity rather than speed. . . .

Fulton's success fired so many rivals that by 1815 steamboats were plying the principal rivers of the country and the public had accepted them as a godsend. . . . The Fulton party's preference for New York left the western traffic to builders who specialized in simple, high-pressure engines ideally suited to the Mississippi. Profits of steamboating at the outset were sometimes as high as 50 percent.

Curtis P. Nettels, *The Emergence of a National Economy, 1775–1815,* 1962.

making four miles an hour. He built the boat in 1798, but since it made only three miles an hour, the monopoly lapsed.

In 1801, Livingston was appointed United States Minister to the Court of Napoleon in France, and in this year the trails of Fulton and Livingston joined. Fulton was in Paris trying to interest Napoleon in his newest hobby, a submarine that actually submerged itself in the Seine, moved about under water, and rose again.

Fulton was considered by everybody a brilliant young man. His time was his own. Livingston, who was more determined than ever to build steamboats, went to Fulton. The result of their conversations was an agreement whereby Livingston was to advance £500 ($2,500) and Fulton was to build a trial boat on the Seine.

The trial boat, on the whole, was not successful. Fulton built the first hull too weak and it broke in two, sinking to the bottom of the Seine. The rebuilt boat, with a steam engine installed, was tried out on the Seine on August 9, 1803, and made a speed of only three and one-half miles an hour.

After this experience, Fulton decided to inspect the work of others. He took a short trip in a Scotch boat and made sketches of its machinery. He visited the consul, Aaron Vail, who had induced Fitch to come to France ten years before. Fulton borrowed Fitch's plans and kept them for several months. Finally, very wisely, he ordered a twenty-four horsepower steam engine from the foremost engine builders in the world, Matthew Boulton and James Watt of England.

That completes the pattern of clues behind the building of the *Clermont*. Isolated facts, many of them, but they show that the genius of many men went into the building of America's first commercially successful steamboat. Fulton's contribution was in selecting the best of what others had done, adding his own ideas, and combining them in one craft.

From Albany to New York and Back Again

The boat was tested on the East River on August 9, 1807, and began its historic trip to Albany at one o'clock on Monday afternoon, August 17. Forty men—investors in the company, Livingston and Fulton and their friends—stood in groups on the deck as the boat left its moorings in North River, near State's Prison.

Thousands of people lined the shore, craned their necks from windows, and sat perched upon the housetops. This immense New York crowd had heard about steamboats for seventeen years. They had read about one experiment after another. Their minds had changed from skepticism to doubt, and now, as the boat chuffed out into the Hudson, black smoke pouring from its thirty-foot stack, the last doubt disappeared and a roar of enthusiasm tumbled over the waters.

Here is the exact itinerary of that first voyage. The boat arrived at Clermont-on-the-Hudson, Chancellor Livingston's home 110 miles up the river, at one o'clock, just twenty-four hours after leaving New York. There the boat moored overnight—Tuesday night.

Wednesday morning at nine it left Clermont and arrived in Albany at five in the afternoon, going the forty-plus miles in eight hours. The total running time upstream was thirty-two hours, meaning that the boat had maintained an average speed of five miles per hour against the current.

Thursday morning at nine the boat left Albany, arriving at Clermont at six o'clock. An hour later it departed, arriving in New York at four on Friday morning. The running time downstream, thirty hours.

Robert Fulton

Although the boat must have appeared both awesome and magnificent to those thunderstruck men and women who lined the shore, it was in reality rather crude. The machinery in the center of the boat was entirely uncovered. The paddle wheels were unprotected. There were no cabins and no guardrails to prevent one from falling overboard.

As is usual with trial trips, this first voyage indicated changes to be made, and for several weeks Fulton was busy lengthening the boat, putting in cabins and berths, and decking over the boiler. An accurate description of the *Clermont* as she appeared on her first commercial trip, September 4, follows:

Her overall length was 150 feet and her beam 13 feet. She displaced 100 tons of water. Her prow was 26 feet high, of which all but two feet was above the water line. The bottom of the boat was of yellow pine plank, 1.5 inches thick, tongued and grooved and set together with white lead. Floors of oak and spruce were laid across the slightly curving hull. Two masts rose from the deck so that sail could be used to augment the engine when the wind was favorable.

Twelve berths were installed for the first voyage and all of them were taken at seven dollars per person. . . .

A Profitable Enterprise

Before winter set in that year, the boat, its accommodations enlarged, embarked with as many as ninety paying passengers. Since the expense of running the boat was not much more than twenty-five dollars a day, and a single passenger paid seven dollars for his ticket to Albany, it can be understood why the venture was considered profitable from the start.

The enlarged *Clermont* had a fore cabin containing sixteen berths, a great cabin with twenty-four berths, and a back cabin for ladies with twelve berths. Overflow passengers were accommodated on sofas. The regulations forbade passengers to go to bed with their shoes on, sit on tables, or smoke in any cabin except the fore cabin.

The age of the steamboat was under way.

Cyrus McCormick and the Mechanical Reaper

H.W. Brands

H.W. Brands is a professor of history at Texas A&M University in College Station and the coordinator of the History of the Americas Research Program. He is also the author of more than a dozen books on U.S. history and foreign relations, including *The Reckless Decade: America in the 1890s* and *The First American: The Life and Times of Benjamin Franklin.*

The following selection is taken from Brands's *Masters of Enterprise: Giants of American Business from John Jacob Astor and J.P. Morgan to Bill Gates and Oprah Winfrey.* He writes that Cyrus McCormick was the first inventor to apply the factory system to the manufacture of farm equipment. By greatly reducing the number of workers needed to harvest grain, the mechanical reaper enabled the United States to become the top producer of food in the world, the author concludes.

Over the course of more than two centuries, the United States would lead the world in any number of industries, from the fundamental (railroads, steel) to the sophisticated (microelectronics, pharmaceuticals). But in no industry was American preeminence more persistent than in the most fundamental industry of all: agriculture. From the middle of the nineteenth century to the end of the twentieth, America's farms proved a cornucopia of food and fiber that fed and clothed the American people and millions in other countries as well. This bounty, which made possible the modernization

Excerpted from *Masters of Enterprise: Giants of American Business from John Jacob Astor and J.P. Morgan to Bill Gates and Oprah Winfrey,* by H.W. Brands (New York: The Free Press, 1999). Copyright © 1999 by Simon and Schuster, Inc. Reprinted with permission.

of American society, was the work of ten million hands—and might have been the work of ninety million more if not for the cussedness of Cyrus McCormick. . . .

McCormick came by his orneriness honestly. His ancestors were Scotch-Irish, of those clans that had fought the English in Scotland, the Irish in Ireland, and the Indians on the American frontier. Cyrus' grandfather Robert, finding life into the Pennsylvania hinterland too confining, had moved southwest into the Valley of Virginia, as the Shenandoah Valley was then called. There he sired a son, also called Robert, who in turn produced a son, Cyrus, in 1809. Committed Calvinists, McCormick's people adhered to the doctrine that God helps those who help themselves; molded by generations of borderland conflict, they helped themselves to whatever they could lay hold of and defend. By 1830, when Cyrus turned twenty-one, his father had secured twelve hundred acres, which produced a profitable diversity of grain, fruit, timber and stone. Five children, including Cyrus, amplified Robert's own labor power; nine slaves magnified it still more.

But not enough. Robert, and now Cyrus, ran up against the fundamental problem of American economic life during the eighteenth and nineteenth centuries: Although blessed with abundant natural resources, the American colonies and then the American states were chronically short of labor. Native-born Americans did their best to alleviate the shortage by reproducing at a breathtaking pace; meanwhile immigrants poured in from overseas. But so immense were the resources available for development—the land area within American borders doubled in 1783 at the end of the American Revolutionary War, and again in 1803 with the Louisiana Purchase—that labor remained the critical constraint on the growth of the economy.

In such circumstances, a single invention could have an enormous effect. Eli Whitney's cotton gin, which in the 1790s mechanized the separation of cotton fibers from cotton seeds, opened up vast new reaches of the American South to cotton culture (a culture that included slavery, which thereby gained a new lease on life).

The Need for Large-Scale Cultivation

What the cotton gin was to the South, a mechanical reaper would be to the North. The principal impediment to the spread of commercial agriculture across the Ohio Valley and beyond was the inability of farm workers to cut more than about half an acre of wheat per laborer per day. Because wheat had the inconvenient habit of ripening all at once, and of falling to the ground and being lost within ten days or two weeks of coming ripe, wheat growers faced an annual harvest-time problem. In Europe, where hands were plentiful and labor correspondingly cheap, the problem could be solved by hiring more workers for the harvest. In America, where hands were few, the expense of hiring more workers drove costs to such levels as to prohibit large-scale cultivation. A person who could devise a method to multiply the labor power of the harvest workers would become a national hero, and wealthy besides.

Cyrus McCormick wasn't the only person to reach this conclusion, nor the first. Tinkerers in sheds and blacksmith shops all across the wheat-growing regions from New York to Illinois, and abroad as well, tried to improve on the sickle and the scythe, tools only marginally modified since the days when the Egyptians built their pyramids. Various inventors approximated success, but until the 1830s none had overcome the combined obstacles of bumpy, sloping and rock-strewn fields; horses and mules that took fright at the clattering contraptions chasing their tails; and skeptical customers—that is, farmers unwilling to bet the farm, in many cases literally, on expensive and as-yet-unproven machinery.

Cyrus McCormick had haunted the blacksmith shop on his father's farm from youth, both out of innate curiosity and as a way of avoiding field work; now he hammered together a working reaper. In 1831 he tested it on a neighbor's farm. Those who saw it accounted it "a right smart curious sort of thing"; McCormick, with the hindsight that comes from having several million dollars in one's pocket, later declared that he knew at once that this device would make his fortune. . . .

He tinkered further with his reaper, then sought a patent, which he received in 1834. New demonstrations went even better than the first; after one successful show, a U.S. senator from South Carolina and a future governor of Virginia jointly declared: "The cutting was rapid and extremely clean, scarcely a stalk of grain being left, and little, if any, being lost by shattering from the work of the machine." Other observers predicted that McCormick's reaper would be "an acquisition of value and importance to the general husbandry."

Curiously, the inventor's vision clouded. Part of the fog followed from bad harvests in the Shenandoah Valley, which for the next few years left farmers struggling to carry the debt load they already bore; new capital purchases were out of the question. Part of the problem was McCormick's quick mind, which spun off other novelties and schemes for making money. A plow designed especially for hillside work performed to favorable reviews and promising sales. An iron mine and smelter seemed a natural for a young man who grew up beating iron at his father's forge. But the plows never caught on outside McCormick's neighborhood, and, in the wake of the Panic of 1837, the iron mine turned out to be a hole in the ground down which his money disappeared.

Only in 1839 did McCormick go back to his reaper, and then chiefly under the pressure of a rival. Obed Hussey wore a patch over his left eye and a stern look on his face; whether one or both were the consequence of his earlier career whaling out of Nantucket, Massachusetts, this Ahab-looking Maine native didn't say. In time, Cyrus McCormick would become his Moby Dick; for now he honed his land-harpoon, a competing reaper. While McCormick was wasting time and money in iron, Hussey was winning customers in grain.

When McCormick learned of Hussey's success, he dusted off his reaper and bought advertising in the Richmond *Enquirer*. He declared that he was back in business and would be able to fill all orders in time for the 1840 harvest. The initial response was disappointing; in 1840 he sold just two machines. By his later admission—albeit not his contemporary claims—these models really weren't worth much, and he retired to his shop to craft improvements. When he reentered the market in 1842 he had a better product. He sold six reapers that year, twenty-nine the next.

Discovering the Western Market

In 1844 he took a trip that changed his life—and altered the course of American history. Until then his horizons had been limited, quite literally, by the ridges that enclosed the Valley of Virginia and framed the Allegheny–Appalachian uplift. In his thirty-sixth year he crossed the mountains onto the prairies that stretched to the Missouri River, and traversed that stream onto the plains that extended from there to the Rocky Mountains. As he gazed out across this vast open territory, the scales fell from his eyes. A reaper could be a convenience in the tight, enclosed fields of Virginia; on the ocean-like tracts of the West, it would be a necessity.

If McCormick had suffered from bad timing before, now he benefited from the opposite. Subsistence farmers had been living in the trans-Appalachian region since colonial times, but only with the opening of the Erie Canal in 1825 had market-minded farmers begun moving into the area. The arrival of the railroads in the 1830s and 1840s augmented the farmers' ability to get crops to market and encouraged additional settlement. Before the canals and especially the railroads, the most profitable way to market grain was often in a jug: Farmers distilled it into whiskey, which commanded a much higher price per pound. . . . The arrival of mechanized transport held out the possibility of shipping raw grain, or grain ground into flour, to the burgeoning cities of the East.

Events outside the grain-growing districts also conspired in McCormick's favor. The failure of the Irish potato crop drove up European demand for food imports from the United States. Partly as a result, the British government in 1846 repealed the Corn Laws, the protectionist measures that heretofore had kept out American grain ("corn," in the generic British sense). The discovery of gold in California in 1848 sent a flood of bullion back East, swelling the money supply and raising farm prices, even as it siphoned labor West, thereby making mechanization all the more imperative. . . .

To capture the rapidly growing western market, McCormick relocated to Chicago in 1848. He set up a factory in a three-story brick building of 10,000 square feet on the north bank of the Chicago River, with convenient access to both water and rail transport. In his factory he adopted the principle of interchangeable parts pioneered by Eli Whitney (to make guns rather than cotton gins), and he installed a steam engine to drive his lathes, saws and grinders. The result was one of the first examples of mass production—and one of the most impressive. . . .

McCormick's entry into mass production was a gamble, but a necessary one. His original patent was about to expire after a normal fourteen-year run; although he sought an extension, success in that endeavor could hardly be taken for granted. Indeed, his rivals, led by Hussey, did their best to block him. The case became a cat fight for editors and a growth industry for lawyers. "McCormick can be beaten in the Patent Office, and must be beaten now or never," asserted an attorney drumming up business for the opposition. "If funds are furnished us, we shall surely beat him; but if they are not furnished, he will as certainly beat us. Please, therefore, take hold and help us to beat the *common enemy.* The subscriptions have ranged from $100 to $1,000." McCormick's opponents in the press contended that he had made enough money from his monopoly, and that to extend it would, as one indignant writer put it, "impose a tax of $500,000 a year upon the starving people of the world." McCormick battled on, even as the odds against him mounted; years elapsed while the future of an emerging industry hung in the balance. Finally the commissioner of patents delivered praise and an unfavorable verdict: "He will live in the grateful recollection of mankind as long as the reaping-machine is employed in gathering the harvest. But the Reaper is of too great value to the public to be controlled by any individual, and the extension of his patent is refused."

A less determined individual than McCormick might have retreated under this blow; instead he redoubled his efforts and drove forward. To the surprise of many—although apparently not McCormick—his short-run defeat became the basis for his long-term success, even as it vindicated the wisdom of the patent system. In his fourteen years of exclusive rights, McCormick had been able to perfect his design; now he had to best the competition by superior production, distribution and service. His ability to do so was what separated him from most other inventors and made his success not merely a technological triumph but an industrial one. Indeed, McCormick's accomplishment (and that of those who followed him) was nothing less than to industrialize agriculture. He was the first to bring the factory system to the production of farm equipment; this, in turn, by making the reaper and its successors available to millions of farmers, brought the factory system to the production of farm crops. When machines replaced humans in the fields, productivity rose, prices fell and consumers—meaning everyone who ate— benefited. . . .

Politics and Business

McCormick's growing fame, together with his success in creating an organization that ran without his direct oversight, allowed him to broaden his activities. As one of the leading citizens of Chicago he was frequently mentioned as a mayoral candidate; in 1860 he agreed to throw his hat into the ring. He lost his race, but not so badly that he didn't make a run for Congress in 1864—also unsuccessfully.

The chief political issue of the early 1860s was, of course, the Civil War. As a Southerner transplanted to the North (in 1860 he still owned slaves in Virginia), not to mention a businessman with sales on both sides of the Mason-Dixon Line, McCormick found his loyalties divided. He at first opposed the forcible preservation of the Union, an attitude that caused the *Chicago Tribune* to brand him a "rebel." Expedience, if not necessarily conviction, eventually prompted him to print a public declaration of allegiance to the Union. . . .

Even as it raised questions about his politics, the Civil War worked wonders for McCormick's business. By 1868 production reached 8000 machines per year, and it continued to grow. Yet what the Civil War did for McCormick Harvester was no more—and in some ways much less—than what McCormick Harvester did for the Civil War. Ironically for a Southern sympathizer who abhorred the idea of conflict between his native region and his adopted one, Mc-

Cormick contributed materially to the North's ability to crush the South. Abraham Lincoln's secretary of war, Edwin Stanton, explained: "The reaper is to the North what slavery is to the South. By taking the place of regiments of young men in the western harvest fields, it releases them to do battle for the Union at the front and at the same time keeps up the supply of bread for the Nation and the Nation's armies. Thus without McCormick's invention, I fear the North could not win and the Union would be dismembered.". . .

In 1871 McCormick's factory burned down, along with the rest of Chicago. Retirement tempted, but McCormick resisted. He rebuilt the factory, larger than before, and pushed production to new records. In the process he became famously rich. Company profits rose from $65,000 in 1849 to $1.2 million in 1880. By his death in 1884 he was one of the wealthiest persons in America.

Until the end, he was as combative as always. "Nettie," he told his wife, "life *is* a battle." No victory could be complete; the struggle never ended. Yet as he rode across the prairies and plains in his private rail car, he must have allowed that he had triumphed as far as anyone could in a continually evolving economy. One measure of his success was what were aptly called "factory farms," enormous spreads where hundreds of machines worked tens of thousands of acres, producing millions of bushels of wheat that would never have been planted, let alone harvested, without the kinds of machines McCormick made.

Another measure of his accomplishment awaited him on his return to Chicago. By bringing industry to the farm, Mc-Cormick also brought the farm to industry. Cheap food fueled the growth of Chicago and other cities, where those ninety-million hands that might have been working on farms were employed in shops and factories. McCormick's machines harvested grain; in the bargain they sowed modern America.

Samuel Morse and the Telegraph

Brooke Hindle

In the following excerpt from his book *Emulation and Invention*, Brooke Hindle relates the story of Samuel Morse's invention of the telegraph, the first device that allowed for instantaneous communication over long distances. According to the author, Morse's accomplishment is even more spectacular because he was not a scientist or technician but a prominent artist who turned to technological experimentation relatively late in his career. Historian emeritus for the National Museum of American History of the Smithsonian Institution in Washington, D.C., Hindle is the author of *The Pursuit of Science in Revolutionary America, 1735–1789* and the coauthor of *Engines of Change: The American Industrial Revolution, 1790–1860*.

The electromagnetic telegraph, like the steamboat, was something new under the sun. It was not an improvement within an existing technology, and it was not a combination of existing capabilities put together in answer to a clear social need. It appeared when it did because not until then had it been possible. The door was opened by the new knowledge of electricity developed by André-Marie Ampère and Hans Christian Oersted and of electromagnetism by William Sturgeon and Joseph Henry. This understanding was the precondition for the telegraph, and consequently it has been labeled the first science-based invention, although scientists were outnumbered by others who sought to rush through the door opened by the new knowledge. Indeed, in the United States and throughout the non-British world, an

Excerpted from *Emulation and Invention*, by Brooke Hindle (New York: New York University Press, 1981). Copyright © 1981 by New York University Press. Reprinted with permission.

artist became identified with the invention of the telegraph, Samuel Finley Breese Morse.

Morse's system of telegraphy was the first to succeed in America where it rapidly overcame competing systems, and it spread to much of the rest of the world. Yet Morse was neither a scientist nor a mechanic; he might be described as the most prominent American artist of his day. A talented painter with accomplishments and potential well beyond those of Robert Fulton, he was president of the National Academy of Design and professor of the literature of the arts of design at New York University—the first professor of art in the country. How could a recognized art professor turn away from art and succeed in using new scientific capabilities to create a genuinely new technology? . . .

Beginnings as an Artist

To begin with, Morse had a favored background, although not one that ostensibly encouraged either art or technology. His father, the Reverend Jedediah Morse, was one of the intellectual leaders of the Congregational church. Yet he had also achieved creative success in a distinctly visual or spatial field—geography. His pioneering American geographies so captured the school market that his son was nicknamed "Geography" Morse. Moreover, when Finley, as he was known in the family, manifested an early talent for art, his father supplied him with drawing paper and then with a camera obscura. Both parents were warm, supportive of Finley and his two younger brothers, and flexible in their own expectations. From this home, all the boys emerged with religious conviction, patriotic dedication, and a strong sense of rectitude; Finley was especially marked by an irrepressible drive to succeed.

At Yale College, he developed in unexpected directions. In contrast to his brothers who followed him there, Finley was never a good student, especially not in Latin or literature, graduating a year late in 1810. He did enjoy his science courses: chemistry with Benjamin Silliman, in which he made models of the batteries demonstrated; electricity with Jeremiah Day; and formal assistance in electrical experiments under Sereno Dwight. Even more he enjoyed hunting, brandy, cigars, and dancing, with the unavoidable result of continuing indebtedness. He also made extracurricular excursions into art, painting a mural in his room depicting *Freshmen Climbing the Hill of Science* and undertaking a series of miniatures for college friends and townspeople, spurred by the opportunity to apply the proceeds to the reduction of his debts.

Morse left college knowing the road he wanted to travel; he was, he reported, "made for a painter.". . . Morse's parents demurred for a time, convincing him to try employment with a bookseller in their hometown of Charlestown, Massachusetts. . . .

As he fretted, he painted: a watercolor of his family, an oil of *The Landing of the Pilgrims at Plymouth*, and a couple of others. They were enough to convince his parents that his talent might be developed. [He] sailed for England, funded by his father. In London, all he had hoped for seemed confirmed, especially when he came under the tutelage of Benjamin West, who appeared to Morse, as he had to Fulton, the ideal model of American success in art. . . .

This expanding dream came to an abrupt end when, after four years, Jedediah wrote that he could no longer support his son's studies. Morse returned home to engage in what by then had come to seem an improbable quest. . . . In America, no earlier artist had made a successful career of historical painting, the only pursuit Morse saw as acceptable. He believed that this was not merely a personal goal but one that his country must make possible for its own fulfillment.

With all his vigor and imagination, both of which he possessed in large measure, Morse launched a heroic effort, but the exhibition of his *Dying Hercules* in Boston and in his rented studio in Charlestown did not awaken the support he needed. The direct approach failing, he undertook, as a temporary reliance for subsistence, what turned out to be a long career in portraiture. In Boston, Concord, the Connecticut Valley, and Charleston, South Carolina, he found good markets for his portraits. . . .

Through several years after his return from Europe, Morse remained uncertain whether or not he was gaining on his goal. Once he thought of studying for the ministry but decided against it. Then he did carry through some serious efforts in a wholly different field—mechanical invention. Wealth from patenting an invention had become an appealing dream to many. For a time, for example, a rash of truss bridge patents was granted to inventors who recognized the financial rewards that might come to the man who designed a cheaper way to make railroad bridges. Morse and his brother Sidney experimented briefly with steamboat designs and then turned to a new pump, intended primarily for use in hand-operated fire engines. He had little success in selling this "flexible-piston pump.". . .

Inventing remained a possible route to wealth and acclaim, but, sticking with art for the moment, Morse in 1825 transferred his base to New York City, by then the great metropolis and the center of the largest American art community. . . . He moved easily into the circle of William Cullen Bryant, James Fenimore Cooper, and Richard Henry Dana, and he quickly became the leader of a vigorous group of young, practicing artists. . . .

He became active in the New York Athenaeum and was asked to deliver its annual series of lectures for 1826 in the Chapel of Columbia College. These he worked upon assiduously, conscious that they were the first course of lectures on art ever given in the country, and he was rewarded with general approbation. Always linking acclaim with wealth, he reported, "reputation in abundance is flowing in upon me which in the end will, with the Blessing of Providence, be wealth." Indeed, by 1829 his portrait painting and teaching permitted him to pay off most of his debts and to collect enough advance commissions to sail again for Europe, where he studied and worked for nearly three years.

He returned in 1832 with refreshed spirit and renewed hope for developing the support required to paint great paintings. . . .

Transition from Art to Science

Then the brightest opportunity yet to appear arose with the decision in 1837 to embellish architect Charles Bulfinch's new

Rotunda in the national Capitol with four giant historical canvases, each painted by a different artist. In Morse's mind, and indeed in the minds of his peers, there was little reason to doubt that he must be one of the four—but the congressional committee passed him by in a crushing blow to all of his dreams. He lost much more than the $10,000 commission, retiring to his bed from which he could see no hope through the blackness. Not even his friends' private subscription of $3,000 toward any painting he might choose to do roused him more than temporarily. His son Edward insisted that this disaster gave the "Death blow to his artistic ambition."

It might not have been so except that another enthusiasm had already begun to capture him. Morse always believed that the "flash of genius" in which he conceived the idea of the telegraph occurred aboard the *Sully* during his 1832 return voyage to the United States. Under the impression that he was the first to whom the idea of the electric telegraph had occurred, he was able to describe the moment of conception precisely and to find fellow passengers who fully confirmed his memory. A shipboard conversation on Ampère's experiments with the electromagnet had led to the question of whether the speed of electricity was retarded by the length of the wire. Dr. Charles T. Jackson, Boston chemist and later claimant to the discovery of anesthesia, was in a position to reply. He responded that it was not, that electricity passed instantly over any length of wire.

Morse immediately saw his vision and declared, "I see no reason why intelligence might not be instantaneously transmitted by electricity to any distance." This he believed to be the true invention—although he later learned that others had seen substantially the same possibility before him and that experimentation with forms of an electric telegraph was even then under way. . . .

Morse came to electricity with some understanding of the field and with an awakened interest. Most recently, he had enjoyed the 1827 lectures on electromagnetism given by James Freeman Dana of Columbia College in the same New York Athenaeum series in which he had lectured. But he did not bring the set of mind of a scientist and did not seek to study electricity as a science. He approached the telegraph as he had the steamboat and the water pump, seeking to discover only enough of the principles involved to design a good, working system. The primary strength he brought to the telegraph was an excellent design capability based upon a mind practiced in forming and re-forming multiple elements into varying complexes. This sort of synthetic-spatial thinking is required in its most unalloyed form in painting or in sculpture where analytic, logical, verbal, or arithmetic thinking plays almost no role. Synthetic-spatial thinking is, of course, involved in most intellectual activity including science, but in technology it has to be central. Morse's mind was well practiced in this essential.

The balance of the ocean crossing he spent thinking about a system composed of elements that his limited knowledge opened to him. He did not then explore the "state of the art": how to build the best battery, how to design the best electromagnet, or how best to insulate the wire; he asked himself the big questions. What form of intelligence, for example, was it possible to transmit by electricity? First he thought of transposing directly the kind of code used in the 1792 Chappe semaphore telegraph. Instead of different semaphore arm settings, each equated with a number and combinations of numbers keyed to words, Morse saw that he might transmit short bursts of electricity and longer bursts, separated by intervals between the bursts. He called the bursts dots and lines, later rendered as dots and dashes, and played around with different combinations that might stand for each number. The possibility of coding each letter in dots and dashes did occur to him, but the notebook in which he recorded his thoughts gives no evidence that he then experimented with letter coding.

This form of intelligence transmission opened the way to the simplest possible circuitry. A single circuit would do, with some means for opening and closing it at one end and for detecting and reading or recording the signal at the other end. Thus he avoided the multiplication of circuits other telegraphic systems required, in some cases a separate circuit for each letter. . . .

Morse's shipboard sketches, recorded in a small notebook, display graphically the character of his thinking. They show his ability to conceptualize all the elements of a complete telegraphic system and to design alternative components. They reveal at this stage no input of analytic science or projected circuit parameters and quantitative performance. Indeed, they resemble remarkably the spatial images recorded in his travel notebooks of the scenes, costumes, and technology he encountered.

Making the Vision Reality

Morse had reason to congratulate himself upon having designed an electromagnetic telegraph before the ship docked—even though he had given little attention to the materials or manner of construction of the electrical components. To his brothers, he spilled over with enthusiasm, convincing Sidney that, at last, fortune might be within their grasp. . . .

Over several years, Morse and his colleagues worked on numerous trials, experiments, and designs—although at a very uneven rate. He was nearly always hobbled for funding. A concentrated development effort and an extended trial were imperative, but Morse might have attained neither without the large outside support finally provided by Congress. In 1840 Morse patented the telegraph. . . . Washington demonstrations went well and good responses were received, but the seemingly endless waiting stretched again into months. Finally on March 3, 1843, the act was signed granting Morse $30,000 for a trial of his telegraph between Washington and Baltimore. . . .

The actual construction of the line from Washington to Baltimore was a continuing learning experience, most of it unplanned. The whole process was difficult precisely because there was no significant pool of electrical technology to draw upon. Morse had learned that he did not need two wires to complete the circuit but could ground his system and use the earth for the return. He did not, however, know how to construct the line economically, and the initial decision to bury insulated wire encased in lead pipes turned out to be wrong. A patent pipe was contracted for, and Ezra Cornell [was brought] into the enterprise at this point. Cornell was a roving plow salesman with a contriving mind that led him to design a plow on the spot that would open the ground, lay the lead pipe, and close the trench in one operation.

By the time contracting, personal, and personnel problems were overcome and nine miles of encased wire laid, $23,000 of the $30,000 had been spent. Then only was it discovered that the wire in the pipe shorted out uncontrollably and that there was no way to insulate it satisfactorily. Cornell urged stringing uninsulated wire on poles—an old idea—but apparently Charles G. Page, examiner in the Patent Office, was the first to try to convince Morse of it. This solution worked well, the unneeded pipe was sold, and the wire already on hand was applied to the task. The line was completed within the appropriation.

It was complete from Washington to Annapolis Junction by May 1, 1844, when the Whig party National Convention met in Baltimore. Morse made the most of a dramatic opportunity by stationing his colleague Alfred Vail at Annapolis Junction to telegraph news to him in Washington as soon as received by train from Baltimore. He thus was able to break to the sitting Congress word of the Clay-Frelinghuysen ticket—word very quickly confirmed when the train got to town. The first message over the completed line from Washington to Baltimore was sent on May 24, "What hath God wrought?" opening the way to still further drama when the Democratic Convention met in Baltimore the following day. Morse in this case was able to report to Congress the unexpected nomination of James K. Polk and to the convention the unexpected declination of the vice-presidential nominee, Silas Wright. Now at last the telegraph was a success before the world. Surely the obvious benefits would follow and the fortune Morse always sought seemed within reach.

Even then, nothing came to him automatically. After the agonizing difficulties of designing and redesigning the telegraph, of painfully pursuing the Congress, and of fighting on all fronts to put the trial system together, Morse was anxious to sell the telegraph to Congress and withdraw. . . . He believed that the best social use of the telegraph called for government ownership and operation.

He therefore plotted a new course designed to permit him to withdraw from the immediate frictions of planning and management while the government purchase was pursued. He readily accepted Amos Kendall's offer to take over these tasks he so disliked. Kendall, an astute and honest man, had been a member of Andrew Jackson's "kitchen cabinet" and then postmaster general. . . . After Congress voted $8,000 to permit Morse to run the telegraph for a year, Kendall gave one more try at selling the telegraph to the government.

When he, too, failed, he turned to the founding of a network of companies to build and operate lines, most of them radiating out of New York. . . . The Magnetic Telegraph Company was formed on May 15, 1845, to build the line from New York to Philadelphia, and others followed, providing links from New York to Boston, New York to Buffalo, Philadelphia to Pittsburgh, and Washington to Mobile. The traffic rose slowly on the early lines, but it was enough to extend a handsome promise. Brokers, lottery agents, various businessmen, and newspapers began to realize their great need for instant communication.

The networks were filled in amid financial conflict, patent suits, and a continuing evolution of the technology. The telegraph that came to prevail in the United States and most of the world was founded on the simple, durable system contrived by Morse.

Thomas Edison and the Electrical Lighting System

Thomas Parke Hughes

Thomas Parke Hughes is a professor emeritus in the department of the history and sociology of science at the University of Pennsylvania in Philadelphia. His books include *Thomas Edison: Professional Inventor*, *American Genesis: A Century of Invention and Technological Enthusiasm, 1870–1970*, and *Networks of Power: Electrification in Western Society, 1880–1930*. In the following article, he describes Thomas Edison's invention of the incandescent electrical lightbulb. Edison's electric light was vastly superior to gas lighting, the author notes, but since most buildings were not yet wired for electricity, Edison realized that he also needed to create an entire system of electrical power stations to encourage the widespread adoption of his new device.

At the same time that Thomas Alva Edison flourished, the United States emerged upon the world scene as the great technological nation. This simultaneity was not altogether accidental, for Edison drew upon the sustaining environment and, at the same time, helped create it. His most fruitful years were those spent at Menlo Park, New Jersey, from 1876 to 1886, which was about the time America rose to preeminence in invention and industry. By 1890 the United States led the world in the number of patents granted and in its iron and steel production. Furthermore, its production of coal—the basic fuel and an important chemical—ranked second to none. Of the many inventive Americans in this productive era, Edison was the most prolific with no less than 500 patents by 1885 and with hundreds more to follow. Not

Excerpted from "Thomas Alva Edison and the Rise of Electricity," by Thomas Parke Hughes, *Technology in America: A History of Individuals and Ideas*, edited by Carroll W. Pursell (Cambridge, MA: The MIT Press, 1990). Copyright © 1990 by The MIT Press. Reprinted with permission.

only did he have the largest number of patents, but the devices and processes they covered were financially rewarding and technologically impressive.

No wonder that Edison was the American hero of the Gilded Age. Newspaper coverage showed him to be one of the most interesting of men to Americans, and a popular poll conducted during his lifetime revealed him as the man that Americans most admired. Americans of his generation liked and admired him because he had risen from humble circumstances to a position of affluence and fame and because he provided them the material needs and pleasures for which many had come to the New World.

Humble Beginnings

Born in 1847 in Milan, Ohio, a Midwestern town earning its living from a canal and from the processing and shipping of agricultural products, Edison was the son of a small manufacturer of wood shingles and of a schoolteacher. Later, the family moved to Port Huron, Michigan, and there, at age 12, he became a traveling candy and newspaper "butcher" (salesman) on the railway to Detroit, setting up his small laboratory for science experiments in the baggage car. This episode and other activities of young Edison became national folklore after his world fame provoked a host of biographies. Parents urged their children to emulate him, and, through him, these parents lived vicariously the American dream.

The anecdotes, once so well known, now recede into the background of the American past as a more worldly America seeks other representative types and even anti-heroes. So we should briefly recall that the laboratory on the car to Detroit had a fire that compelled young Edison to experiment elsewhere. Also we might remember that he was introduced to the telegraph by a grateful operator whose small son Edison had pushed from the path of an oncoming train. And that his partial deafness began to isolate the young man from his immediate environment and turned him toward introspection. To understand him, we should note his *Wanderjahre* [time of wandering] as journeyman telegraph operator, for he learned not only the art of survival in a tumultuous and demanding world, but a great deal about electricity. He was thought a bit odd by his fellow operators for choosing to stage experiments according to the precepts of the great Michael Faraday, whom Edison much admired and deeply read, instead of joining his fellows in a night on the town, wherever that might have been for the highly mobile telegraphers.

By 1868 he was working for Western Union in Boston, and there he committed himself to invention. At first his inventing could only be during off hours, but he found time to build and patent an automatic vote recorder for which he could find no market. (He later said that it was then he decided to identify a market always before he invented—an obvious strategy employed by most professional inventors, then and now.) No amateur, and determined to live by his new profession, Edison journeyed to New York in 1869. With him he carried ideas for improvements in telegraph systems and a sharp eye and a clear head for opportunity. Opportunities opened to him shortly when chance allowed him to repair a Wall Street printing telegraph at a time when its price quotations were badly needed. Subsequent support from the grateful owner, who was well connected in the telegraph business, gave Edison an entree. Less familiar are accounts of the intricate business and technological activities in which he became involved as he invented telegraph improvements, including a quadruplex design, for several, even competing, telegraph companies. When Western Union fell into the hands of Jay Gould, the notorious financier and waterer of stock, Edison said his kind of inventiveness was no longer needed there, so he became an independent inventor, choosing his own problems, making his own inventions, and forming new companies to market them. In 1870 he had set up a telegraph manufacturing shop and laboratory in Newark, New Jersey; in 1876 when he decided to become an independent inventor, he drew upon his capital and his growing reputation to fulfill a vision—the establishment of an invention enterprise or, as some said, an invention factory.

He chose Menlo Park, a lonely site on the Pennsylvania Railroad between New York City and Philadelphia, which as bases of supply and ready markets were only an hour or so away by train. But at Menlo Park, unlike the cities, there was a freedom from worldly distraction and an invitation to concentration. Edison realized this as he moved old experienced aides such as John Kreusi, the machinist and ingenious model maker, from the Newark shop and brought in new ones who would have to learn the Edison style and absorb the deep commitment to inventing a method of invention.

The compound at Menlo Park was both cozy and workmanlike. The buildings provided the resources needed by a professional inventor, and Edison soon became known as the Wizard of Menlo Park. Within a few years of settling at the new site, Edison had a building for an office and a technical and scientific library (long series of the world's leading journals were housed there for the seekers of ideas about the state of the art), as well as another large building that housed on its two floors a remarkably well-provided chemical laboratory, an electrical testing facility, and, initially, a machine shop. (Later, the machine shop—the producer of electrical and mechanical models, small and full-scale—was separately housed.) After Edison concentrated upon the invention of a system of electric light, small buildings for blowing the glass bulbs and for obtaining the filament carbon were added. A carpentry shop rounded out the facilities. When the invention factory was built and full of life, a number of watercolors and drawings captured the public imagination by portraying it snow-covered, suggestive of a bountiful Santa Claus and his busy elves. In fact, the place worked more like a center for advanced invention. . . .

Choosing a Project

Edison was the leader of an invention and development group (today it would be labelled research and development), but he was also something more—an inventor-entrepreneur. Only a few men today attempt to carry such a broad range of responsibilities as designated by the term inventor-entrepreneur. Edison not only presided over invention and development, but he also took part in financing, publicizing, and marketing for the project. His most famous project, the electric light system, serves well to illustrate the point.

To choose a problem or a project is a critical decision for an independent inventor; an inventor hired by a corporation usually has guidelines explicitly defined or implicitly revealed by the vested interests of the corporation or agency for which he works. Edison decided, for complex reasons, to expend his resources upon the electric light project in 1878. Friends in science and engineering told him that the state of the art in incandescent lighting suggested that practical achievement might be near. Technical periodicals and patents also signalled activity in incandescent lighting. Such information alerted Edison to the possibility that he might solve the remaining critical problems—such as a durable filament—that would make the difference between ingenious tinkering and commercial success. He had confidence in his ability to solve electric lighting problems because, like so many professional inventors, he knew his characteristics and drew upon the experiences that had helped shape them. In short, he was, after years of work on the telegraph, an expert on electrical matters. The electromagnetic phenomena of the telegraph, the electrochemistry of the battery, the fine mechanics of the relay, and the laws of circuitry, all had relevance to the new endeavor, if one could transfer, adapt, and invent by analogy.

Another reason for working on electric light was the nature of Menlo Park itself, both its physical and personnel resources. For its day Menlo Park represented a considerable investment of resources and, as a result, it had substantial momentum. It had mass, movement, and direction. Therefore, certain problems could be solved best at Menlo Park, and others better elsewhere. Edison and his advisers realized that the problem of inventing and developing an electric lighting system suited Menlo Park, for a system involved electromagnetic machines (generators), delicate apparatus (switches, fixtures, controls, incandescent lamps, and so on), and complex circuitry. Because of the diversity of problems posed by the varied components, the complex of facilities and people at Menlo Park could be advantageously employed. The system required the repeated testing and experimentation for which Menlo Park and its men were also well suited. Most important, a system of electric lighting needed vision, planning, and coordination for which Edison had a genius and for which Menlo Park was designed.

Before finally committing himself, he had to define the market and to identify the financial resources. Edison, who often thought in analogies, saw that an incandescent lighting system was like a gas one, and he knew that gas lighting thrived commercially. Therefore he would be following the less risky course of improving, instead of introducing, a product or service. To make sure, he commissioned a survey of gas lighting use in the thickly populated Wall Street district of New York City. There the deep, man-made canyons between the office buildings and the thousands of offices within needed artificial light. It was not by coincidence that he focused upon offices owned by men such as J.P. Morgan, who had the funds to finance Edison's project—and did.

The Edison Electric Light Company

The project needed a business and financial structure as well as the technological one provided by Menlo Park. So with the advice of Grosvenor P. Lowrey, whose strong characteristics as an experienced business and financial entrepreneur nicely rounded out his own, Edison established in the fall of 1878 the Edison Electric Light Company. Its purpose was to fund the inventive enterprise of Edison insofar as it pertained to electric light and power, and to promote throughout the world the adoption of the patented inventions. There is much to be learned about the art of technological innovation from the constitution of this company. Edison's investment, for which he received stock, was his form of capital—his patents. He assigned to the company for five years all of his patents in the general category of electric lighting and power. J.P. Morgan and other financiers contributed their resources—cash. He awarded his most valued staff members stock in other companies which were soon established. These companies manufactured components and performed services that would be needed in the Edison system of electric lighting. (Unlike some organizers, Edison did not impose an administrative structure upon the creative concept.) The companies institutionalized the various components, or functions, of the system: the Edison Electric Illuminating Company of New York (1880), founded to preside over the first demonstration central station; the Edison Machine Works (1881) to manufacture the generators; the Edison Lamp Works (1880); the (Edison) Electric Tube Company (1881) to make the underground conductors for the distribution systems; and Bergmann & Company to produce electric light accessories. Other inventors who came into the lighting field were often willing to modify the designs of existing generators or to turn over manufacture of components to companies not under their direction and control.

The history of the invention of the Edison electric lighting system is well known and need not be repeated in detail

---

Better Lighting

In the following excerpt from American Made: Men Who Shaped the American Economy, *Harold C. Livesay discusses Thomas Edison's search for a better type of artificial light.*

The arc light had been in use since the 1850s, illuminating streets and lighthouse beacons, but had inherent disadvantages—glare, obnoxious fumes, and the need for frequent adjustment—that made it impractical for use indoors. Inventors on both sides of the Atlantic struggled to eliminate these quirks, but Thomas Edison's nimble mind leapt to another track altogether. He would make light not through an electrical arc—that is, passing a current across a gap from one conductor to another—but by incandescence: that is, passing a current through a continuous conductor of sufficient resistance to glow. . . .

When Edison started his search, indoor lighting depended on the burning of candles, coal gas, or kerosene. Only the latter two were economical on a large scale, but both had objectionable features. They shed a feeble light and smelled. Both were fire hazards. . . .

So, the market was there and Edison went after it.

Harold C. Livesay, *American Made: Men Who Shaped the American Economy,* 1979.

here. It should be pointed out, however, that far too much emphasis in most accounts has been placed on the search for—and testing of—the lamp filament. This stress distracts attention from the essence of Edison's genius. He wrote of his approach:

> It was not only necessary that the lamps should give light and the dynamos generate current, but the lamps must be adapted to the current of the dynamos, and the dynamos must be constructed to give the character of current required by the lamps, and likewise all parts of the system must be constructed with reference to all other parts, since, in one sense, all the parts form one machine, and the connections between the parts being electrical instead of mechanical. Like any other machine the failure of one part to cooperate properly with the other part disorganizes the whole and renders it inoperative for the purpose intended.
>
> The problem then that I undertook to solve was stated generally, the production of the multifarious apparatus, methods and devices, each adapted for use with every other, and all forming a comprehensive system. . . .

Rarely does one find so succinctly stated a systematic approach to invention.

By September 1882 the system had been conceived, designed, patented, and tested on a small scale at Menlo Park. The equipment had been manufactured by the various Edison companies. The first Edison central station for public supply was then placed into operation, serving, as planned, New York's Wall Street district with about a one-mile radius. The Pearl Street Station had six steam engines, driving six Edison Jumbo generators, each capable of supplying 1,200 16-candlepower lamps. Within a year, about 8,000 Edison lamps were being supplied from a 110-volt distribution system. The world celebrated its first central station's technical success.

Financial reports show, however, that for the first few years the Pearl Street Station sold electricity at a loss. This was sustained for several reasons. Foremost was the consideration that Pearl Street served as a demonstration plant to interest local civic leaders and financiers throughout the country and abroad in buying the licenses to operate an exclusive franchise and the equipment of a central station similar to Pearl Street. Another reason was the valid assumption that as service was improved, customers were added, unit fixed-costs were lowered, and various economies were achieved through rationalization, the operation would then become profitable. It did, before fire destroyed the historic station in January 1890. By then, there were Edison stations in large cities and small towns throughout the world. The era of the Edison direct-current station had been established; this era in the 1890s gave way to that of the alternating or polyphase station serving a larger area with both power and light over high-voltage systems. Thomas Edison did not demonstrate the flexibility to make the transition.

Later Years

Edison's period of brilliance passed with the triumph at Pearl Street. He lived and worked on until 1931, adding to this long list of inventions and patents, and making substantial innovations, but his later contributions to the technology of motion pictures, magnetic ore separation, portland cement manufacture, the storage battery, and the derivation of rubber from indigenous American plants lacked the incisive insight and the dramatic rendition of his work on quadruplex telegraph, the telephone transmitter, and the early phonograph, all of which—like the lighting system— came before 1882. . . .

Between 1882 and 1892 he lost influence in his electrical manufacturing companies, and he finally sold out his stock in the enterprises and saw them consolidated in 1892 not as Edison General Electric, but as simply General Electric. . . .

Despite the lack of brilliance surrounding later projects such as the storage battery, Edison rode the crest of public acclaim until, by the time of his death, he approached the status of a secular saint, a representative to masses of Americans of the best in the American character. They saw him as a plain-spoken, self-educated, practical-minded, eminently successful, native genius. They believed him an inspired empiricist, both an experimenter and tinkerer. He was an American success story—that of a hardworking, hard-nosed, down-to-earth man who provided material in abundance for an upwardly mobile society. The public wanted more of him than inventions; his pronouncements about education, religion, and other general questions commanded front-page newspaper space and became oracular statements for countless admirers.

In fact, Edison was more complex. He spoke plainly when raising money from Wall Street financiers who distrusted long-haired scientists; he was self-educated, but his reading included the classics of Western literature and the notebooks of Michael Faraday; he was eminently successful, but not simply because he had inventive genius; and, truly, he practiced the art of the experimenter with consummate skill, but he also knew the science of his day and used it to formulate hypotheses and organize experimental data. . . . Long before professional public relations perfected image-making, Edison presented to the world an inventor whom it would support and a hero whom it needed.

During his lifetime the center of industrial research moved from Menlo Park into the General Electric, Bell Telephone, and DuPont Laboratories. Men with advanced degrees in science working in the laboratories did not simply use the available science to solve their technological problems; they generated the science as needed. Americans, by the time of Edison's death, began to look to men in white coats bending over microscopes as images of the new research and development bringing "better things for better living."

Despite his limitations, however, Edison was nonetheless a representative American and a key to understanding its late 19th-century character, when it became the world's leading technological and industrial power. America, then, had moved beyond steamboats, railroads, and textile mills; it had not yet reached the stage of automatic controls, missiles, and computers. Edison possessed just the touch to provide the lights and sounds that brought a sense of well-being, even affluence, to hard-working people still laboring on the construction site that was young America.

Henry Ford and the Automobile

Thomas V. DiBacco

In the following selection from his book *Made in the U.S.A.: The History of American Business*, Thomas V. DiBacco traces the remarkable career of Henry Ford, who popularized the automobile in the United States. At the beginning of the twentieth century, DiBacco explains, automobiles were still considered luxury items to be enjoyed only by the rich. However, the author writes, Ford wanted to make an affordable and durable car that would appeal to the average American. He came up with an innovative idea—the moving assembly line—which greatly reduced production costs while maintaining the high quality that his customers expected. Formerly a professor of business history at American University in Washington, D.C., DiBacco contributes frequently to such periodicals as the *Wall Street Journal*, the *Washington Times*, and *USA Today*.

Henry Ford was the classic example of the American tinkerer. And no American would be more well-known in his lifetime: Russians marveled in the 1920s over "Fordizatzia," Germans over "Fordismus," and Americans simply over the word *Ford*. Born on a farm outside Dearborn, Michigan, in the midst of the Civil War, Ford was at war with the monotony and drudgery of farm work during his formative years. His mental highs came when he could fix various appliances or wander to other nearby farms for the same purpose. But there were only so many things that needed fixing in rural areas, so in 1879 Ford decided to head for Detroit to become a machinist and repair more things in a day than he had contemplated during a long, dreary winter. For eight years Ford worked as a machinist of marine engines, both steam and gasoline. It should have been a good life in a city that was conspicuous for its rising industrial prominence, but Ford exhibited the kind of mental restlessness that was more indicative of a creative artist than a blue-collar machinist. He returned home to the farm at age twenty-four, gladly accepted a forty-acre plot from his father, got married, and appeared to settle down to the life that his parents had always wanted for him. To be sure, Ford was busy with his farm chores—eking out an existence wasn't easy—but he also found some time to do tinkering. For two years he sweated the details of what might be called a mechanical plow, a device he was absolutely certain would revolutionize American farming. It did not work, however, and back to the big city Ford, now twenty-eight, headed, this time with a wife and a sense of both failure and relief. Landing a job with Detroit's Edison Illuminating Company, Ford stayed with the firm for eleven years, rising to the post of chief engineer and taking in all the mechanical contraptions that the metropolis illustrated in this age of inventiveness. Indeed, Ford may well have become an ex-inventor turned secure with a good blue-collar job. Then something caught Ford's fancy, something far more attractive than a mechanical plow, something that he would develop as no other American before and after him. That something was the automobile.

The Origins of the Automobile

The motor car that made its debut in Detroit during Ford's years in the city laid little claim to American ingenuity. A European by the name of Gottlieb Daimler devised and displayed the internal combustion engine in 1886, and a French firm pioneered in putting the motor into a frame that could be sold to consumers. And the automobile was sold in France in large numbers before the turn of the century. The first American to get in on the auto act in a leading role was Ransom E. Olds, who began a mass-production scheme in Detroit in 1899. One company, the Dodge brothers, made the engine, another firm the transmission, and then Olds used his plant to assemble the final product. The Oldsmobile was a quality product far cheaper and better than the autos that would be produced by nearly 180 competitors that eventually tried their luck in the industry. Even before Olds had begun his enterprise, Henry Ford was absolutely fascinated with the possibilities of the automobile, an excitement that was fanned by his friendship with Charles B. King, a Detroit businessman who assembled a motor car. Ford soon built his own model and for the next five years tried to get the kinks out of it, exasperating Detroit residents with his frequent breakdowns and rush back to home base for spare parts. He joined forces with several investors to form the Detroit Automobile Company in 1899, the same year that Olds led the field. But Ford's product was a bomb that had no market. His model was a high-speed racer that was mostly designed to break speed records on barren stretches of roads. By 1900 Ford left the company to put more time and energy into his race car, which he demonstrated as its "chauffeur" (note the influence of the French) for the next three years.

In sum, Ford was on his way to becoming the nation's speed demon, a somewhat unusual role for a middle-aged man, one that was almost certain to give him rich historical obscurity. Fortunately, a Detroit coal dealer interfered with Ford's plans; Alex Y. Malcomsen wanted Ford to be his chief honcho at a new automobile plant. In 1903 the two men cut a deal, with the Ford Motor Company coming into existence. As with Ford's earlier economic decisions, this one was nothing to write home about, at least initially. However, Malcomsen was smart to bring outside contractors into the picture: as the Dodge brothers brought forth excellent parts that were assembled at the Ford plant, Henry in the first year continued to race his own special models. However, he soon began to pay attention to the need to produce his cars with dispatch so as to be affordable to average Americans. His first model, priced at $850, was a two-cylinder car that sold well, priced $100 below what Olds charged. Then Malcomsen urged that a high-priced, luxury car be produced, selling from $1,000 to $2,000, depending on model. That was done by 1906, but the result was calamitous in terms of reduced sales. So Ford campaigned for producing a good, inexpensive model—a campaign that led to Malcomsen's selling out in July 1906 and the reintroduction of a 1903-type car in 1907, a depression year. The strategy paid off, and Ford Motor Company made a profit of $1,250,000 as other automakers were flush with red ink.

Henry Ford next set his sights on production. A Ford car contained about 5,000 parts and was ordinarily assembled by men in the same way that construction workers built a house. Observing the overhead trolley system that Chicago meatpackers used in dressing beef, Ford experimented with the assembly line. "It must not be imagined," he wrote in retrospect, "that all this worked out as quickly as it sounds. The speed of the moving work had to be carefully tried out; in the fly-wheel magneto we first had a speed of sixty inches per minute. That was too fast. Then we tried eighteen inches per minute. That was too slow. Finally we settled on forty-four inches per minute. The idea is that a man must not be hurried in his work—he must have every second necessary but not a single unnecessary second. We have worked out speeds for each assembly, for the success of the chassis assembly caused us gradually to overhaul our entire method of manufacturing and to put all assembling in mechanically driven lines. . . . Some men do only one or two small operations, others do more. The man who places a part does not fasten it—the part may not be fully in place until after several operations later. The man who puts in a bolt does not put on the nut; the man who puts on the nut does not tighten it. On operation thirty-four the budding motor gets its gasoline; it has previously received lubrication; on operation number forty-four the radiator is filled with water, and on operation forty-five the car drives onto John R. Street." Within a year of Ford's introducing the assembly line, the time required to put together a car was reduced from twelve hours, twenty-eight minutes to two hours, thirty-eight minutes. In another year the time was cut to one hour, thirty-three minutes.

The low-priced car that Ford introduced after Malcomsen left was called the Model N. Its secret was tough vanadium steel, that is, strong and yet light so as to permit the car to be economically run. Steel makers in America could not produce this type of steel, however. It required a temperature of 3,000 degrees when the maximum employed in United States furnaces was 2,700. Ford hired an Englishman with a knowledge of vanadium production and guaranteed a small steel company against any loss from making the product. Instead of a tensile strength of 70,000 pounds for regular steel, vanadium reached 170,000. . . .

Fresh from the moving assembly line, a Model T's engine is started for the first time at the Ford Motor Company.

In 1908 Ford announced that his company henceforth would build only one car, the Model T, which was a distillation of the best features of his previous models. "I cannot say that any one agreed with me," said Ford of his decision. "The selling people could not of course see the advantages that a single model would bring about in production. More than that, they did not particularly care. They thought our production was good enough as it was and there was a very decided opinion that lowering the sales price would hurt sales, that the people who wanted quality would be driven away and that there would be none to replace them." When Henry

Ford was right, as he was about the early attraction of the Model T, he was absolutely right. Praise about the car came from all quarters, even the U.S. Board of Tax Appeals writing in retrospect in 1928: the Model T, it said, "was a utility car. It was a good car. It had a good reputation and a thoroughly accepted standing in 1913. It was used by all classes of people. It was the cheapest car on the market and was a greater value for its price than any other car. Because of its low price it had a much larger field of demand than any other car. It was within the purchasing power of the greatest number of people and they were rapidly availing themselves of it. There was a greater demand for it than the car of any other company." Until World War I, each year saw the number of Model Ts increase. . . . And each year saw the price fall. . . .

Ford set up assembly plants in twenty-seven areas by 1915; shipping parts from factories located in the Detroit area to the assembly plants was cost effective because they were less bulky and hence much easier to ship than a finished automobile. . . .

Critical also to Ford's success were the strategies of business manager James Couzens. As the firm's sales increased, Couzens negotiated the best terms from manufacturers of parts in order to keep costs down, sometimes even getting parts below cost from manufacturers who hoped to make their profits from sales to other companies. Couzens also saw to it that the freight costs priced into each auto were considerably reduced in practice, thereby assuring an additional source of profits. Most important, Couzens got 7,000 dealers to market Ford cars by 1912. He went to various towns, made a nice deposit in the local bank, and urged the institution to lend money to the newly emerging Ford dealer in his community. Then Couzens shipped an overload of cars to the dealer, ensuring that he would have to work like the dickens to sell them all. . . .

Dealing with Labor

Ford Motor Company was not without its problems in these heady years. Labor was the most difficult to handle. The usual working day for the firm's assembly-line employees was nine hours, the maximum daily wage $2.34 in 1913—

both indexes quite respectable. Not so respectable was the regimentation and speed of the assembly-line routine, which gave rise to a 10-percent daily absentee rate and an enormous turnover, nearly 400 percent in 1913 alone. Ford, in sum, had done what any prudent business at the time would have done, that is, put its money into machines, and scarcely a working day went by without the introduction of another laborsaving piece of machinery. By 1913 serious attention had to be given to Ford's working force not only because of absenteeism and turnover but also labor radicalism, best illustrated by the Industrial Workers of the World, who hoped to take advantage of the situation. Yet Henry Ford's solution was more radical than the ideology of the IWW: in January 1914 he announced a $5-a-day wage plan, based upon a profit-sharing formula and a reduction of the workday to eight hours. Although some editorial opinion was critical because of the fear that other workers would strike their employers for similar wages, the immediate reaction of Ford's employees was positive. In fact, in spite of bone-chilling cold at the Highland Park, Michigan, plant at the time of the announcement, some 10,000 men created a mob scene in hopes of gaining employment, ultimately having to be dispersed by police with fire hoses. This incident aside, worker productivity increased, absenteeism and turnover plummeted, and Ford profits skyrocketed—from $24 million in 1915 to $60 million a year later.

However, the $5-a-day scheme had its underside. Ford Motor Company expected the worker to be productive *and* accept the firm's rules; otherwise, the employee would get the boot or never come close to attaining the maximum wage. For instance, a worker would have to move through probationary status before being eligible for the $5 wage. Next he would have to satisfy Ford's Sociology Department, whose staff would visit his home, advise him on saving money, buying reasonable and nutritious foods, abstaining from liquor, and turning away male boarders on the grounds that they might violate the females of the residence. Families found deficient in the Ford rules were ineligible for the big bucks, even though those receiving the maximum wage helped to fuel inflation for the entire community in which the plant was located. But to most workers, the benefits of Ford's paternalistic program outweighed the liabilities, and most believed that the scheme devised to judge eligibility for profit sharing was fair. . . .

Between Farm and City

Henry Ford was more than a tinkerer. He was the embodiment of the American caught between farm and city. His values were rooted in the farm, as were the values of most Americans of his day. City values with their mass-produced goods made sense to Ford so long as the products were increasingly affordable (the Model T reached a low price of $290 in 1925), unencumbered by gimmickry, and illustrative of a handshake between seller and buyer as to longevity. "A manufacturer is not through with his customer when a sale is completed," wrote Ford. "He has then only started with his customer. In the case of an automobile the sale of the machine is only something in the nature of an introduction. If the machine does not give service, then it is better for the manufacturer if he had never had the introduction, for he will have the worst of all advertisements—a dissatisfied customer. There was something more than a tendency in the early days of the automobile to regard the selling of a machine as the real accomplishment and thereafter it did not matter what happened to the buyer." To give service was also being neighborly in the good farm tradition. Some city and farm values did not mix for Ford, however. Bringing down the price of the car had limits that rarely applied to the low-cost goods sold by Sears, Penney, Rockefeller, and Carnegie. For the automobile by the 1920s became an extension of the American's personality. With more people living in the city than on the farm for the first time, Americans cried for the individuality that they had known on the farm but was stifled amongst the huddled masses yearning to breathe free on urban streets. The sameness of the Model T ("Any customer can have a car painted any color that he wants so long as it is black" was the way Ford put it) was all right until consumers were exposed to different styles and models affordably provided by General Motors ("A car for every purse and purpose" was GM's slogan). Ford's notion of credit, like that of Sears and Penney, was country bred. Don't go in debt, he admonished for a long time. Sure, that worked for watches and underwear, as Sears and Penney demonstrated, but not for cars. Like country people, Ford detested banks and bankers; he was anti-Semitic, antiunion, and antimilitaristic. War promoted government to the forefront of an economy that it was ill equipped to handle, unionism emphasized collectivism instead of the individualistic spirit, and Jews were sharp city slickers who manipulated money and credit. . . .

Torn between farm and city, Ford let the farm end of his personality win out, which made him an enormously popular American—a folk hero of sorts—in the 1930s and 40s and a less-than-successful businessman.

Chapter 3

Laborers and Robber Barons

The Industrial Revolution Lowered Laborers' Standard of Living

J.L. Hammond and Barbara Hammond

British journalist J.L. Hammond and his wife Barbara Hammond coauthored several books on the effects of the Industrial Revolution in England, including *The Rise of Modern Industry* and *The Age of the Chartists, 1832–1854: A Study of Discontent.* In the following excerpt from *The Skilled Labourer, 1760–1832*, the Hammonds admit that the life of the ordinary worker prior to the Industrial Revolution was not ideal. However, they argue, the introduction of the industrial system greatly worsened the condition of the working class. Most laborers received little material benefit from the Industrial Revolution, the authors maintain, while at the same time they lost the freedom to control their own work environment. The demands of the factory system also weakened community bonds and placed new stresses on lower-class families, the Hammonds contend, which shattered the workers' traditional way of life.

The history of England between 1760 and 1832 reads like a history of civil war. This is the impression produced by the speeches and the policy of Ministers, the letters and the conduct of magistrates, the records of the Courts of Justice, the system on which our military forces were organised and the purposes they were designed to serve. . . .

What was this civil war about? It was not a quarrel over religion nor a quarrel over rival claims of Parliament and Crown. The issue that now divided the English people was in one sense less simple, in another sense it was simpler than

Excerpted from *The Skilled Labourer, 1760–1832*, by J.L. Hammond and Barbara Hammond (London: Longmans, Green, and Co., 1920).

the issue that had provoked the better known civil wars of the seventeenth century. It was less simple because it assumed various and changing aspects and one side in the struggle was not always articulate. Yet it was simpler because it arose from the fundamental instincts of human nature, for the question that it put was this, whether the mass of the English people were to lose the last vestige of initiative and choice in their daily lives. . . .

Losing Their Freedom

In the medieval village all over Europe, here as elsewhere, the normal man had certain rights. On the dissolution of that old village society in England these rights were lost, and the peasant disappeared in a social revolution that created a proletariate ready for the service of the owners of capital, whether they employed their capital in agriculture or in one of the new industries. . . .

Within certain limits the ordinary workman had still a large margin of freedom in his daily life at the beginning of the period discussed in this essay. We have Felkin's picture of the Frame-work Knitters of Leicester: 'Each had a garden, a barrel of home-brewed ale, a week-day suit of clothes and one for Sundays, and plenty of leisure.'. . . The domestic worker was not like the modern domestic worker who usually supplies the worst examples of sweated conditions. He was not hopelessly and despairingly poor. He had some say in his own life: he could go out and dig in his garden or smoke as he pleased: he was in some cases a farmer as well as a weaver or a spinner: he was in short not quite disinherited from the old village economy in which a man did not merely sell his labour but had some kind of holding and independence of his own.

The industrial changes that occurred at this time destroyed this social economy with its margin of freedom and choice for the worker. To the upper-class observer those changes seemed to promise a great saving of human labour. To the worker they seemed to threaten a great degradation of human life. And the worker was right, because the saving of human labour did not mean that the worker worked less or received greater compensation for his toil, but that the capitalist could draw greater profits from the labour of the workers he employed. What happened during this period was that the power of the owners of capital to control the energy of mankind was so immensely increased by the industrial changes that in many parts of England it spread over the entire life of a society. The worker had to surrender his freedom to this power: he had to surrender his home as well. His wife who in the old days brewed the ale, cleaned and cooked, and helped with the loom, had now to spend the day in the mill: the child had to be sent or carried to the mill as soon as it could walk. Welsh social reformer Robert Owen told Peel's Committee [the Select Committee on the State of Children Employed in Manufactures, headed by Sir Robert Peel] in 1816 that he could remember in the days before the advent of factories that the children looked as well fed as at that time, though few of them were employed before they were twelve or thirteen. A few years' experience of the new system made this seem incredible, for it was supposed that no home could be kept going unless the children of five or six went to the mill. Under that system the owners of capital could decide not only how the worker spent his life, but how he brought up his children. In other words the weaver or spinner or carder could call less of his life or his time his own than the humblest peasant in the old village, who worked so many days for his lord and so many days as farmer or as weaver for himself.

Fighting for Home and Hearth

The workers were in the main ignorant men, but they were not so perverse or so foolish as they appeared to the philosophers who wrote *The Results of Machinery*. They felt that the grasp of the new power was closing on them, and they resisted instinctively every change that could hasten that process. They considered about each invention not whether it meant that a piece of work could be done in one hour instead of ten—the only consideration for the reasonable and enlightened people of the time—but whether it brought their final enslavement a day nearer. They were fighting as literally as ever men have fought 'pro aris et focis' [for altars and firesides]. Something of the atmosphere of a tragedy— the tragedy that seemed to set science in the lists against

---

The Drawbacks of Industrial Life

History professor Peter N. Stearns is the provost of George Mason University in Fairfax, Virginia, and the editor of the Journal of Social History. *His books include* Interpreting the Industrial Revolution *and* Lives of Labor: Work in a Maturing Industrial Society. *In the following passage from* The Industrial Revolution in World History, *Stearns describes the various hardships faced by industrial workers, including the hazardous conditions of early manufacturing.*

No regular provision for illness or old age cushioned industrial life, and factory workers, unlike many small farmers, had no plot of land to fall back on for at least a modest food supply if their strength began to fail. The frequent economic slumps often caused unemployment rates, even for skilled workers, to soar as high as 60 percent for several months or even a year, and food prices often went up in these periods. Not surprisingly, many workers, even those capable of improving their earnings, found industrial life extremely unpredictable, even nerve-wracking, and in the worst slumps, death rates rose in the factory centers. Furthermore, and again even for workers whose pay might have increased modestly, the industrial revolution cut into leisure time. The labor force was prodded to work harder than its preindustrial counterpart, and work hours inched up as employers sought to maximize use of the expensive machinery. Some textile factories drove their workers sixteen hours a day, Saturdays included. Traditional festival days, when rural workers had taken time off, came under attack as the new factories fined workers for unauthorized absences. Finally, factory jobs exposed many workers to new physical dangers: dust from textile fibers, accidents in the coal mines, and maimings from the fast-moving—usually unprotected—machinery.

Peter N. Stearns, *The Industrial Revolution in World History*, 1998.

happiness, and knowledge against freedom—clings to the villages and the grey hills of the West Riding. The bleak and sombre landscape seems to speak of the destinies of that world of combers and croppers and spinners and weavers on whom the Industrial Revolution fell like a war or a plague. For of all these classes of workers it is true that they were more their own masters, that they had a wider range of initiative, that their homes and their children were happier in 1760 than they were in 1830. Surely never since the days when populations were sold into slavery did a fate more sweeping overtake a people than the fate that covered the hills and valleys of Lancashire and the West Riding with the factory towns that were to introduce a new social type for the world to follow.

It was not only those workers whose art or skill was superseded by the developments of the factory system that suffered in these changes. The strengthening of the power of capital, which followed the introduction of machinery told disastrously on the position of those home workers whose industry remained a domestic industry. The hand-loom weaver sank steadily more and more as the power-looms increased, until, as one of them said to factory reformer Richard Oastler, they were reduced to living on their children. . . . Felkin gives a most interesting review of the changes in the conditions of the Frame-work Knitters as recalled by an old man who had been apprenticed in 1755: 'When a lad, the work-people laboured ordinarily ten hours a day, five days a week, the Saturday being always left open for taking in work to Nottingham, gardening, etc.: through the middle of his life they worked about twelve hours a day; but of late years they work by necessity fourteen to sixteen hours a day. . . . For the first thirty years or thereabouts of his being in the trade, or from 1755 to 1785, fluctuation in wages was almost unknown; taking work in, he describes as being as regular and well understood in the general rate of wages, as to be like going and paying 1d. [one penny] for a penny loaf.' It is interesting to note that a Leicester witness, speaking of the conditions of this trade in 1833, said, 'We have no factory bell: it is our only blessing.'

Unrelenting Work

The new industrial system which robbed this society of its freedom robbed it also of its pleasures. If the introduction of machinery had taken place under a system that allowed the workers to control it, that system would have increased leisure and so made the life of man happier: it would in fact have done what the philosophers claimed for it. But machinery was introduced under a system that placed the workers at the disposal of the owners of capital, who valued machinery as a means, not to a larger and richer life for the workers, but to greater and quicker profits for their enterprise. There were of course many thinkers, politicians, and magistrates before the Industrial Revolution who thought that the mass of men and women ought to spend their lives in hard toil without relief or distraction. But the Industrial Revolution gave a great momentum to this view and increased the power of those who held it. Take for example the way in which the average manufacturer regarded the introduction of labour-saving machinery. He never thought of it as a means to increasing leisure. On the contrary; if one machine could do ten men's work, there was all the more reason for not allowing so valuable an instrument to be idle a moment longer than was necessary: in other words, the machine was an argument for lengthening rather than shortening the working day. There were honourable employers, chief among them the illustrious John Fielden, who contended as ardently as any workmen's leader against this vicious monomania, but the spectacle of the immense and sudden expansion of trade was so intoxicating that the educated classes were led to forget every other side of life.

This aspect of industry, as an unrelenting and slave-driving master, was emphasised by the general atmosphere of competition that dominated this new world. During a war a nation is obliged to concentrate all its resources on one aim, to regard everything in its bearing on the efficiency of a society for one particular purpose. Everything is seen in a special perspective which is false if once you take your eyes off that exclusive end. The Industrial Revolution had an effect like this on the imagination of England, for it made people think that their society was to be judged solely by its commercial success in a struggle of which the whole world was now the arena. The test of success was the test of profits: if a society could make its social and political conditions favourable to the earning of high profits that society was prosperous.

Under this influence there grew up the idea which more than any other branded the workers as servile: the idea that they were to be treated as the instruments of this power, and not as citizens with faculties and interests of their own for which society should make some provision. This fixed idea rules the outlook of the age on religion, politics, philosophy, and all the arts and pleasures of social life. The optimism created by the new discoveries mingled with as dark a disbelief in a wide range of happiness and freedom as the world had ever known. The majority of educated men renounced the hope of adapting human life and human power to their new surroundings in such a way as to satisfy the nobler instincts of human character, content to think of the mass of their fellow-countrymen as concerned only with a routine of working, eating, and sleeping. It was as if men had deliberately turned their backs on 'the master task of civilised mankind.'

The Disappearance of Recreation

The towns that belonged to this age are steeped in its character: they are one aspect of an industrial system that refused to recognise that the mass of mankind had any business with education, recreation, or the wide and spiritual interests and purposes of life. The age that regarded men, women, and children as hands for feeding the machines of the new industry had no use for libraries, galleries, playgrounds, or any of the forms in which space and beauty can bring comfort or nourishment to the human mind. The new towns were built for a race that was allowed no leisure. Education, it was believed, would make the workers less passive and therefore less useful instruments: therefore they were not to be educated, or to be educated only within the narrowest limits. Recreation was waste: the man who was kicking a football or playing a fiddle might be wielding a hammer at a forge or superintending a spinning machine. In some parts of Lancashire it was the custom to forbid music in the public-houses, and parsons and magistrates were found who thought that the worker would be demoralised by hearing an oratorio in a church on a Sunday. A witness before the Factory Commission gave his impressions of the factory system in a vivid phrase: 'Thinks they are not much better than the Israelites in Egypt and their life is no pleasure to them.' It is significant that we find in the pages of the poet George Crabbe, of the political writer William Cobbett, and of the radical working-class reformer Samuel Bamford the same lament that the games and happiness of life are disappearing. The rich might win their Waterloos on the playing-fields of Eton, but the rivals who were trying to shake our grasp of the new wealth could only be conquered by a nation that shut up its workers in mill or mine or workshop from the rising to the setting of the sun.

For with the Industrial Revolution the long working day becomes the rule in all industries, factory or domestic, old or new. We have an example of a new domestic industry in the case of lace-running, which employed over 180,000 women and children in 1832. In this industry the worker paid the penalty of these hours in blindness. A girl worker before the Factory Commission, who worked from six in the morning to ten at night, with two hours off for meals, described the trade as one that made you subject to headache, and said in contrast to another witness who was no longer able to see the clock at all, that she could see the clock but could not distinguish the figures from the hands. . . .

The Struggle Between Rich and Poor

Thus there is a growing strain and tension, the workers finding their lives more and more hemmed in, their surroundings more and more forbidding, their place in the society that regulated their arrangements more and more insignificant. Their rulers were becoming at the same time more and more preoccupied with the danger of yielding any point to their impatience. They sought to maintain every monopoly, to keep Manchester under the rule of the county magistrates, to preserve a system which gave two members of Parliament

to a ditch in Wiltshire and left the large industrial towns un-
represented, to strengthen and perpetuate by every device
the control of the new world and the new wealth by a small
class. They seemed bent on withholding from the workers all
initiative in every direction, politics, industry, education,
pleasure, social life. For they had come to look on civilisation
as depending on the undisputed leadership of this small class
and on the bondage of the workers in the service of the new
power by means of which they hoped to make and keep England the mistress of the commerce of the world. . . .

Here were all the elements of a mortal struggle. And so
we see on one side strikes, outbursts of violence, agitations,
now for a minimum wage, now for the right to combine, attempts, sometimes ambitious and far-sighted, to co-operate
for mutual aid and mutual education, the pursuit from time
to time of projects for the reform of Parliament: on the
other, Ministers and magistrates replying with the unhesi-
tating and unscrupulous use of every weapon they can find:
spies, *agents provocateurs*, military occupation, courts of justice used deliberately for the purposes of a class war, all the
features of armed government where a garrison is holding its
own in the midst of a hostile people. It is not surprising that
a civil war in which such issues were disputed and such
methods were employed was fierce and bitter at the time or
that it left behind it implacable memories.

The Industrial Revolution Raised Laborers' Standard of Living

Ludwig von Mises

In the following selection from his book *Human Action: A Treatise on Economics*, Ludwig von Mises takes issue with the theory that the Industrial Revolution negatively impacted the laborers of England. In actuality, according to von Mises, prior to the Industrial Revolution, most members of the working class lived miserable and desperate lives, one step away from destitution and starvation. The rise of the factory system provided thousands of new jobs for these poor laborers and ultimately brought about a general increase in their standard of living and material well-being, the author asserts.

During his long career, von Mises taught economics at the University of Vienna in Austria, the Graduate Institute for International Studies in Switzerland, and New York University in the United States. He also served as an academic adviser to the Foundation for Economic Education in New York for more than twenty-five years. His books include *The Anti-Capitalistic Mentality* and *Nation, State, and Economy: Contributions to the Politics and History of Our Time.*

It is generally asserted that the history of modern industrialism and especially the history of the British "Industrial Revolution" provide an empirical verification of the "realistic" or "institutional" doctrine and utterly explode the "abstract" dogmatism of the economists.

The economists flatly deny that labor unions and govern-

Excerpted from *Human Action: A Treatise on Economics*, by Ludwig von Mises (New Haven, CT: Yale University Press, 1949). Copyright © 1949 by McGraw-Hill. Reprinted with permission.

ment prolabor legislation can and did lastingly benefit the whole class of wage earners and raise their standard of living. But the facts, say the anti-economists, have refuted these fallacies. The statesmen and legislators who enacted the factory acts displayed a better insight into reality than the economists. While laissez-faire philosophy, without pity and compassion, taught that the sufferings of the toiling masses are unavoidable, the commonsense of laymen succeeded in quelling the worst excesses of profit-seeking business. The improvement in the conditions of the workers is entirely an achievement of governments and labor unions.

The Myth and the Truth

Such are the ideas permeating most of the historical studies dealing with the evolution of modern industrialism. The authors begin by sketching an idyllic image of conditions as they prevailed on the eve of the "Industrial Revolution." At that time, they tell us, things were, by and large, satisfactory. The peasants were happy. So also were the industrial workers under the domestic system. They worked in their own cottages and enjoyed a certain economic independence since they owned a garden plot and their tools. But then, in the words of historians J.L. Hammond and Barbara Hammond, "the Industrial Revolution fell like a war or a plague" on these people. The factory system reduced the free worker to virtual slavery; it lowered his standard of living to the level of bare subsistence; in cramming women and children into the mills it destroyed family life and sapped the very foundations of society, morality, and public health. A small minority of ruthless exploiters had cleverly succeeded in imposing their yoke upon the immense majority.

The truth is that economic conditions were highly unsatisfactory on the eve of the Industrial Revolution. The traditional social system was not elastic enough to provide for the needs of a rapidly increasing population. Neither farming nor the guilds had any use for the additional hands. Business was imbued with the inherited spirit of privilege and exclusive monopoly; its institutional foundations were licenses and the grant of a patent of monopoly; its philosophy was restriction and the prohibition of competition both domestic and foreign. The number of people for whom there was no room left in the rigid system of paternalism and government tutelage of business grew rapidly. They were virtually outcasts. The apathetic majority of these wretched people lived from the crumbs that fell from the tables of the established castes. In the harvest season they earned a trifle by occasional help on farms; for the rest they depended upon private charity and communal poor relief. Thousands of the most vigorous youths of these strata were pressed into the service of the Royal Army and Navy; many of them were killed or maimed in action; many more perished ingloriously from the hardships of the barbarous discipline, from tropical diseases, or from syphilis. Other thousands, the boldest and most ruthless of their class, infested the country as vagabonds, beggars, tramps, robbers, and prostitutes. The authorities did not know of any means to cope with these individuals other than the poorhouse and the workhouse. The support the government gave to the popular resentment against the introduction of new inventions and labor-saving devices made things quite hopeless.

The factory system developed in a continuous struggle against innumerable obstacles. It had to fight popular prejudice, old established customs, legally binding rules and regulations, the animosity of the authorities, the vested interests of privileged groups, the envy of the guilds. The capital equipment of the individual firms was insufficient, the provision of credit extremely difficult and costly. Technological and commercial experience was lacking. Most factory owners failed; comparatively few succeeded. Profits were sometimes considerable, but so were losses. It took many decades until the common practice of reinvesting the greater part of profits earned accumulated adequate capital for the conduct of affairs on a broader scale.

That the factories could thrive in spite of all these hindrances was due to two reasons. First there were the teachings of the new social philosophy expounded by the economists. They demolished the prestige of Mercantilism, paternalism, and restrictionism. They exploded the superstitious belief that labor-saving devices and processes cause unemployment and reduce all people to poverty and decay. The laissez-faire economists were the pioneers of the unprecedented technological achievements of the last two hundred years.

Then there was another factor that weakened the opposition to innovations. The factories freed the authorities and the ruling landed aristocracy from an embarrassing problem that had grown too large for them. They provided sustenance for the masses of paupers. They emptied the poorhouses, the workhouses, and the prisons. They converted starving beggars into self-supporting breadwinners.

The factory owners did not have the power to compel anybody to take a factory job. They could only hire people

Child Labor

Lawrence W. Reed is the author of Lessons from the Past: The Silver Panic of 1893 *and the president of the Mackinac Center for Public Policy, a free-market research and education organization located in Midland, Michigan. In the following passage, Reed addresses the issue of child labor during the Industrial Revolution. He contends that for many poor children who needed to work to survive, employment in the factories was one of the best options available.*

The evidence strongly suggests that whatever benefits the British factory legislation may have produced by preventing children from going to work (or raising the cost of employing them) were marginal, and probably were outweighed by the harm the laws actually caused. . . .

Conditions of employment and sanitation were best, as the Factory Commission of 1833 documented, in the larger and newer factories. The owners of these larger establishments, which were more easily and frequently subject to visitation and scrutiny by inspectors, increasingly chose to dismiss children from employment rather than be subjected to elaborate, arbitrary, and ever-changing rules on how they might run a factory employing youths. The result of legislative intervention was that these dismissed children, most of whom needed to work in who were ready to work for the wages offered to them. Low as these wage rates were, they were nonetheless much more than these paupers could earn in any other field open to them. It is a distortion of facts to say that the factories carried off the housewives from the nurseries and the kitchens and the children from their play. These women had nothing to cook with and to feed their children. These children were destitute and starving. Their only refuge was the factory. It saved them, in the strict sense of the term, from death by starvation.

It is deplorable that such conditions existed. But if one wants to blame those responsible, one must not blame the factory owners who—driven by selfishness, of course, and not by "altruism"—did all they could to eradicate the evils.

order to survive, were forced to seek jobs in smaller, older, and more out-of-the-way places where sanitation, lighting, and safety were markedly inferior. Those who could not find new jobs were reduced to the status of their counterparts a hundred years before, that is, to irregular and grueling agricultural labor, or worse. . . .

Child labor was relieved of its worst attributes not by legislative fiat, but by the progressive march of an ever more productive, capitalist system. Child labor was virtually eliminated when, for the first time in history, the productivity of parents in free labor markets rose to the point that it was no longer economically necessary for children to work in order to survive. The emancipators and benefactors of children were not legislators or factory inspectors, but factory owners and financiers. Their efforts and investments in machinery led to a rise in real wages, to a growing abundance of goods at lower prices, and to an incomparable improvement in the general standard of living.

Of all the interpretations of industrial history, it would be difficult to find one more perverse than that which ascribes the suffering of children to capitalism and its Industrial Revolution.

Lawrence W. Reed, "Child Labor and the British Industrial Revolution," in *The Industrial Revolution and Free Trade*, ed. Burton W. Folsom Jr., 1996.

What had caused these evils was the economic order of the precapitalistic era, the order of the "good old days."

In the first decades of the Industrial Revolution the standard of living of the factory workers was shockingly bad when compared with the contemporary conditions of the upper classes and with the present conditions of the industrial masses. Hours of work were long, the sanitary conditions in the workshops deplorable. The individual's capacity to work was used up rapidly. But the fact remains that for the surplus population which had been reduced to dire wretchedness and for which there was literally no room left in the frame of the prevailing system of production, work in the factories was salvation. These people thronged into the plants for no reason other than the urge to improve their standard of living.

The Benefits of Mass Production

The laissez-faire ideology and its offshoot, the "Industrial Revolution," blasted the ideological and institutional barriers to progress and welfare. They demolished the social order in which a constantly increasing number of people were doomed to abject need and destitution. The processing trades of earlier ages had almost exclusively catered to the wants of the well-to-do. Their expansion was limited by the amount of luxuries the wealthier strata of the population could afford. Those not engaged in the production of primary commodities could earn a living only as far as the upper classes were disposed to utilize their skill and services. But now a different principle came into operation. The factory system inaugurated a new mode of marketing as well as of production. Its characteristic feature was that the manufactures were not designed for the consumption of a few well-to-do only, but for the consumption of those who had hitherto played but a negligible role as consumers. Cheap things for the many, was the objective of the factory system. The classical factory of the early days of the Industrial Revolution was the cotton mill. Now, the cotton goods it turned out were not something the rich were asking for. These wealthy people clung to silk, linen, and cambric. Whenever the factory with its methods of mass production by means of power-driven machines invaded a new branch of production, it started with the production of cheap goods for the broad masses. The factories turned to the production of more refined and therefore more expensive goods only at a later stage, when the unprecedented improvement in the masses' standard of living which they caused made it profitable to apply the methods of mass production also to these better articles. Thus, for instance, the factory-made shoe was for many years bought only by the "proletarians" while the wealthier consumers continued to patronize the custom shoemakers. The much talked about sweatshops did not produce clothes for the rich, but for people in modest circumstances. The fashionable ladies and gentlemen preferred and still do prefer custom-made frocks and suits.

The outstanding fact about the Industrial Revolution is that it opened an age of mass production for the needs of the masses. The wage earners are no longer people toiling merely for other people's well-being. They themselves are the main consumers of the products the factories turn out. Big business depends upon mass consumption. There is, in present-day America, not a single branch of big business that would not cater to the needs of the masses. The very principle of capitalist entrepreneurship is to provide for the common man. In his capacity as consumer the common man is the sovereign whose buying or abstention from buying decides the fate of entrepreneurial activities. There is in the market economy no other means of acquiring and preserving wealth than by supplying the masses in the best and cheapest way with all the goods they ask for.

Blinded by their prejudices, many historians and writers have entirely failed to recognize this fundamental fact. As they see it, wage earners toil for the benefit of other people. They never raise the question who these "other" people are.

Mr. and Mrs. Hammond tell us that the workers were happier in 1760 than they were in 1830. This is an arbitrary value judgment. There is no means of comparing and measuring the happiness of different people and of the same people at different times. . . .

The early industrialists were for the most part men who

had their origin in the same social strata from which their workers came. They lived very modestly, spent only a fraction of their earnings for their households and put the rest back into the business. But as the entrepreneurs grew richer, the sons of successful businessmen began to intrude into the circles of the ruling class. The highborn gentlemen envied the wealth of the parvenus and resented their sympathies with the reform movement. They hit back by investigating the material and moral conditions of the factory hands and enacting factory legislation.

The history of capitalism in Great Britain as well as in all other capitalist countries is a record of an unceasing tendency toward the improvement in the wage earners' standard of living. This evolution coincided with the development of prolabor legislation and the spread of labor unionism on the one hand and with the increase in the marginal productivity of labor on the other hand. The economists assert that the improvement in the workers' material conditions is due to the increase in the per capita quota of capital invested and the technological achievements which the employment of this additional capital brought about. As far as labor legislation and union pressure did not exceed the limits of what the workers would have got without them as a necessary consequence of the acceleration of capital accumulation as compared with population, they were superfluous. As far as they exceeded these limits, they were harmful to the interests of the masses. They delayed the accumulation of capital, thus slowing down the tendency toward a rise in the marginal productivity of labor and in wage rates. They conferred privileges on some groups of wage earners at the expense of other groups. They created mass unemployment and decreased the amount of products available for the workers in their capacity as consumers.

The apologists of government interference with business and of labor unionism ascribe all the improvements in the conditions of the workers to the actions of governments and unions. Except for them, they contend, the workers' standard of living would be no higher today than it was in the early years of the factory system.

Biased Historians

It is obvious that this controversy cannot be settled by appeal to historical experience. With regard to the establishment of the facts there is no disagreement between the two groups. Their antagonism concerns the interpretation of events, and this interpretation must be guided by the theory chosen. . . .

Most of the authors who wrote the history of the conditions of labor under capitalism were ignorant of economics and boasted of this ignorance. However, this contempt for sound economic reasoning did not mean that they approached the topic of their studies without prepossession and without bias in favor of any theory. They were guided by the popular fallacies concerning governmental omnipotence and the alleged blessings of labor unionism. It is beyond question that a host of authors were at the very start of their studies imbued with a fanatical dislike of the market economy and an enthusiastic endorsement of the doctrines of socialism and interventionism. They were certainly honest and sincere in their convictions and tried to do their best. Their candor and probity exonerates them as individuals; it does not exonerate them as historians. However pure the intentions of a historian may be, there is no excuse for his recourse to fallacious doctrines. The first duty of a historian is to examine with the utmost care all the doctrines to which he resorts in dealing with the subject matter of his work. If he neglects to do this and naïvely espouses the garbled and confused ideas of popular opinion, he is not a historian but an apologist and propagandist.

The Rise of Organized Labor

Carl N. Degler

Historian Carl N. Degler traces the origins of the labor movement in the following excerpt from *The Age of the Economic Revolution, 1876–1900*. He writes that many industrial laborers were dissatisfied with the low wages, long hours, and harsh working conditions present in most factories. Realizing that they could not bring about meaningful change individually, they began to band together in trade unions designed to promote workers' rights, Degler explains. Formerly the Margaret Byrne Professor of American History at Stanford University in California, Degler won the Pulitzer Prize in history in 1972 for his book *Neither Black Nor White: Slavery and Race Relations in Brazil and the United States*.

Even if wages had been high and hours short, the adjustment of erstwhile European peasants and American farmers to industrial labor would have been hard. Work on the farm, to be sure, had been physically demanding, but work in the factory was no less so, and its pace was often faster and more rigorous under the relentless pressure of the clock, the foreman, and the tireless machine. Paid holidays and summer vacations, now commonplace among all workers, were virtually unknown in the nineteenth century. The work week was six full days, so that Sunday was truly a day of rest.

For the newcomers from farms, the world of the factory was not only strange, it was often poorly paying. It is not easy to generalize about the wages and hours of industrial labor, since they varied according to location and occupation. Nevertheless, for many workers the hours were certainly long, the pay low, and the work exhausting. . . .

Excerpted from *The Age of the Economic Revolution, 1876–1900*, by Carl N. Degler (Glenview, IL: Scott, Foresman, 1967). Copyright © 1967 by Carl N. Degler. Reprinted with permission.

Despite the many examples of low wages and long hours that might be cited, the general picture, taking in the whole country, was less grim and suggests that the workers were sharing in the spectacular industrial growth. Real wages for industrial workers—that is, the actual buying power of the money the workers earned—rose significantly between 1870 and 1900. Moreover, hours declined for the average worker from 66 per week in 1860 to 59 in 1900. . . .

Reasons for the Growth of Unions

If, in the long run, conditions for most workers were improving, in the short run, as the tripling of the number of strikes and other measures of labor dissatisfaction in the 1880's attest, workers had a number of reasons to be discontented with their lot. Wages might be adequate in a given industry, but long periods of layoff reduced a good hourly wage to an inadequate annual income. A survey made in Massachusetts in 1885 reported that 30 per cent of the state's wage earners lost one third of their potential income because they were unemployed four months of the year. Even if the annual income was adequate, working conditions might be intolerable, and there were few government regulations of labor conditions designed to improve them. Workingmen's compensation for injuries on the job was only a twentieth-century innovation, and even sanitary inspection and sanitary codes came slowly during the 1880's and 1890's.

The power of the boss over most workers was almost unlimited, and the prevailing view among employers was that labor was a commodity to be purchased when needed and to be laid off when business declined. Most employers pressed their employees to produce as much as possible for their wages. A witness before the Industrial Commission of 1901 reported that in the textile industry the machines were run at a much faster rate than they had been 40 years before. Some employers even charged the workers for the machinery on which they worked. Anyone caught organizing a protest committee or a union was usually fired and then "blacklisted" from other jobs in the vicinity. As a consequence, early unions, like the Knights of Labor, often operated secretly in order to protect their members against reprisals. Unions were a direct response of the workers to the impact of the factory system. Only by collective action could workers expect to contest the power of the growing business enterprises of the time.

Despite the many sound reasons that can be adduced for the growth of unions in the late nineteenth century, the trade union movement in the United States developed slowly. (Even today, unionization in the United States lags behind that of many European countries. In 1956, for instance, less than 34 per cent of those people employed in nonagricultural jobs in the United States were members of unions as compared with 90 per cent in Sweden, 66 per cent in Austria, and 50 per cent in the United Kingdom.) Part of this slowness undoubtedly stemmed from the hostility of employers to trade unions, but a comparable hostility in European countries suggests that such an explanation is far from the whole story. In fact, two other factors were more influential. One was the great diversity of nationalities in the American working class, which spawned antagonisms and suspicion within the house of labor that European unions did not have to contend with. The second influence was the strong sense of individualism in the American worker, which probably resulted from his recent rural background. Most American workers simply lacked that sense of identification with their fellow workers which acceptance of a labor union requires. They believed that social mobility and financial advancement would come more rapidly to them as individuals.

The small size of the unions also meant that they were too weak to withstand downswings in the business cycle. In periods of prosperity, workers joined unions, only to leave during hard times when jobs became scarce. Such had been the case in the panics of 1837 and 1857 and again after the Civil War. In America, unionism has been so vulnerable to economic crisis that not until the 1890's could organized labor be sure that a majority of its unions would be able to weather a severe depression. When the long depression of 1873 struck, the promising union movement across the country collapsed under the impact. In 1878, labor union membership in the

United States was estimated by union leader Samuel Gompers to be 50,000 as against 300,000 in 1872. Throughout the nation during the depression, wages plummeted and hours lengthened as unemployment mounted. In the building trades in New York City, for example, wages fell from a high of three dollars a day in 1872 to a low of $1.50 in 1875, while the working day jumped from eight to ten hours. Not until the middle eighties was organized labor able to regain the position it had held prior to the depression.

Because employers often refused to deal with a union, workers sometimes resorted to violence to gain recognition or to protest poor working conditions and low pay. The most extreme example of violence in labor relations took place in the anthracite coal fields of Pennsylvania in the late 1860's and early 1870's, where Irish miners organized themselves into a secret labor organization popularly known as the Molly Maguires. Very little has ever been learned about the organization, except that it probably grew out of the Irish fraternal society of the Ancient Order of Hibernians and that it carried on a fierce struggle against the mine owners; this violence included the extensive burning of mine property and even the murder of company officials. Although the terrorism of the Mollies attracted wide attention at the time and eventually resulted in the hanging of 19 of the organization's leaders, it brought no substantial gains for the workers. It did, however, leave in the public mind an association between violence and labor organization that was reinforced by the great railroad strike of 1877 and the Haymarket riot of 1886.

The association of unions with violence was essentially unjust because the philosophy of the major labor organizations of the time clearly repudiated violence or lawlessness. Broadly speaking, two philosophies of trade unionism dominated the thought of organized labor. The first type, idealistic, sometimes Utopian, sought through the union to improve not only the worker's position, but the condition of society in general. This kind of union advocated a comprehensive membership including all types of workers. It also supported broad social reforms, such as education, temperance, women's rights, and cheap money, and not merely those which would be beneficial to labor. The second type took the view that unions existed not to improve the lot of all, but to gain advantages for their members. Such unions accepted the economic and social system of their time, but wanted to increase their own returns from that system. They would have nothing to do with broad programs for social amelioration and confined their membership to skilled workers who could negotiate from strength with employers. The National Labor Union (NLU) and the Knights of Labor represented the first kind, and the American Federation of Labor (A.F. of L.), the Railroad Brotherhoods, and the craft unions represented the second.

The Utopian Approach

The National Labor Union, founded in 1866, was the first truly nation-wide organization of labor unions in the United States. Its leading figures, William Sylvis of the Iron Molders Union and Richard A. Trevellick of the Ship Carpenters, were skilled workers who had long been active in labor organization. Just before the depression of 1873, the NLU boasted a membership of 300,000 and some success in gaining better conditions for its members. Moreover, in 1868 it influenced Congress to repeal the Contract Labor Law of 1864, which, in the opinion of the NLU, had encouraged the importation of cheap, competitive immigrant labor. But like many of the unions before the Civil War, the NLU also believed in the use of government action to aid the cause of labor. For example, it advocated cheap paper money (though it is questionable whether a wage earner actually gained anything from inflation). The NLU also agitated, with some success, for a working day limited by law to eight hours. Six states passed laws limiting working hours, and the federal government ordered an eight-hour day for workers at its workshops and arsenals. However, only the federal government's response to the NLU's agitation proved effective, since the state laws were riddled with loopholes. By the 1870's and even before the depression of '73, the reformist interests of the NLU split it asunder. To many workers and to craft union leaders within the organization, general reform was of relatively little interest. The onset of the depression finished off even the remnants of the NLU.

One labor organization that did survive the panic of 1873 was the Noble Order of the Knights of Labor, founded in 1869 by a Philadelphia tailor, Uriah Stephens. Destined to be a much more important union than the NLU, the Knights, nevertheless, reflected a similar reformist ideology. Stephens' reformist bent was evident in the Knights' practice of opening membership to any gainfully employed workers, including farmers, and excluding only lawyers, stockholders, liquor dealers, and physicians. To emphasize the fraternal, almost mystical unity of all working men, the Knights insisted upon an elaborate ritual, and for a time operated as a secret society.

In some respects, the Knights anticipated the modern industrial union in which all workers in a given factory are members of the same union, regardless of their craft or occupation. The basic unit of the Knights was the district, a kind of territorial "local," to which all workers of a given locale belonged, even including members of the traditional craft unions, if they wished to join. Unquestionably, Stephens wanted to obtain better working conditions for his Knights, but his central purpose was more far-reaching, looking to a renovation of society and the economy. On principle, the Knights opposed "the wage system," which they believed was transforming the independent craftsman into a dependent and degraded proletarian. To Stephens and his followers, the proper course for labor was the formation of workers' cooperatives in which each member could be at once a worker and an employer, sharing in the profits as well as receiving wages. Between 1884 and 1886, when the Knights were at their peak of membership and success, some 135 producers' cooperatives were in operation; a third of them in mining, coopering (making or repairing wooden casks and tubs), and shoemaking.

Certainly in retrospect and even in the light of conditions evident at the time, a cooperative approach to the problems of industrial labor was exceedingly Utopian. Business enterprise was fast moving in the direction of larger units of production; to have expected the small, weak cooperatives of the Knights to compete successfully with the giant corporations already in the field was illusory if not foolhardy. American labor unions took a long time to evolve the "bread and butter" unionism that today is axiomatically considered the purpose of labor organization.

Frustrated with long hours, low wages, and harsh working conditions, many laborers united to form trade unions designed to promote workers' rights.

Exclusive attention to economic issues may well have been the key to any labor organization's success in America, as shown by the history of the Knights in the 1880's. After 15 years of activity as a Utopian union, the Knights could count no more than 52,000 members throughout the country. But in 1884 and 1885, the Order's energetic organizer, Joseph Buchanan, carried off successful strikes against the Union Pacific and the Wabash railroads, thereby bringing thousands of new members into the ranks. Never before had an industrial giant like Jay Gould, the financier who controlled the Wabash Railroad, been forced to engage in collective bargaining. By 1886, membership in the Knights reached

700,000, making it the largest and strongest national labor organization the United States was to see during the entire nineteenth century. (It was ironic that the Knights' greatest success should result from strikes, for the Order's Constitution of 1884 condemned strikes as affording "at best . . . only temporary relief" for the difficulties of labor; cooperatives were judged to be the only permanent help.)

The spectacular success of the Knights, however, was only temporary. Most American workers were still not prepared to bear the risks and costs of unionization. A new strike on Gould's southwestern system of railroads in 1886 failed. With the winning streak of the Knights over, many workers left the union as abruptly as they had joined only a few months earlier. Moreover, many workers were scared away from the Knights because several of the anarchists hanged for the Haymarket bombing had been members of the Order. But perhaps most important in accounting for the decline in membership was the refusal of the Knights to abandon their strong interest in reform and to confine themselves to issues of direct concern to the ordinary workingman. Skilled workers, for example, discovered that the rising craft or trade unions were much more suited to their needs; even the unskilled workers, who really had nowhere else to go, found the Knights unsatisfactory because the Order was reluctant to support the movement for an eight-hour day. Furthermore, continued support for the producers' cooperatives, which the public did not patronize, drained the resources of the Knights. By 1890, membership in the Order had fallen to 100,000 and was still decreasing. . . .

The Triumph of Bread-and-Butter Unionism

As the Knights declined, the membership of the trade unions continued to rise steadily. With the trade union, labor organization had reached its final stage of evolution in meeting the needs and outlook of the ethnically heterogeneous and individualistically minded working class in the United States. The essential character of the trade or craft union was typified by the Cigar Makers Union, reorganized on its modern lines by Samuel Gompers and Adolph Strasser, both of whom would later be active in the formation and leadership of the American Federation of Labor. Gompers and Strasser were immigrants, who, though once interested in socialism as an ideology for labor, soon abandoned the idea as impractical for American conditions. Instead, they turned to strong union organization. In accordance with their conception of the trade union, the locals were put under tight control of the national officers; and dues, deliberately set high to permit the accumulation of substantial funds for strikes and organizing activities, were also given over to the national office. Backed by such a structure, labor would have a fighting chance in controversies with employers. As a further inducement to membership, the new craft unions of the 1880's, which followed the Cigar Makers' model, usually offered accident, sickness, and death benefits.

In 1886, a group of trade unions formed the American Federation of Labor, which, as the word "federation" in its title implies, was really a loose association of strong unions, free from centralized control. Unlike the NLU or the Knights, the A.F. of L. was made up of national unions in which each trade in North America (there were a few locals of some unions in Canada) was represented by a single union only, thereby avoiding rival groups whose conflicts in the past had often shattered attempts at national organization. For the most part, the constituent unions of the A.F. of L. were craft unions composed of skilled workers, though in the 1890's, the United Mine Workers, an industrially organized union, also affiliated with it.

At its founding, the A.F. of L., with a mere 140,000 members in its dozen or so national unions and lesser organizations, was distinctly weaker than the Knights, who were then at a peak of membership five times greater than the A.F. of L. But the newer labor organization was destined to survive and grow in the United States, while the Knights would pass from the scene entirely within a decade. Thus an examination of the differences between the two great rival national organizations reveals something of the institutional requirements for success in labor organization in America.

Aside from the differences in organization that have already been mentioned, there were important differences in membership. The A.F. of L. concentrated on organizing the skilled trades, and, though professing to recognize no barriers against women and Negroes, it in fact mobilized few of these marginal workers. The Knights, on the other hand, included unskilled workers and thousands of women and Negro workers. Such an approach, while it was democratic, endangered survival, both because such marginal workers were easily replaced during a strike, and, as objects of the prejudice of other workers, they created internal dissension. By limiting its membership to the skilled and the "acceptable," the A.F. of L. built a strong union for a few rather than a weak union for the many. As practical men, Gompers and his A.F. of L. members saw survival as the first test of validity.

It was in their philosophies that the two labor organizations differed most radically. The Federation, for example, would have nothing to do with the kind of long-range social goals that the Knights had long and proudly stood for. Gompers and the A.F. of L. even opposed any government interference in the conflicts between capital and labor, simply asking that government treat each side equally. Primarily concerned with preserving the worker's job, the trade unions of the A.F. of L. were eminently, if narrowly, practical. That practicality stood in clear contrast with the fraternalism of the Knights, who, by taking in all workers, sacrificed survival to principle. Gompers instinctively recognized what labor historian Selig Perlman later described as the deadliest disease of American labor unions: their fragility, their inability to endure. Only by the elimination of as many divisive elements as possible, Gompers reasoned, could a national labor movement of consequence be created. And it worked.

Gomper's practical approach, in pragmatic and materialistic America, worked better than the idealism of the Knights, but it exacted a price. The resulting labor movement was narrowly based. By failing to organize the unskilled, immigrant workers in the growing mass industries, the A.F. of L. ignored the great majority of American industrial workers.

Indeed, not even all of organized labor was affiliated with the Federation. As late as 1900, a third of the organized workers of the country had not joined the A.F. of L., and some of these unaffiliated unions were strong and influential, like the Railroad Brotherhoods, the bricklayers, and the plasterers. By the First World War, however, the principal unions and the overwhelming majority of unionized workers were a part of the Federation. Yet only 15 per cent of non-agricultural workers in the United States, even in 1914, were members of any union.

Thus by the opening of the new century, the American working class had at last determined the permanent form of its response to the impact of the industrial system.

An Indictment of the Robber Barons

Howard Zinn

Howard Zinn is a professor emeritus of political science at Boston University in Massachusetts and former chair of the department of history and social science at Spelman College in Atlanta, Georgia. His books include *The Politics of History, Declarations of Independence: Cross-Examining American Ideology*, and *Three Strikes: Stories of American Labor*. In the following excerpt from *A People's History of the United States, 1492–Present*, Zinn discusses the industrial entrepreneurs who came to power after the Civil War. Often called "robber barons" in reference to their ruthless attainment of wealth, these industrialists exploited their workers and harmed American society, in Zinn's view. The robber barons amassed their personal fortunes by unscrupulous means, the author asserts, frequently with the tacit consent of the U.S. government.

In the year 1877, the signals were given for the rest of the century: the black would be put back; the strikes of white workers would not be tolerated; the industrial and political elites of North and South would take hold of the country and organize the greatest march of economic growth in human history. They would do it with the aid of, and at the expense of, black labor, white labor, Chinese labor, European immigrant labor, female labor, rewarding them differently by race, sex, national origin, and social class, in such a way as to create separate levels of oppression—a skillful terracing to stabilize the pyramid of wealth.

Excerpted from *A People's History of the United States, 1492–Present*, by Howard Zinn (New York, HarperCollins, 1999). Copyright © 1980 by Howard Zinn. Reprinted by permission of HarperCollins Publishers, Inc.

The Acceleration of Production

Between the Civil War and 1900, steam and electricity replaced human muscle, iron replaced wood, and steel replaced iron (before the Bessemer process, iron was hardened into steel at the rate of 3 to 5 tons a day; now the same amount could be processed in 15 minutes). Machines could now drive steel tools. Oil could lubricate machines and light homes, streets, factories. People and goods could move by railroad, propelled by steam along steel rails; by 1900 there were 193,000 miles of railroad. The telephone, the typewriter, and the adding machine speeded up the work of business.

Machines changed farming. Before the Civil War it took 61 hours of labor to produce an acre of wheat. By 1900, it took 3 hours, 19 minutes. Manufactured ice enabled the transport of food over long distances, and the industry of meatpacking was born.

Steam drove textile mill spindles; it drove sewing machines. It came from coal. Pneumatic drills now drilled deeper into the earth for coal. In 1860, 14 million tons of coal were mined; by 1884 it was 100 million tons. More coal meant more steel, because coal furnaces converted iron into steel; by 1880 a million tons of steel were being produced; by 1910, 25 million tons. By now electricity was beginning to replace steam. Electrical wire needed copper, of which 30,000 tons were produced in 1880; 500,000 tons by 1910.

To accomplish all this required ingenious inventors of new processes and new machines, clever organizers and administrators of the new corporations, a country rich with land and minerals, and a huge supply of human beings to do the back-breaking, unhealthful, and dangerous work. Immigrants would come from Europe and China, to make the new labor force. Farmers unable to buy the new machinery or pay the new railroad rates would move to the cities. Between 1860 and 1914, New York grew from 850,000 to 4 million, Chicago from 110,000 to 2 million, Philadelphia from 650,000 to 1½ million.

In some cases the inventor himself became the organizer of businesses—like Thomas Edison, inventor of electrical devices. In other cases, the businessman compiled other people's inventions, like Gustavus Swift, a Chicago butcher who put together the ice-cooled railway car with the ice-cooled warehouse to make the first national meatpacking company in 1885. James Duke used a new cigarette-rolling machine that could roll, paste, and cut tubes of tobacco into 100,000 cigarettes a day; in 1890 he combined the four biggest cigarette producers to form the American Tobacco Company.

While some multimillionaires started in poverty, most did not. A study of the origins of 303 textile, railroad, and steel executives of the 1870s showed that 90 percent came from middle- or upper-class families. The Horatio Alger stories of "rags to riches" were true for a few men, but mostly a myth, and a useful myth for control.

Bribes and Fraud

Most of the fortune building was done legally, with the collaboration of the government and the courts. Sometimes the collaboration had to be paid for. Thomas Edison promised New Jersey politicians $1,000 each in return for favorable legislation. Daniel Drew and Jay Gould spent $1 million to bribe the New York legislature to legalize their issue of $8 million in "watered stock" (stock not representing real value) on the Erie Railroad.

The first transcontinental railroad was built with blood, sweat, politics and thievery, out of the meeting of the Union Pacific and Central Pacific railroads. The Central Pacific started on the West Coast going east; it spent $200,000 in Washington on bribes to get 9 million acres of free land and $24 million in bonds, and paid $79 million, an overpayment of $36 million, to a construction company which really was its own. The construction was done by three thousand Irish and ten thousand Chinese, over a period of four years, working for one or two dollars a day.

The Union Pacific started in Nebraska going west. It had been given 12 million acres of free land and $27 million in government bonds. It created the Credit Mobilier company and gave them $94 million for construction when the actual cost was $44 million. Shares were sold cheaply to Congressmen to prevent investigation. This was at the suggestion of Massachusetts Congressman Oakes Ames, a shovel manufacturer and director of Credit Mobilier, who said: "There is no difficulty in getting men to look after their own property." The Union Pacific used twenty thousand workers—war veterans and Irish immigrants, who laid 5 miles of track a day and died by the hundreds in the heat, the cold, and the battles with Indians opposing the invasion of their territory.

Both railroads used longer, twisting routes to get subsidies from towns they went through. In 1869, amid music and speeches, the two crooked lines met in Utah.

In 1869, the Union Pacific and the Central Pacific lines met in Utah. The majority of laborers were immigrants who endured strenuous and often hazardous working conditions.

The wild fraud on the railroads led to more control of railroad finances by bankers, who wanted more stability—profit by law rather than by theft. By the 1890s, most of the country's railway mileage was concentrated in six huge systems. Four of these were completely or partially controlled by the House of Morgan, and two others by the bankers Kuhn, Loeb, and Company.

J.P. Morgan had started before the war, as the son of a banker who began selling stocks for the railroads for good commissions. During the Civil War he bought five thousand rifles for $3.50 each from an army arsenal, and sold them to a general in the field for $22 each. The rifles were defective and would shoot off the thumbs of the soldiers using them. A congressional committee noted this in the small print of an obscure report, but a federal judge upheld the deal as the fulfillment of a valid legal contract.

Morgan had escaped military service in the Civil War by paying $300 to a substitute. So did John D. Rockefeller, Andrew Carnegie, Philip Armour, Jay Gould, and James Mellon. Mellon's father had written to him that "a man may be a patriot without risking his own life or sacrificing his health. There are plenty of lives less valuable."

It was the firm of Drexel, Morgan and Company that was given a U.S. government contract to float a bond issue of $260 million. The government could have sold the bonds directly; it chose to pay the bankers $5 million in commission.

On January 2, 1889, as Gustavus Myers reports in *History of the Great American Fortunes:*

> . . . a circular marked "Private and Confidential" was issued by the three banking houses of Drexel, Morgan & Company, Brown Brothers & Company, and Kidder, Peabody & Company. The most painstaking care was exercised that this document should not find its way into the press or otherwise become public. . . . Why this fear? Because the circular was an invitation . . . to the great railroad magnates to assemble at Morgan's house, No. 219 Madison Avenue, there to form, in the phrase of the day, an iron-clad combination . . . a compact which would efface competition among certain railroads, and unite those interests in an agreement by which the people of the United States would be bled even more effectively than before.

There was a human cost to this exciting story of financial ingenuity. That year, 1889, records of the Interstate Commerce Commission showed that 22,000 railroad workers were killed or injured.

In 1895 the gold reserve of the United States was depleted, while twenty-six New York City banks had $129 million in gold in their vaults. A syndicate of bankers headed by J.P. Morgan & Company, August Belmont & Company, the National City Bank, and others offered to give the government gold in exchange for bonds. President Grover Cleveland agreed. The bankers immediately resold the bonds at higher prices, making $18 million profit.

A journalist wrote: "If a man wants to buy beef, he must go to the butcher. . . . If Mr. Cleveland wants much gold, he must go to the big banker.". . .

John D. Rockefeller started as a bookkeeper in Cleveland, Ohio, became a merchant, accumulated money, and decided that, in the new industry of oil, who controlled the oil refineries controlled the industry. He bought his first oil refinery in 1862, and by 1870 set up Standard Oil Company of Ohio, made secret agreements with railroads to ship his oil with them if they gave him rebates—discounts—on their prices, and thus drove competitors out of business.

One independent refiner said: "If we did not sell out. . . . we would be crushed out. . . . There was only one buyer on the market and we had to sell at their terms." Memos like this one passed among Standard Oil officials: "Wilkerson & Co. received car of oil Monday 13th. . . . Please turn another screw." A rival refinery in Buffalo, New York, was rocked by a small explosion arranged by Standard Oil officials with the refinery's chief mechanic.

The Standard Oil Company, by 1899, was a holding company which controlled the stock of many other companies. The capital was $110 million, the profit was $45 million a year, and John D. Rockefeller's fortune was estimated at $200 million. Before long he would move into iron, copper, coal, shipping, and banking (Chase Manhattan Bank). Profits would be $81 million a year, and the Rockefeller fortune would total two billion dollars.

Andrew Carnegie was a telegraph clerk at seventeen, then secretary to the head of the Pennsylvania Railroad, then broker in Wall Street selling railroad bonds for huge commissions, and was soon a millionaire. He went to London in 1872, saw the new Bessemer method of producing steel, and returned to the United States to build a million-dollar steel plant. Foreign competition was kept out by a high tariff conveniently set by Congress, and by 1880 Carnegie was producing 10,000 tons of steel a month, making $1½ million a year in profit. By 1900 he was making $40 million a year, and that year, at a dinner party, he agreed to sell his steel company to J.P. Morgan. He scribbled the price on a note: $492,000,000.

Morgan then formed the U.S. Steel Corporation, combining Carnegie's corporation with others. He sold stocks and bonds for $1,300,000,000 (about 400 million more than the combined worth of the companies) and took a fee of 150 million for arranging the consolidation. How could dividends be paid to all those stockholders and bondholders? By making sure Congress passed tariffs keeping out foreign steel; by closing off competition and maintaining the price at $28 a ton; and by working 200,000 men twelve hours a day for wages that barely kept their families alive.

And so it went, in industry after industry—shrewd, efficient businessmen building empires, choking out competition, maintaining high prices, keeping wages low, using government subsidies. These industries were the first beneficiaries of the "welfare state." By the turn of the century, American Telephone and Telegraph had a monopoly of the nation's telephone system, International Harvester made 85 percent of all farm machinery, and in every other industry resources became concentrated, controlled. The banks had interests in so many of these monopolies as to create an interlocking network of powerful corporation directors, each of whom sat on the boards of many other corporations. According to a Senate report of the early twentieth century, Morgan at his peak sat on the board of forty-eight corporations; Rockefeller, thirty-seven corporations.

Governmental Favoritism

Meanwhile, the government of the United States was behaving almost exactly as Karl Marx described a capitalist state: pretending neutrality to maintain order, but serving the in-

terests of the rich. Not that the rich agreed among themselves; they had disputes over policies. But the purpose of the
state was to settle upper-class disputes peacefully, control
lower-class rebellion, and adopt policies that would further
the long-range stability of the system. The arrangement between Democrats and Republicans to elect Rutherford Hayes
in 1877 set the tone. Whether Democrats or Republicans
won, national policy would not change in any important way.

When Grover Cleveland, a Democrat, ran for president
in 1884, the general impression in the country was that he
opposed the power of monopolies and corporations, and
that the Republican party, whose candidate was James
Blaine, stood for the wealthy. But when Cleveland defeated
Blaine, Jay Gould wired him: "I feel . . . that the vast business interests of the country will be entirely safe in your
hands." And he was right.

One of Cleveland's chief advisers was William Whitney, a
millionaire and corporation lawyer, who married into the
Standard Oil fortune and was appointed Secretary of the
Navy by Cleveland. He immediately set about to create a
"steel navy," buying the steel at artificially high prices from
Carnegie's plants. Cleveland himself assured industrialists
that his election should not frighten them: "No harm shall
come to any business interest as the result of administrative
policy so long as I am President . . . a transfer of executive
control from one party to another does not mean any serious disturbance of existing conditions.". . .

In 1887, with a huge surplus in the treasury, Cleveland ve-
toed a bill appropriating $100,000 to give relief to Texas
farmers to help them buy seed grain during a drought. He
said: "Federal aid in such cases . . . encourages the expectation of paternal care on the part of the government and
weakens the sturdiness of our national character." But that
same year, Cleveland used his gold surplus to pay off wealthy
bondholders at $28 above the $100 value of each bond—a
gift of $45 million.

The chief reform of the Cleveland administration gives
away the secret of reform legislation in America. The Interstate Commerce Act of 1887 was supposed to regulate the

railroads on behalf of the consumers. But Richard Olney, a lawyer for the Boston & Maine and other railroads, and soon to be Cleveland's Attorney General, told railroad officials who complained about the Interstate Commerce Commission that it would not be wise to abolish the Commission "from a railroad point of view." He explained:

> The Commission . . . is or can be made, of great use to the railroads. It satisfies the popular clamor for a government supervision of railroads, at the same time that that supervision is almost entirely nominal. . . . The part of wisdom is not to destroy the Commission, but to utilize it.

Cleveland himself, in his 1887 State of the Union message, had made a similar point, adding a warning: "Opportunity for safe, careful, and deliberate reform is now offered; and none of us should be unmindful of a time when an abused and irritated people . . . may insist upon a radical and sweeping rectification of their wrongs."

Republican Benjamin Harrison, who succeeded Cleveland as president from 1889 to 1893, was described by Matthew Josephson, in his colorful study of the post–Civil War years, *The Politicos:* "Benjamin Harrison had the exclusive distinction of having served the railway corporations in the dual capacity of lawyer and soldier. He prosecuted the [railroad] strikers [of 1877] in the federal courts . . . and he also organized and commanded a company of soldiers during the strike. . . ."

Harrison's term also saw a gesture toward reform. The Sherman Anti-Trust Act, passed in 1890, called itself "An Act to protect trade and commerce against unlawful restraints" and made it illegal to form a "combination or conspiracy" to restrain trade in interstate or foreign commerce. Senator John Sherman, author of the Act, explained the need to conciliate the critics of monopoly: "They had monopolies . . . of old, but never before such giants as in our day. You must heed their appeal or be ready for the socialist, the communist, the nihilist. Society is now disturbed by forces never felt before. . . ."

When Cleveland was elected president again in 1892, Andrew Carnegie, in Europe, received a letter from the manager of his steel plants, Henry Clay Frick: "I am very sorry for President Harrison, but I cannot see that our interests are going to be affected one way or the other by the change in administration." Cleveland, facing the agitation in the country caused by the panic and depression of 1893, used troops to break up "Coxey's Army," a demonstration of unemployed men who had come to Washington, and again to break up the national strike on the railroads the following year.

The Supreme Court

Meanwhile, the Supreme Court, despite its look of somber, black-robed fairness, was doing its bit for the ruling elite. How could it be independent, with its members chosen by the president and ratified by the Senate? How could it be neutral between rich and poor when its members were often former wealthy lawyers, and almost always came from the upper class? Early in the nineteenth century the Court laid the legal basis for a nationally regulated economy by establishing federal control over interstate commerce, and the legal basis for corporate capitalism by making the contract sacred.

In 1895 the Court interpreted the Sherman Act so as to make it harmless. It said a monopoly of sugar refining was a monopoly in manufacturing, not commerce, and so could not be regulated by Congress through the Sherman Act (*U.S. v. E.C. Knight Co.*). The Court also said the Sherman Act could be used against interstate strikes (the railway strike of 1894) because they were in restraint of trade. It also declared unconstitutional a small attempt by Congress to tax high incomes at a higher rate (*Pollock v. Farmers' Loan & Trust Company*). In later years it would refuse to break up the Standard Oil and American Tobacco monopolies, saying the Sherman Act barred only "unreasonable" combinations in restraint of trade. . . .

Very soon after the Fourteenth Amendment became law, the Supreme Court began to demolish it as a protection for blacks, and to develop it as a protection for corporations. However, in 1877, a Supreme Court decision (*Munn v. Illinois*) approved state laws regulating the prices charged to farmers for the use of grain elevators. The grain elevator company argued it was a person being deprived of property, thus violating the Fourteenth Amendment's declaration "nor shall any State deprive any person of life, liberty, or property without due process of law." The Supreme Court disagreed, saying that grain elevators were not simply private property but were invested with "a public interest" and so could be regulated.

One year after that decision, the American Bar Association, organized by lawyers accustomed to serving the wealthy, began a national campaign of education to reverse the Court decision. Its presidents said, at different times: "If trusts are a defensive weapon of property interests against the communistic trend, they are desirable." And: "Monopoly is often a necessity and an advantage."

By 1886, they succeeded. State legislatures, under the pressure of aroused farmers, had passed laws to regulate the rates charged farmers by the railroads. The Supreme Court that year *(Wabash* v. *Illinois)* said states could not do this, that this was an intrusion on federal power. That year alone, the Court did away with 230 state laws that had been passed to regulate corporations.

By this time the Supreme Court had accepted the argument that corporations were "persons" and their money was property protected by the due process clause of the Fourteenth Amendment. Supposedly, the Amendment had been passed to protect Negro rights, but of the Fourteenth Amendment cases brought before the Supreme Court between 1890 and 1910, nineteen dealt with the Negro, 288 dealt with corporations.

The justices of the Supreme Court were not simply interpreters of the Constitution. They were men of certain backgrounds, of certain interests. One of them (Justice Samuel Miller) had said in 1875: "It is vain to contend with Judges who have been at the bar the advocates for forty years of railroad companies, and all forms of associated capital. . . ." In 1893, Supreme Court Justice David J. Brewer, addressing the New York State Bar Association, said:

It is the unvarying law that the wealth of the community will be in the hands of the few. . . . The great majority of men are unwilling to endure that long self-denial and saving which makes accumulations possible . . . and hence it always has been, and until human nature is remodeled always will be true, that the wealth of a nation is in the hands of a few, while the many subsist upon the proceeds of their daily toil.

This was not just a whim of the 1880s and 1890s—it went back to the Founding Fathers, who had learned their law in the era of *Blackstone's Commentaries*, which said: "So great is the regard of the law for private property, that it will not authorize the least violation of it; no, not even for the common good of the whole community."

Buffers Against a Popular Revolt

Control in modern times requires more than force, more than law. It requires that a population dangerously concentrated in cities and factories, whose lives are filled with cause for rebellion, be taught that all is right as it is. And so, the schools, the churches, the popular literature taught that to be rich was a sign of superiority, to be poor a sign of personal failure, and that the only way upward for a poor person was to climb into the ranks of the rich by extraordinary effort and extraordinary luck.

In those years after the Civil War, a man named Russell Conwell, a graduate of Yale Law School, a minister, and author of best-selling books, gave the same lecture, "Acres of Diamonds," more than five thousand times to audiences across the country, reaching several million people in all. His message was that anyone could get rich if he tried hard enough, that everywhere, if people looked closely enough, were "acres of diamonds." A sampling:

> I say that you ought to get rich, and it is your duty to get rich. . . . The men who get rich may be the most honest men you find in the community. Let me say here clearly . . . ninety-eight out of one hundred of the rich men of America are honest. That is why they are rich. That is why they are trusted with money. That is why they carry on great enterprises and find plenty of people to work with them. It is because they are honest men. . . .

. . . I sympathize with the poor, but the number of poor who are to be sympathized with is very small. To sympathize with a man whom God has punished for his sins . . . is to do wrong . . . let us remember there is not a poor person in the United States who was not made poor by his own shortcomings. . . .

Conwell was a founder of Temple University. Rockefeller was a donor to colleges all over the country and helped found the University of Chicago. Henry Edwards Huntington, of the Central Pacific, gave money to two Negro colleges, Hampton Institute and Tuskegee Institute. Carnegie gave money to colleges and to libraries. Johns Hopkins was founded by a millionaire merchant, and millionaires Cornelius Vanderbilt, Ezra Cornell, James Duke, and Leland Stanford created universities in their own names.

The rich, giving part of their enormous earnings in this way, became known as philanthropists. These educational institutions did not encourage dissent; they trained the middlemen in the American system—the teachers, doctors, lawyers, administrators, engineers, technicians, politicians—those who would be paid to keep the system going, to be loyal buffers against trouble.

A Defense of the Robber Barons

Burton W. Folsom Jr.

The industrial entrepreneurs of the post–Civil War era have been unfairly denigrated, argues Burton W. Folsom Jr. in the following excerpt from his book *The Myth of the Robber Barons*. In Folsom's opinion, the so-called robber barons were actually innovative leaders who masterminded America's rise to dominance of the global market. Through hard work and personal sacrifice, he contends, these entrepreneurs ensured that the United States would emerge as the world's leading industrial power, thereby improving life on the whole for all U.S. citizens. Folsom is historian in residence with the Center for the American Idea in Houston, Texas, and the editor of *Continuity: A Journal of History*.

One reason for studying history is to learn from it. If we can discover what worked and what didn't work, we can use this knowledge to create a better future. Studying the rise of big business, for example, is important because it is the story of how the United States prospered and became a world power. During the years in which this took place, roughly from 1840 to 1920, we had a variety of entrepreneurs who took risks and built very successful industries. We also had a state that created a stable marketplace in which these entrepreneurs could operate. However, this same state occasionally dabbled in economic development through subsidies, tariffs, regulating trade, and even running a steel plant to make armor. When the state played this kind of role, it often failed. This is the sort of information that is useful to know when we think about planning for the future.

The Misconceptions of Historians

The problem is that many historians have been teaching the opposite lesson for years. They have been saying that entrepreneurs, not the state, created the problem. Entrepreneurs, according to these historians, were often "robber barons" who corrupted politics and made fortunes bilking the public. In this view, government intervention in the economy was needed to save the public from greedy businessmen. This view, with some modifications, still dominates in college textbooks in American history.

American history textbooks always have at least one chapter on the rise of big business. Most of these works, however, portray the growth of industry in America as a grim experience, an "ordeal" as one text, *The National Experience*, calls it. Much of this alleged grimness is charged to entrepreneurs.

Thomas Bailey, in *The American Pageant*, is typical when he says of Cornelius Vanderbilt: "Though ill-educated, ungrammatical, coarse, and ruthless, he was clear-visioned. Offering superior railway service at lower rates, he amassed a fortune of $100 million." If this second sentence is true, to whom was Vanderbilt "ruthless?" Not to consumers, who received "superior service at lower rates," but to his opponents, such as Edward Collins, who were using the state to extort subsidies and impose high rates on consumers. This distinction is vital and must be stressed if we are to sort out the impact of different types of entrepreneurs.

I have systematically studied three of the best-selling college textbooks in American history: *The American Pageant*, by Thomas Bailey and David Kennedy of Stanford University; *The American Nation*, by John Garraty of Columbia University; and *The National Experience*, by John Blum of Yale University, Edmund Morgan of Yale University, William S. McFeely of the University of Georgia, Arthur Schlesinger, Jr., of the City University of New York, Kenneth Stampp of the University of California at Berkeley, and C. Vann Woodward of Yale University. These works have been written by some of the most distinguished men in the historical profession; all three books have sold hundreds of thousands of copies. In all three, John D. Rockefeller receives more attention than any other entrepreneur. This is probably as it should be. His story is a crucial part of the rise of big business: he dominated his industry, he drastically cut prices, he never lobbied for a government subsidy or a tariff, and he ended up as America's first near-billionaire.

The three textbooks do credit Rockefeller with cutting costs and improving the efficiency of the oil industry, but they all see his success as fraudulent. In *The National Experience*, Woodward says that:

> Rockefeller hated free competition and believed that monopoly was the way of the future. His early method of dealing with competitors was to gain unfair advantage over them through special rates and rebates arranged with the railroads. With the aid of these advantages, Standard became the largest refiner of oil in the country. . . . In 1881 [Standard Oil] controlled nearly 90 percent of the country's oil refining capacity and could crush any remaining competitors at will.

In *The American Nation*, John Garraty commends Rockefeller for his skill but adopts roughly the same line of reasoning as does Woodward:

> Rockefeller exploited every possible technical advance and employed fair means and foul to persuade competitors either to sell out or to join forces. . . . Rockefeller competed ruthlessly not primarily to crush other refiners but to persuade them to join with him, to share the business peaceably and rationally so that all could profit. . . . Competition almost disappeared; prices steadied; profits skyrocketed. By 1892 John D. Rockefeller was worth over $800 million.

In these views the cause and effect are clear: the rebates and "unfair competition" were the main causes of Rockefeller's success; this success gave him an alleged monopoly; and the alleged monopoly created his fortune. Yet, Rockefeller's astonishing efficiency was the main reason for his success. He didn't get the largest rebates until he had the largest business. Even then, the Vanderbilts offered the same rebates to anyone who shipped as much oil on the New York

Central as Rockefeller did. In any case, the rebates went largely to cutting the price of oil for consumers, not to Rockefeller himself.

Perhaps even more misleading than the faulty stress on the rebates is the omitting of the most important feature of Rockefeller's career: his thirty-year struggle with Russia to capture the world's oil markets. Not one of the three texts even mentions this oil war with Russia.

Three facts show the importance of Rockefeller's battle with the Russians. First, about two-thirds of the oil refined in America in the late 1800s was exported. Second, Russia was closer than the U.S. to all European and Asian markets. Third, Russian oil was more centralized, more plentiful, and more viscous than American oil. If Rockefeller had not overcome Russia's natural advantages, no one else could have. America would have lost millions of dollars in exports and might have even had to import oil from Russia. The spoils of victory—jobs, technology, cheap kerosene, cheap by-products, and cheap gas to spur the auto industry—all of this might have been lost had it not been for Rockefeller's ability to sell oil profitably at six cents a gallon. The omitting of the Russo-American oil war was so striking that I checked every college American history text that I could find (twenty total) to see if this is typical. It is. Only one of the twenty textbooks even mentions the Russian oil competition.

John D. Rockefeller

Obviously textbooks can't include everything. Nor can their authors be expected to know everything. Textbook writers have a lot to cover and we can't expect them to have read much on Rockefeller. Unfortunately, they also don't seem to be very familiar with the books on Vanderbilt, James J. Hill, Charles Schwab and other entrepreneurs. None of the twenty texts that I looked at describe the federal aid to steamships and the competition between the subsidized lines and Vanderbilt. Similarly, none of the textbooks mentions Schwab's triumph over the government-run armor plant in West Virginia.

Some of the textbook authors do talk about Hill and his accomplishments. In fact, large sections of Bailey's, Garraty's, and Woodward's books tell us about the transcontinental railroads. But the problem of the government subsidies is often not well-reasoned. Bailey, for example, admits that Hill was "probably the greatest railroad builder of them all." Bailey even displays a picture of all four transcontinentals and says that Hill's Great Northern was "the only one constructed without lavish federal subsidies." But from this, he does not consider the possibility that federal subsidies may not have been needed. Instead, he says, "Transcontinental railroad building was so costly and risky as to require government subsidies." However, when the federal aid to railroads came, so did political entrepreneurship and corruption. Bailey describes some of this boondoggling and blames not the government, for making federal aid available, but the "grasping railroads" and "greedy corporations," for receiving it.

Bailey later applauds the passing of the Sherman Anti-trust Act and the creation of the Interstate Commerce Commission.

> Not until 1914 were the paper jaws of the Sherman Act fitted with reasonably sharp teeth. Until then, there was some question whether the government would control the trusts or the trusts the government. But the iron grip of monopolistic corporations was being threatened. A revolutionary new principle had been written into the law books by the Sherman Anti-Trust Act of 1890, as well as by the Interstate Commerce Act of 1887. Private greed must henceforth be subordinated to public need.

However, the efficient Hill was the one who got hurt by these laws: The Hepburn Act, which strengthened the Interstate Commerce Commission, throttled his international railroad and shipping business; the Sherman Act was used to break up his Northern Securities Company.

Organizational Historians

Not all historians accept the modified robber-baron view dominant in the textbooks. Specialists in business history have been moving away from this view since the 1960s. Instead, many of them have adopted an interpretation called the "organizational view" of the rise of big business. Where the authors of these textbooks say that entrepreneurs cheated us, organizational historians say that entrepreneurs were not very significant. Business institutions, and their evolution, were more important than the men who ran them. To organizational historians, the rise of the corporation is the central event of the industrial revolution. The corporation—its layers of specialized bureaucracy, its centralization of power, and its thrust to control knowledge—evolved to meet the new challenges in marketing, producing, and distributing goods. In this view, of course, moral questions are not so relevant. The entrepreneur's strategy was almost predetermined by the structure of the industry and the peculiarities of vertical integration. The corporation was bigger than the entrepreneur.

The organizational historians have contributed much to the writing of business history. Their amoral emphasis on the corporation is a refreshing change from the Robber Baron model. Yet, this points up a problem as well. Amoral organizational history has a deterministic quality to it. The structure of the corporation shapes the strategy of the business. In this setting, there is little room for entrepreneurship. Whatever happened had to happen. And if any entrepreneur had not done what he did, another would have come along and done roughly the same thing.

This point of view is perhaps most boldly stated by Robert Thomas:

> Individual entrepreneurs, whether alone or as archetypes, *don't matter!* (Thomas's emphasis) And if indeed they do not matter, the reason, I suggest, is that the supply of entrepreneurs throughout American history, combined with institutions that permitted—indeed fostered—intense competition, was sufficiently elastic to reduce the importance of any particular individual. . . . This is not to argue that innovations

don't matter, only that they do not come about as the product of individual genius but rather as the result of more general forces acting in the economy.

Thomas illustrates his view in the following way:

> Let us examine an analogy from track and field; a close race in the 100-yard dash has resulted in a winner in 9.6 seconds, second place goes to a man whose time is 9.7, and the remaining six runners are clustered below that time. Had the winner instead not been entered in the race and everyone merely moved up a place in the standings, I would argue that it would only make a marginal difference to the spectators. To be sure they would be poorer because they would have had to wait one-tenth of a second longer to determine the winner, but how significant a cost is that? That is precisely the entrepreneurial historian's task, to place the contributions of the entrepreneur within a marginal framework.

It is only when we extend Thomas' logic that we see its flaws. For, in fact, small margins are frequently the crucial difference between success and failure, between genius and mediocrity. To continue the sports analogies, the difference between hitting the ball 311 feet and 312 feet to left field in Yankee Stadium is probably the difference between a long out and a home run. The difference between a quarterback throwing a pass forty yards or forty-one yards may be the difference between a touchdown and an incompleted pass. When facing a ten-foot putt, any duffer can hit the ball nine or eleven feet; it takes a pro to consistently sink it.

In the same way small margins can reveal the differences between an entrepreneur, with his creative mind and innovative spirit, and a run-of-the-mill businessman. John D. Rockefeller dominated oil refining primarily by making a series of small cuts in cost. For example, he cut the drops of solder used to seal oil cans from forty to thirty-nine. This small reduction improved his competitive edge: he gained dominance over the whole industry because he was able to sell kerosene at less than eight cents a gallon.

A better illustration would be the small gradual cost-cutting that allowed America to capture foreign steel markets. When Andrew Carnegie entered steel production in 1872, England dominated world production and the price of steel was $56 per ton. By 1900, Carnegie Steel, headed by Charles Schwab, was manufacturing steel for $11.50 per ton—and outstripping the entire production of England. That allowed railroad entrepreneur James J. Hill to buy cheap American rails, ship them across the continent and over the ocean to Japan, and still outprice England. The point here is that America did not claim these markets by natural advantages: they had to be won in international competition by entrepreneurs with vision for an industry and ability to improve products bit by bit.

It would be silly for someone to say that if Carnegie had not come along, someone else would have emerged to singlehandedly outproduce the country that had led the world in steel. Yet some organizational historians say exactly this. They are right in claiming that the rise of the corporation made some of Carnegie's success possible. But Carnegie was the only steel operator before Schwab to take full advantage of this rise. They are also right in saying that the environment (*e.g.* location and resources) plays some role in success. But Carnegie rose to the top *before* the opening of America's Mesabi iron range. American steel companies began outdistancing the British even when the Americans had to import some of their raw material from Cuba and Chile, manufacture it in Pennsylvania, and ship it across the country and over oceans to foreign markets.

This is not to denigrate the organizational view, but only to recognize its limitations. By focusing on the rise of the corporation, organizational historians have shown how corporate structure pervaded and helped to shape American economic and social life. However, the organizational view, like all other interpretations, can't explain everything. Specifically, it tends to ignore or downgrade the significant and unique contributions that entrepreneurs made to American economic development.

The "organizational" and "robber baron" views both have some merit. The rise of the corporation did shape economic development in important ways. Also, we did have industrialists, such as Jay Gould and Henry Villard, who mulcted government money, erected shoddy enterprises, and ran them into the ground. What is missing are the builders who took the risks, overcame strong foreign competition, and pushed American industries to places of world leadership. These entrepreneurs are a major part of the story of American business.

Many historians know this and teach it, but the issue is often muddled because textbooks tend to lump the predators and political adventurers with the creators and builders. Therefore, the teaching ends up like this: "Entrepreneurs cut costs and made many contributions to American economic growth, but they also marred political life by bribing politicians, forming pools, and misusing government funds. Therefore, we needed the federal government to come in and regulate business."

Studies of Social Mobility

Historians' misconceptions about entrepreneurs have led to problems in related areas as well. This is nowhere more apparent than in the studies of social mobility, which have become very popular among historians ever since the 1960s. Naturally, historians of social mobility have not operated in a vacuum. They have often been influenced by the prevailing historical theories denigrating the role of entrepreneurs and championing the role of government regulation. Put another way, if America's industrial entrepreneurs were a sordid group of replaceable people, then they could not have helped, and may have hindered, upward social mobility in cities throughout America. This is the implicit assumption in many social mobility studies conducted in the last generation.

Influenced by these prevailing views, many historians have argued two basic ideas about social mobility under American capitalism. First is the notion of low social mobility for manual laborers. In *Poverty and Progress: Social Mobility in a Nineteenth Century City*, Stephan Thernstrom finds that "the common workman who remained in Newburyport, [Massachusetts, from] 1850 to 1880 had only a slight chance of rising into a middle class occupation." As for the captains of industry at the opposite end of the spectrum, the second idea is that they usually got rich because they were born rich. This again suggests little mobility. For example, in a November 1949 article in the *Journal of Economic History*, William Miller recorded the social origins of 190 corporation presidents between 1900–1910. He found that almost 80 percent of them had business or white collar professionals as fathers. More recently, Edward Pessen argued in a 1971 *American Historical Review* article that 90 percent of the antebellum elite in New York, Philadelphia, and Boston was silk-stocking in origin.

Fortunately, more careful research has discredited this negative view of social mobility. Newburyport, for example, was a stagnant town during the thirty years covered by Thernstrom's research. If new industries were rare and if opportunities were few, then, of course, we would expect social mobility to be low. Michael Weber sensed this and did a study of social mobility in Warren, Pennsylvania, an oil-producing boom town from 1880 to 1910, in his 1976 book *Social Change in an Industrial Town*. In Warren, population multiplied every decade as market entrepreneurs created a climate for opportunity and growth. Growth and opportunity seem to have gone together: Warren residents were much more upwardly mobile than those living in Thernstrom's Newburyport.

Flaws are also apparent in William Miller's analysis of the social origins of America's corporate elite in 1910. Miller traced the background of 190 corporate presidents and board chairmen. But as diligent as his research was, he could not discover the social origins of 23 (12 percent) of these men. Miller draws no inference from this lack of evidence. If they left no record, however, the fathers were probably artisans at best, crooks at worst. Furthermore, 60 percent of Miller's industrialists came from farms or small towns (under 8,000 population). This almost certainly makes their fathers country merchants rather than urban capitalists. And the ascent from son of a country merchant to corporate president is indeed sensational. Miller's statistics do not "speak for themselves": they need careful thought and imaginative interpretation. . . .

There is another realm of misunderstanding, too: some historians have implied that the economic pie was fixed. This is a weakness in many historical studies of social stratification. Edward Pessen, for example, tells how only one percent of the population held about forty percent of the wealth in many industrial cities in the 1840s. His research is careful, and he insists this share increased over time. Along similar lines, in his 1962 book *Wealth and Power in America*, Gabriel Kolko has recorded the distribution of income from 1910 to 1959. He points out that the top one-tenth of Americans usually earned about thirty percent of the national income and that the lowest one-tenth consistently earned only about one percent. This may be true, but Pessen and Kolko also need to emphasize that the total amount of wealth in American society increased geometrically after 1820. This means that American workers improved their standard of living over time even though their percentage of the national income may not have increased. We must also remember that there was constant individual movement up and down the economic ladder. Therefore, the pattern of inequality may have persisted, but the categories of wealth-holding were still fluid in our open society. Finally, it needs to be stressed that one percent of the population often *created* not only their own wealth, but many of the opportunities that enabled others to acquire wealth.

The Two Types of Industrialists

To sum up, then, we need to divide industrialists into two groups. First, were market entrepreneurs, such as Vanderbilt, Hill, Schwab, Rockefeller, and Mellon, who usually innovated, cut costs, and competed effectively in an open economy. Second, were political entrepreneurs, such as Edward Collins, Henry Villard, Elbert Gary, and Union Pacific builders, all of whom tried to succeed primarily through federal aid, pools, vote-buying, or stock speculation. Market entrepreneurs made decisive and unique contributions to American economic development. The political entrepreneurs stifled productivity (through monopolies and pools), corrupted business and politics, and dulled America's competitive edge.

The second point is that, in key industries, the state failed as an economic developer. It failed first as a subsidizer of industrial growth. Vanderbilt showed this in his triumph over the Edward Collins' fleet and the Pacific Mail Steamship Company in the 1850s. James J. Hill showed this forty years later when his privately built Great Northern outdistanced the subsidized Northern Pacific and Union Pacific. The state next failed in the role of an entrepreneur when it tried to build and operate an armor plant in competition with Charles Schwab and Bethlehem Steel. The state also seems to have failed as an active regulator of trade. The evidence is far from conclusive; but we can see problems with the Interstate Commerce Commission and the Sherman Anti-trust Act, both of which were used against the efficient Hill and Rockefeller.

A third point is that the relative absence of state involvement—either through subsidies, tariffs, or income taxes—may have spurred entrepreneurship in the 1840–1920 period. . . .

Low taxes often spur entrepreneurs to invest and take risks. If the builders can keep most of what they build, they will have an incentive to build more. It is true that the state lost the revenue it could have raised if it had taxed large incomes. This was largely offset, however, by the philanthropy of the entrepreneurs. When the income tax became law in 1913, the most anyone had to pay was seven percent of that year's income. Most people paid no tax or only one percent of their earnings. In the years before and after 1913, however, John D. Rockefeller sometimes gave over 50 percent of his annual income to charitable causes. He almost always gave more than ten percent. Hill, Vanderbilt, and Schwab were also active givers. Sometimes they gave direct gifts to specific people. Usually, though, they used their money to create opportunities that many could exploit. In academic jargon, they tried to improve the infrastructure of the nation by investing in human capital. A case in point consisted of the many gifts to high schools and universities, north and south, black and white, urban and rural. Cheap, high-quality education meant opportunities for upwardly mobile Americans, and was also a guarantee that the United States would have quality leadership in its next generation. Vanderbilt University, the University of Chicago, Tuskegee Institute, and Lehigh University were just some of the dozens of schools that were supported by entrepreneurs.

Libraries were also sources of support. Not just Andrew Carnegie, but also Hill and Rockefeller were builders and suppliers of libraries. The free public library, which became an American institution in the 1800s, gave opportunities to rich and poor alike to improve their minds and their careers.

Finally, America has always been a farming nation: Rockefeller attacked and helped conquer the boll weevil in the South; Hill helped create dry farming and mixed agriculture in the North. America's cotton and wheat farmers took great advantage of these changes to lead the world in the producing of these two crops.

Passing On the Wealth

All of these men (except for Schwab) tried to promote self-help with their giving. They gave to those people or institutions who showed a desire to succeed and a willingness to work. Rockefeller and Hill both paid consultants to sort out the deadbeats and the gold diggers. They sympathized with the needy, but supported only those needy imbued with the work ethic.

Each entrepreneur, of course, had his own variations on the giving theme. Vanderbilt, for example, plowed a series of large gifts into Vanderbilt University and helped make it one of the finest schools in the nation. He almost never gave to individuals, though, and said if he ever did he would have people lined up for blocks to pick his pockets. Schwab, by contrast, was a frivolous giver and had dozens of friends and hangers-on who tapped him regularly for handouts. Rockefeller concentrated his giving in the South and the Midwest; Schwab focused on the East; Hill gave mainly in the Northwest. . . .

If we seriously study entrepreneurs, the state, and the rise of big business in the United States we will have to sacrifice the textbook morality play of "greedy businessmen" fleecing the public until at last they are stopped by the actions of the state. But, in return, we will have a better understanding of the past and a sounder basis for building our future.

Chapter 4

The Impact of the Industrial Revolution

Turning|Points

IN WORLD HISTORY

An Increase in Black Migration and Foreign Immigration to Industrial Centers

Harold U. Faulkner

In the following excerpt from his book *The Decline of Laissez Faire, 1897–1917*, Harold U. Faulkner describes the influx of new workers to the manufacturing centers that arose in the United States due to the Industrial Revolution. According to the author, the industrial jobs available in these cities were especially attractive to black agricultural laborers from the South. African Americans moved to the North in large numbers during the early years of the twentieth century, he writes, partly to escape the pervasive racism in the South and partly to find better-paying jobs in the factories of the northern cities.

During these same years, European immigration to America greatly increased, Faulkner notes. Whereas previous waves of European immigrants came primarily from England and Germany, he explains, these "new immigrants" were predominately from southern and eastern Europe. Typically less educated than earlier immigrants, these workers gravitated to semiskilled industrial occupations in America's manufacturing centers.

Faulkner served for two decades as the Dwight Morrow Professor of History at Smith College in Northampton, Massachusetts. His books include *American Economic History*, *Labor in America*, and *The Quest for Social Justice: 1898–1914*.

One of the most important movements of population during the two decades 1897–1917 was the northward migration of

Negroes, particularly after the opening of the First World War. This migration was not a new phenomenon, for Negroes, like the white population, have sought new homes and opportunities. What was new about the movement were its predominating direction, its acceleration, and its size. From the days of the "Underground Railroad," Negroes have moved toward the North but never before had this been the predominating direction. Up until the decade 1910–1920 the direction had generally been toward the West or the Southwest, where new areas had been opened adaptable to Southern crops.

Another trend was also obvious. Up to this time Negro migration was almost entirely local, that is, from one state to the next. About half of those who had moved across Mason and Dixon's line and the Ohio River had come from Virginia and Kentucky. Now the migration began to come from the cotton belt states of Georgia, Alabama, Mississippi, Louisiana, and Texas. And it was a straight-line movement "roughly along meridians of longitude," as historian Emmet J. Scott writes.

Migration to the Northern Cities

The sudden acceleration of the northward migration of Negroes aroused great interest in the North and also produced exaggerated estimates of its size. Actually the Negro migration to the North had not been great between 1870 and 1910 except for the decade 1890–1900. From 1910 to 1920, the migration to the North and West showed a net gain of about 334,000. Even so the percentage of Negroes born in the United States and living in a state other than that of birth increased only from 15.6 per cent in 1900 to 19.9 per cent in 1920. The second decade of the century was the great period of regional redistribution of Negro population.

It was not only the acceleration of migration that emphasized the movement, but also the concentration of Negroes in the cities of the Middle Atlantic and East North Central states. Whether they came from the urban or rural districts in the South, the Negroes, when they reached the North, concentrated in the cities. Sixty per cent of the Negro population of Illinois lived in Chicago, 68 per cent of those in Michigan were in Detroit, and more than 75 per cent of the Negroes in New York State lived in New York City. The per cent of urban Negroes in 1900 was 22.7; in 1920, it was 34.

Many reasons account for the northward migration. Both contemporary observers and later students agree that the economic were the most important. Negro students have also rightly emphasized the social disabilities under which the Negro suffered in the South. The decline of European immigration after 1914, combined with increased production of war goods and, after America's entry into the war, the draft of workers into the army, created a labor shortage in the North. Rumors of high wages in munitions factories spread by advertisements and labor agents did much to start the movement. Low wages in the South, unsatisfactory tenant conditions, and economic exploitation everywhere, added to Mississippi floods and devastation wrought by the boll weevil, gave a push that helped turn the Negro toward the North. Wages in northern munitions factories were triple those in the South and were paid once a week in cash and not once a year in credit at the country store.

Other causes which in a greater or less degree influenced this migration include political disfranchisement, racial discrimination in education and in the carrying out of many civic laws and government services, segregation of all types, and lynchings. . . .

Whatever the causes for this migration, the effects were significant. Only one, and that economic, will be noted here—the increasing participation of Negro wage earners in the industrial life of the nation. In 1900, agriculture and domestic and personal service, traditional Negro work, occupied 86.7 per cent of those gainfully employed; by 1920, the percentage of Negroes engaged in these two occupations had declined to 67.06. By 1920, about 1,506,000 Negroes, 31.2 per cent of those gainfully employed, were engaged in manufacturing, the mechanical industries, and trade and transportation. The developing participation of the Negro in industrial life was caused not alone by the migration to northern factories, but also by the movement of Negroes to southern cities where the increasing industrialization of the South was evident. . . .

The New Immigration

Two aspects of immigration during the two decades after 1897 immediately catch the attention of the student—its tremendous size and the continued shift in origin. In the entire history of American immigration only the decade 1840–1850 showed a larger inflow relative to the population already in the United States. In actual number of immigrants, however, the years 1900–1909 showed a higher total than any similar period. Beginning in 1900, the tide of immigrants passed the 400,000 mark; it did not fall under that figure again until 1915. During six of these years (1905, 1906, 1907, 1910, 1913, 1914) over 1,000,000 immigrants reached the United States. More than 8,000,000 came in the years 1900–1909 and another 5,000,000 in the period 1910–1914.

A search for an explanation of this inundation reveals, first of all, a culmination of causes which had operated for many years. Jews, Armenians, and others suffered religious persecution. Subject peoples, such as the Finns, Poles, and various

In the early twentieth century, many African Americans migrated to northern cities seeking new opportunities and higher-paying industry jobs.

groups of Slavs, were denied political equality. A low standard of living, accentuated by occasional crop failures, famines, plagues, depressions, and other misfortunes supplied a major reason. Money wages in southern and eastern Europe, from which more than 80 per cent of the "new immigration" came, were often not more than one third those in the United States. A minor cause was dislike for compulsory military training. As always, the main driving impetus was economic.

Although older causes continued to operate, two particular reasons help to account for this unusual flood of aliens—the greater ease of getting to America and the prosperity enjoyed in the United States, at least up to 1907. The hardships and dangers of earlier years had been largely surmounted. Instead of weeks of weary travel and bitter hardship, any immigrant accessible to railroad and steamship could reach America in fourteen days. Immigrant ships had become mere ferryboats plying between the two continents. Not only was transportation more rapid than in earlier years but steerage accommodations were more comfortable. Moreover, millions of immigrants already in the United States were prepared to remit funds to bring their friends and relatives to America. By this time, also, there had appeared an intricate network of steamship agents to propagandize prospects, immigrant bankers to finance the journey, and labor contractors (*padrones*) to find jobs for the newly arrived immigrant. The American Consul General in Italy reported that "immigrants are generally well informed by foremen, contractor agents, and friends in the United States as to chances of obtaining work.". . .

The pull from America was exceedingly strong. The wave of prosperity which swept the nation after 1897, and only briefly halted by recessions in 1904, 1907, 1911, and 1913, provided expanding opportunities in factories, mines, and railroad construction and in almost every phase of economic life. The sensitivity of immigration and emigration to economic conditions and opportunities can hardly be questioned. Correlations of data pertaining to male immigration, pig iron production, and factory employment during these years reveal this clearly. The influence of major cyclical changes in industrial conditions in the United States was usually apparent in immigration within less than half a year. Immigration increased with prosperity and declined with depression; and such conditions influenced emigration conversely. Moreover, immigration was closely related not only to employment opportunities, but also to the ability of friends and relatives to remit funds for the journey.

Immigration from central, southern, and eastern Europe began to increase rapidly after 1890; by the middle of the decade it surpassed that from northern and western Europe. Before 1883, northern and western Europe (the British Isles, Germany, the Scandinavian peninsula, and other neighboring countries) furnished 95 per cent of the immigrants. By 1907, over 80 per cent of the European immigrants came from Austria-Hungary, Italy, Russia, and the Balkan nations. In 1914, only 10 per cent of the entire immigration came from northern and western Europe. By that time any one of the three countries of Austria-Hungary, Italy, or Russia furnished more immigrants than all the northern European countries put together.

According to the census of 1920 the "new immigration," as it was then called, comprised 46.4 per cent of the foreign-born white population, and the "old immigration" 40.2. A careful examination of immigration statistics, however, reveals the fact that this shift was neither so uniform nor so revolutionary in its effect on American population as many believed. The new immigration had been slowly increasing for some time, and that from certain areas of northern and western Europe declining. . . .

A Different Type of Immigrant

The new immigrants often differed markedly from the old in their tendency to consider America as a temporary abode with the expectation of returning to their home country. Until 1907, immigration records did not tabulate aliens leaving American ports. After that, however, the difference in this respect between the two types of immigrants was evident. Records from 1908 to 1910, for example, show that from every one hundred, 16 of the old immigration, and 38 of the new, returned. The typical immigrant who came to America simply to make a stake and return usually had less interest in learning the English language or American ways of living. His economic aid might be great, but his cultural contribution was slight. At the same time he was more easily exploited by employer and *padrone*. The new immigration, as might be expected from its impermanent character, was predominantly male and single. During the decade 1899–1909, the percentage of females in the old immigration from Europe was 45.5; that of the new immigration, 27. The new immigration was also somewhat younger than the old. Of the new immigrants, about 83.5 per cent were in the age groups 14 to 44 years.

It was also clear that the new immigration as a whole represented a lower economic and cultural background. During the decade 1899–1909, the illiterates among the new immigration at the time of admission amounted to 35.8 per cent and that of the old, 2.7. From south Italy, where the largest group of illiterates originated, the percentage was 54.2 and the number 822,113. This obviously meant an utter lack of formal education for over one third of the new immigrants and a greater difficulty in social assimilation. Since at least two thirds of the new arrivals could not speak English, the tendency to crowd into cities where they could live with their own kind was accentuated. . . .

The tendency of immigrants to remain in urban areas is clear from the census studies. By 1920, at least 71.6 per cent of the entire foreign white stock (foreign born and natives of foreign or mixed parentage) lived in urban regions, and 28.4 per cent in rural. This group comprised 48 per cent of the urban population and 20.1 per cent of the rural. More than 70 per cent of the populations of New York, Boston, Chicago, and Milwaukee were foreign-born whites or native whites of foreign or mixed parentage. Cleveland had a similar population of 69 per cent, and seven other cities had over 60 per cent. It was the thickly populated industrial states of New York, Pennsylvania, and Massachusetts that showed the largest proportions of foreign born, and in general the correlation between the concentration of population and foreign born was close. . . .

Urban Occupations

Urban concentration may have been accentuated by the fact that many immigrants clung to the large cities at the points of debarkation or on main-traveled roads where earlier colonies of immigrants had established themselves. They went where there were jobs and friends. The rapid occupation of western agricultural areas and the end of the frontier undoubtedly backed up the immigrants into the cities; many of them had come from rural areas in eastern Europe and might normally have sought labor on the farms. The urban trend of immigrants was also strengthened by the tendency of industry to follow the labor supply. This helps to explain the concentration of the clothing industry in certain cities, the labor for which was mainly supplied by Jewish immigrants.

Since the foreign born largely massed in urban areas, it is not surprising that the census of 1910 showed that of the 6,588,711 foreign born males having some occupation, five sixths were engaged in essentially urban pursuits. About one third of them were in manufacturing. These immigrants furnished 45.4 per cent of the labor in extracting minerals, 36.0 per cent of that in manufacturing, 27.3 of that in the building and hand trades, and 25.0 in transportation. Of the female foreign born workers in 1910 (1,222,791), about one half were engaged in domestic and personal service and more than one fourth in manufacturing. Although there were many skilled workers among the immigrants, the masses were likely to be engaged in the less skilled work. By 1910 more than half of the coal miners and two thirds of the copper and iron miners were foreign born. In transportation more than half of the longshoremen and laborers in the electric and steam railways were immigrants. In many of the great industries of the country, at least half of the wage earners were foreign born; in some, approximately two thirds or more were in this category. The latter industries included clothing manufacturing, construction work, copper mining and smelting, cotton manufacturing in the North Atlantic states, leather manufacturing, oil refining, and sugar refining.

The Relationship Between Industrialization and Urban Pollution

Martin V. Melosi

Martin V. Melosi is a professor of history at the University of Houston and the director of the' Institute for Public History. He has written *Thomas A. Edison and the Modernization of America*, *Coping with Abundance: Energy and Environment in Industrial America*, and *Garbage in the Cities: Refuse, Reform, and the Environment, 1880–1980*. His most recent book is *Effluent America: Cities, Industry, Energy, and the Environment*. In the following article, Melosi explores the connection between the industrialization of America's cities and the increase in urban pollution. A number of factors contributed to this environmental crisis, he argues, including the unregulated disposal of industrial waste and the overcrowding of factory workers in decrepit tenements.

The industrial city was the most visible sign of the nineteenth-century economic revolution in the United States. Between 1870 and 1920, it became the dominant urban form in the country. As Sam Bass Warner, Jr., has suggested, "The ubiquity of power and machines in the late nineteenth and early twentieth centuries had profound effects on the American urban system." In earlier times, large American cities had chiefly been centers of commerce and finance. As early as 1820, urban development and industrial growth were becoming immutably linked. Relatively new cities, such as Pittsburgh, Cleveland, and Milwaukee, began to experience rapid growth and vast economic prosperity by producing such products as iron and steel, petroleum, and beer. Industrialization also transformed many older commercial cities, such as New York, Boston, and Philadelphia, which attracted major industries of their own.

As the undisputed centers of economic dynamism in the United States, industrial cities flourished. Yet their overcrowded tenements, congested traffic, critical health problems, smoky skies, mounds of putrefying wastes, polluted waterways, and unbearable noise levels attested to the price they had to pay for such success. Unlike the commercial cities, which had not suffered such massive physical defilement (because agriculture, decentralized manufacturing, and trade had dominated the preindustrial economy), the industrial cities were experiencing an environmental crisis on a scale not encountered before in America. . . .

Contributing Factors to the Crisis

The magnitude and nature of industrial expansion in the nineteenth and early twentieth centuries are major reasons for the environmental crisis that occurred. Especially important was the sophistication of manufacturing after 1820. New machinery supplanted hand tools and muscle power in the fabrication of goods, while the harnessing of water power to drive that machinery allowed production to be centered in large factories. In addition, mechanization undercut the need for workers with strong backs but required a large labor force with specialized skills or, at least, the agility to operate the myriad equipment. Rapid increases in the population helped provide this labor force. Technological achievements, ranging from advanced communications and transportation to interchangeable machine parts, encouraged the expansion and concentration of manufacturing. An organizational revolution brought about better coordination between management and production functions in various business enterprises and encouraged the formation of large, integrated companies, which began to exploit regional as well as national markets. Also, by mid-century factories were concentrating in milltowns and other urban areas at an increasingly rapid pace.

Later, between 1870 and 1920, American industry retained the basic features of the preceding decades but underwent substantial changes in detail and scale. In the 1880s, the value added to goods by manufacturing and processing exceeded the value of agricultural products for the first time. About 1890, the United States surpassed Great Britain in the volume of its industrial output, thus becoming a world leader in that field. American economic success in this period can be attributed primarily to superior natural and human resources. Coal, iron ore, lumber, and petroleum were abundant and provided the raw materials necessary for extensive economic growth. Steel production served as a yardstick of industrial primacy, and the United States became a major international producer after 1870. The exploitation of its petroleum resources led to extensive distilling and refining of lubricants, kerosene, and other commercial fuels. By 1914, electricity would revolutionize industry in America and replace water and steam as the major source of commercial power. A vibrant agricultural system, exceptionally adaptable to mechanization, became increasingly productive, even though industrial expansion came to dominate the economy. Population growth continued at a steady pace, and the demands for labor were met without serious setbacks throughout the period.

Many of these factors, which did in fact encourage industrial expansion in the nineteenth century, also contributed directly to the creation or aggravation of urban pollution. Chief among these were the use of coal as a major industrial energy source, the nature of the factory system, the process of industrial specialization and concentration, and the steadily increasing labor force.

Air Pollution

The smoky skies of the industrial city were a constant reminder of the dominance of coal as an energy source in the late nineteenth and early twentieth centuries. The need for a plentiful, inexpensive, and effective source of energy to provide power to run factory machinery and locomotives led to the preeminence of coal. In the early 1830s, the discovery of huge anthracite (or hard) coalfields in Pennsylvania furnished a high-quality fuel for industrial use, especially in the expanding iron (and later steel) industry. After 1850, a growing demand for iron in railroad construction and operation led to the shift from charcoal to mineral coal as a metallurgical fuel. Although wood was abundant and inexpensive west of the Mississippi, it was no longer available in large amounts in the vicinity of the eastern ironworks, especially in Pennsylvania. By 1895, coal consumption began to surpass wood use, because of the high demand for bituminous (or soft) coal by the steel and railroad industries. Wood continued to supply a substantial portion of the energy for domestic heating, but coal became the primary fuel for manufacturing and transportation.

Using coal as a major energy source, industrial development increased markedly, which, in turn, contributed to the severity of air pollution in urban areas. The most serious problem with coal, especially bituminous coal, was its devastating smoke, which left its mark on buildings, on laundry, and in the lungs of urbanites. Since only a small portion of bituminous coal was consumed in the generation of heat or power, much of the residue went directly into the air. The problem was greatest for cities with high concentrations of primary industries, such as Pittsburgh or St. Louis. Without vigorous regulation of pollution standards or the installation of adequate anti-smoke equipment, the smoke menace became critical. The Edison Company, which generated electricity for New York City, was a constant source of smoke pollution in the 1910s and was repeatedly cited by sanitary inspectors. During times when hard coal was in short supply, New York Edison would use soft coal, thereby increasing its smoke output markedly. Often, to deter sanitary inspectors from photographing Edison's smokestacks for use as evidence in legal proceedings, the company placed scouts on the roof who warned the engineers to stop feeding the coal into the furnaces. Even so, the New York Health Department was able to institute twenty-eight actions against the company in the early 1900s. Not until alternative fuels, such as natural gas, replaced coal, did the smoke problem begin to dissipate.

Coal provided the basic source of energy for large-scale industrial development, but the factory system created the managerial and operational means for the mass production of goods. By the 1850s, factories had become the dominant form of industrial enterprise, and they continued to expand in size as well as number into the twentieth century. . . . By its very nature, the factory system encouraged the central-ization of production in or near urban centers. Modern fac-tories produced goods on a large scale, and location was of primary importance. Factories had to be near, or have ready access to, sources of raw materials, a sufficient labor force, and sizeable markets. Efficient transportation could com-pensate for some deficiencies, especially access to raw mate-rials, but for the most part proximity to large cities meant the difference between economic success and failure.

Waste Disposal

These requirements for location of factories and their oper-ational practices, however, contributed greatly to urban pol-lution. Factories, especially those in the textile, chemical, and iron and steel industries, were often constructed near waterways, since large quantities of water were needed to supply steam boilers or for various production processes such as cooling hot surfaces of metals or making chemical solutions. Waterways also provided the easiest and least ex-pensive means of disposing of soluble or suspendable wastes. Studies of the impact of factories upon the environment sug-gest that, in 1900, 40 percent of the pollution load on Amer-ican rivers was industrial in origin. (By 1968 that figure had increased to 80 percent.) The "death" of New Jersey's Pas-saic River in the late nineteenth century was a classic illus-tration of how factories defiled their environment. Before it became badly polluted, the Passaic was a major recreational area and also the basis for a thriving commercial fishing in-dustry. As urbanization and industrialization expanded after the Civil War, the volume of sewage and industrial waste that poured into the river forced the city of Newark to aban-don the Passaic as a water supply. Pollution also ruined com-mercial fishing in the area, and soon homes along the waterway disappeared. During hot weather the river emitted such a stench that many factories were forced to close.

Factories found simple methods of disposal for other forms of waste, too. Rubbish, garbage, slag, ashes, and scrap metals were often indiscriminately dumped on land. . . . Slaughterhouses and meat packers were major land polluters. Meat packing, which began on farms or in small rural slaughterhouses, eventually concentrated in such cities as Chicago and St. Louis. In the New York/Brooklyn area alone, meat packers slaughtered more than 1.5 million animals in 1886. Foul smells permeated the area around the packinghouses, and animal wastes were simply dumped on vacant lots. Slaughterhouses and related animal processing industries such as tanneries, glue factories, and fat and bone boiling companies were often located in residential areas. The tanning industry contributed directly to water pollution, since hides were washed in urban watering places. . . .

The concentration of factories in or near urban areas substantially increased the polluting capability of industrial development. It stands to reason that two factories in close proximity compound the stress on the environment. A single factory may be responsible for tainting a water supply, but two or more may make the water toxic. From the late nineteenth century until 1920, American industry was concentrated in the Northeast. The so-called manufacturing belt included New England, the Middle Atlantic states, and the North Central states. At least three-fourths of American manufacturing was contained within the region bounded by the Great Lakes to the north, the Mississippi River to the west, and the Ohio River and the Mason-Dixon line to the south. Within this area, manufacturing was centered in the cities. As early as 1900, no less than thirty-four of the forty-four states produced more than 50 percent of their manufactured goods in urban rather than rural areas. In eighteen states more than 75 percent of products came from urban factories. The most intense concentration was in New England, where 296 cities contained more than 75 percent of the region's population and 81 percent of the manufacturing establishments. The Middle Atlantic states were not far behind. What made concentration of factories a critical environmental problem, aside from their density, was the fact that neither city authorities nor businessmen did much to confine factories to industrial areas or to segregate the most offensive industries from residential communities.

Industrial specialization in certain urban communities compounded the problems created by factory operations and concentration. Industrial specialization implies specialization of function and location—that is, special types of industry clustered in a single geographic location. Especially after 1870, there was a growing tendency for certain industries to congregate in or near specific urban centers for the sake of efficiency. Although this arrangement was economically sound, it often had disastrous environmental effects, especially if the industry was a blatant polluter. The Pennsylvania cities of McKeesport, Johnstown, and Pittsburgh, which produced large quantities of iron and steel, were inundated with environmental pollution. For instance, Pittsburgh in 1904 produced 63.8 percent of the national total of pig iron and 53.5 percent of the nation's steel. Little wonder that Pittsburgh had the reputation of being "the smoky city." As the chamber of commerce explained during debate over a 1906 anti-smoke ordinance, "With the palls of smoke which darken our sky continually and the almost continuous deposits of soot, our dirty streets and grimy buildings are simply evidences of the difficulty under which we labor in any endeavor to present Pittsburgh as an ideal home city.". . .

Overpopulation in the Cities

Human concentration in the cities matched industrial concentration as a major cause of pollution. The phenomenal increase in the American population in general and the urban population in particular during the nineteenth century is well known. It is staggering to consider that, between 1850 and 1920, the world population increased only 55 percent, while the population of the United States grew 357 percent. In 1850, the total population of the United States was approximately 23 million; by 1920 it was 106 million. As the population continued to enlarge, it concentrated increasingly in the cities. Also by 1920, the number of urban areas rose from 392 to 2,722, and the number of cities with a population of 50,000 or more increased from 16 to 144. . . .

As industrialization advanced, urban population rapidly rose to provide the labor force. Many workers found themselves crammed into deteriorating tenements with inadequate waste disposal.

With the urban population steadily on the rise and the bulk of the working force being attracted to industrial jobs, the cities underwent an incredible physical strain. None suffered the repercussions of the environmental crisis more than the working class. Overcrowding was the worst of the problems. Forced to live close to their places of employment, many workers found themselves crammed into the burgeoning slums in the central city. Housing was at a premium; few could afford to buy single-unit dwellings, so they rented what they could. . . . In a seller's market, landlords did little to upgrade the deteriorating tenements and converted buildings that many workers were forced to use as residences. Often families would share quarters with other individuals or groups. David Brody describes living conditions of Slavic steelworkers in Pennsylvania:

> The inadequate dwellings were greatly overcrowded. The boarding boss and his family slept in one downstairs room in the standard four-room farm house. The kitchen was set aside for eating and living purposes, although it, too, often served as a bedroom. Upstairs the boss crammed double beds which were in use night and day when the mill was running full. Investigators came upon many cases of extreme crowding. Thirty-three Serbians and their boarding boss lived in a five-room house in Steelton. In Sharpsburg, Pennsylvania, an Italian family and nine boarders existed without running water or toilet in four rooms on the third floor of a ramshackle tenement.

Brody went on to state, according to an Immigration Commission report, that the number per sleeping room in immigrant households averaged about three, with quite a few having four or as many as six or more per sleeping room.

Not only were individual dwellings overcrowded, but neighborhood densities were staggering. The average block density in lower Manhattan increased from 157.5 persons in 1820 to 272.5 persons in 1850. New York City's Sanitary District "A" averaged 986.4 people to the acre for thirty-two acres in 1894—or approximately 30,000 people in a space of five or six blocks. In comparison, Bombay, India—the next most crowded area in the world—had 759.7 people per acre, and Prague, the European city with the worst slum conditions, had only 485.4 people per acre.

Such crowded conditions and such limited city services provided fertile ground for health and sanitation problems. Many workers had little choice but to live in the least desirable sections of the city, usually close to the smoke-belching factories where they worked or near marshy bogs and stagnant pools, which speculators could not develop into prime residential communities. City services, especially sewage and refuse collection, failed to keep up with the demand. Smoke from wood-burning and coal-burning stoves and fireplaces fouled the air of the inner city, and the noise level in some areas reached a roar. Contemporary accounts of slum life were filled with horror stories of unsanitary living conditions. . . .

The statistics on health problems, disease, and high mortality rates were even more sobering. In one of the most widely publicized epidemics of its day, Memphis lost almost 10 percent of its population in 1873 to yellow fever, which ostensibly originated in its slums. In New Orleans, typhoid was spread throughout the city by sewage that oozed from the unpaved streets. In "Murder Bay," not far from the White House in Washington, D.C., black families picked their dinners out of garbage cans and dumps. Mortality figures for the area were consistently twice as high as in white neighborhoods; infant mortality in 1900 ranged as high as 317 per thousand. By 1870, the infant mortality rate in New York was 65 percent higher than in 1810. The enumeration of statistics could go on and on; the sad fact is that the personal tragedies of families in the crowded slums of the major cities were part of massive health, sanitation, and pollution problems that could not be corrected without the total commitment of the community.

The Mechanization of Farming

Carroll Pursell

Although the Industrial Revolution is usually associated with urban factories, it also revolutionized farming through the development of new agricultural machines, as Carroll Pursell explains in the following selection from his book *The Machine in America: A Social History of Technology*. Innovative devices such as the mechanical reaper and the electric milker significantly reduced the amount of time and labor needed to perform agricultural tasks, Pursell relates. He notes that these labor-saving machines were both beneficial and detrimental: They enabled farmers to become more productive, but they also led to the elimination of many agricultural jobs. Pursell is the Adeline Barry Davee Distinguished Professor of History at Case Western Reserve University in Cleveland, Ohio.

Agriculture in America in 1800 was the occupation of 80 percent of the American people. It was largely a hand operation, lightened only by the use of horses or oxen in certain limited, though important, tasks such as hauling and plowing. By 1900 a large percentage of the farmer's task was mechanized, and tools were often powered—in most cases still by horses and oxen, but steam, electricity, and internal combustion engines were already available for those who chose them. The primary characteristic of agricultural progress then, at least as far as technology was concerned, was the coming of machines. The second most important, and closely associated change, was the increasing use of horses to power those machines. . . .

With the traditional plow, it took three to five yoke of oxen and two people an entire day to turn just one-half acre of prairie sod. The common plow, as it had come down through the eighteenth century, was made entirely of wood, with perhaps some iron added at the share or with iron strips covering the mouldboard. This was not referred to as a wooden plow (although of course it was) until the introduction and spread of wrought iron plows in the early nineteenth century. In part this change was due to the increasing amount of iron available in the early years of the Industrial Revolution; in part it was a result of the same spirit of improvement that led Thomas Jefferson to try to work out mathematically an improved design for the mouldboard. . . .

Probably the most important breakthrough in plow design, at least for the western states, was the introduction of what came to be called the "steel plow." Prairie plowing involved two separate problems: the breaking of the mat of roots (sod) and the tendency of moist soil to stick to the mouldboard. It seems probable that during the 1830s blacksmiths in the prairie states began, here and there, to nail strips of saw-steel to the face of wooden mouldboards to prevent the soil from sticking. Then in 1837, at Grand Detour, Illinois, John Deere began to manufacture the first of his famous "steel" plows.

The name was somewhat misleading. Apparently what Deere did during these early years was to attach a share of steel to a wrought iron mouldboard and to polish the iron so that soil would be less likely to stick. He made ten of these plows in 1839 and 400 in 1843. Then in 1847, he moved to Moline, Illinois, a site that had better transportation to the growing West. By 1857 he was turning out 10,000 plows a year. It was probably not until about this time—that is, sometime late in the 1850s—that Deere actually began to make plows with a steel mouldboard. The fact that he referred to his plows as steel years earlier merely shows his own flare for advertising and the importance attached to having a share that could cut sod.

Important Inventions

Gathering the grass for hay was another of the great bottlenecks of agricultural technology in the early nineteenth century. To take the hay rake as an example, a whole stream of devices had made their appearance by the time of the Civil War. By hand, it took one day to cut an acre of hay and another half day to pile it into windrows where it could dry without moulding; turning the hay to cure it and then picking it up required still more labor. Under favorable conditions, one person in one day could harvest, with hand tools only, 1 ton of hay; under more usual conditions, a third of a ton was more likely.

Devices designed to dispense with the pitchfork in gathering hay began to appear in the late eighteenth century, and it has been reported that George Washington used a drag rake made of wood with wooden teeth. This type was not efficient and was little used. About 1830 drag rakes with wire teeth appeared on the market. Both types were in use until about 1850, but neither played a significant role in agricultural technology. A more useful device, the revolving horse rake, was apparently of American design and began to appear about 1820. Within thirty years it was standard among progressive farmers who grew large quantities of hay. Costing only $6 to $12, it was an important implement in the progressive application of horse power to agriculture.

The revolving rake eventually evolved into the sulky rake, which a farmer could ride. One of these was noted as early as 1837, but it did not receive wide attention until an improved version was patented by Calvin Delano of Maine in 1849. This machine was essentially perfected by 1870 and was a great labor-saving device: with it one person and a horse could gather 20 to 30 acres of hay a day. . . .

Perhaps the most famous agricultural implement to come out of America in the nineteenth century was the reaper, especially as perfected by Cyrus Hall McCormick. He patented his horse-drawn reaper in 1854, a year after Obed Hussey had patented what is generally accepted as the first successful machine of that type. The attempts to solve the problem, however, had been going on for some time: Cyrus's father, Robert McCormick, had spent years working on a reaper that he never brought to perfection. In 1847 Cyrus moved from Cincinnati to Chicago, where he made an enormous fortune and came to dominate the industry. His great horse-drawn machine, with its revolving blades slicing off the wheat, provided the primary mechanical icon of nineteenth-century American agriculture, and his manufacturing firm, protected by its monopoly on the device, was an early giant among American corporations.

The Growth of Farms

The land given over to farming in the United States more than doubled between 1850 and 1890 and trebled by 1910. The farm population of the nation rose by 50 percent between 1880 and 1910, from 21.9 million to 32.4 million souls, a high figure that was never significantly exceeded. . . .

In areas such as the Red River Valley and the central valley of California, the simple pioneer with perhaps $100 worth of machinery gave way to "bonanza farming," so named for its great scale and rich rewards. Many of these large landholdings were obtained directly from railroads, which, in turn, had obtained them free from the government as an inducement to build. One farm syndicate in the Dakotas in the mid-1870s was 6 miles long and 4 miles wide. In 1879 it had 10,000 acres planted to wheat. In 1877 this farm was equipped with 26 special plows to break the sod, 40 plows for turning over the earth once broken, 21 seeders, 60 harrows, 30 self-binding harvesters, five steam-powered threshers, and 30 wagons. Some idea of the expense of such an operation is suggested by the costs incurred by a similar farm during 1878–80: it had taken $60,100 of investment to prepare for production: $17,000 was for breaking the sod, $9,000 for machinery, $6,500 for buildings, and the rest for miscellaneous costs.

Such farms had appeared in California much earlier. One farm of 8,000 acres near Sacramento in 1856 had 1,000 acres under fence. A nearby farm had 1,600 fenced acres in addition to large unfenced tracts. A thousand acres of wheat and barley were under cultivation, and farm equipment included 20 wagons, 50 plows, 25 harrows, two threshing machines, seven reapers and mowers, and four hay presses. Farms of 11,000 acres were not unknown. McCormick's reaper was a necessity on such farms, of course, as was the steam-powered thresher to remove the grain from the dry stalks. Late in the century, repeated efforts were made to join these two together in what came to be called a combine. . . .

It is not possible to say exactly when the first steam engine was used on a farm, although by 1838 several hundred were at work grinding sugarcane, sawing wood, and being used for other tasks of this kind. Such stationary engines did not provide adequate power for American farmers, however, who needed something more flexible. The first portable engines were built by two firms in 1849. These could be moved about from barnyard to field and were available to do various kinds of belt work. About a dozen firms were making them during the 1850s.

Since plowing accounted for about 60 percent of the labor involved in raising grain, agricultural societies, journals, and inventors concentrated on developing a self-propelled traction engine. Another incentive was that threshing machines of increased capacity (the acreage of wheat doubled between 1866 and 1878) were beyond the efficient capacity of horses to operate. Portable engines built to provide this power cost about $1,000.

Before 1873 scores of companies and individual inventors had tried to make engines self-propelling, but to no avail. It was not until the builders of threshing machines began to make their portable engines self-propelling that real progress was made. These earliest traction engines still depended on horses to steer them, and it was not until 1882 that an Ohio firm produced the first self-steering, self-propelled traction engine. This success greatly stimulated the use of steam on the farm: in 1880 it produced 1.2 million horsepower; in 1890, 2 million; and in 1910 it reached its highest level at 3.6 million. The largest number of steam traction engines in use at any one time was not reached until 1913, when 10,000 were counted. By then, of course, the popularity of the gasoline tractor was eating into this number. In 1920 only 1,700 steam engines were built, and by 1925 their manufacture was largely abandoned. The remaining examples of this machine are still impressive: some of the largest weighed 20 tons (developing 50–100 horsepower) and consumed 3 tons of coal and 3,000 gallons of water a day. They cost anywhere from two to six thousand dollars.

Changes in the Workforce

The productivity of farm workers rose dramatically during the nineteenth century, and the time spent on different tasks changed as well. In 1800 it took an estimated fifty-six person-hours per acre to produce a crop of wheat, and forty of these were taken up by harvesting. By 1880 the total number of hours had dropped to twenty, and of that only twelve were used in harvesting. In 1900 the total required per acre of wheat was fifteen person-hours, of which only eight were for harvesting. Not only did the number of hours fall dramatically, from fifty-six to fifteen, but the proportion needed for harvesting dropped from nearly four-fifths to only slightly more than half. It was a signal example of the oft-boasted fact that farm workers were becoming more productive, which was part of the reason that the food one farm worker could raise increased from an amount for only 4.1 persons in 1820 to 7.0 persons by 1900.

The appearance of labor-saving devices on American farms worked to push down "hired help" from a class of apprentice farmers, often the children of other farmers who were considered almost one of the family, to a permanent class of migrant and part-time workers, socially stigmatized in many districts as "tramps." Some improved machines, like the self-binding harvester, significantly cut labor needs. This device, which first became available in 1878, displaced an estimated 75 percent of the workers needed in harvesting grain.

Not only that, the machine significantly widened the gap between farmer and hired hand. Now the former tended to do the lighter work, and the latter the heavier. Total, or at least seasonal, unemployment meant that hands had to travel to find work, thus weakening local ties and creating a floating body of workers who were strangers wherever they went. One worker testified: "Of one thing we are convinced, that while the improved machinery is gathering our large crops, making our boots and shoes, doing the work of our carpenters, stone sawyers, and builders, thousands of able, willing men are going from place to place seeking employment, and finding none. The question naturally arises, is improved machinery a blessing or a curse?"

In some places strikes were held in an attempt to keep up wages. During the 1878 harvest season, some farmers in Ohio, Indiana, Michigan, and in parts of other states had their machines destroyed. Farmers, usually described as wealthy or well-to-do, received threatening letters warning, as one put it, "if you use one of these G—d——d machines we will burn your wheat stacks." Sometimes the machines themselves were burned, and in other cases farmers who had already purchased self-binding reapers were too fearful to actually put them into the fields, preferring to go back to cradle scythes for that season. A few farmers voluntarily clung to hand methods, acting on an ethic other than that of maximizing profits no matter whom it hurt. "A large class of farmers," one newspaper noted, "has steadily refused to purchase binders for the reason that it deprives the laboring class of work." The other extreme was represented by a Minnesota farmer who shot and killed two men setting fire to his harvester. He surrendered to local authorities but was released without charges, and neighbors formed a rifle club and put up signs declaring "Tramps wanted as a top-dressing [i.e., fertilizer] for the growing crops." Both the rising capital requirements for entering into farming and the disappearance of year-round work opened a widening gulf between those who could successfully farm and those who could never hope for better than inadequate seasonal wage-labor.

Not only the farm laborer but the farm owner, too, began to find technological improvement a two-edged sword. Transportation had always been critical to successful commercial farming, and before the canal era even farms in the East and Midwest went through a pioneer period in which crops that could not be easily transported were grown only for family consumption and cash was provided by the butter and egg business of the farm women. In the West, large crops and vast distances made farmers entirely dependent on railroads for getting produce to market. Refrigerated cars helped cattle-raisers carry beef, but the building of giant storage silos provided yet another opportunity for monopoly practices that cut farmers off from customers and channeled the profit to those who controlled the mediating technology. The power of railroads over farmers was dramatically conveyed in Frank Norris's novel *The Octopus* (1901), which fictionalized an actual violent confrontation between California wheat farmers and the Southern Pacific Railroad. . . .

Electricity

Although horse power was the most significant and widely useful form of energy for the farm, new forms other than steam were also appearing by the end of the century. Electricity was not easily tamed for farm work, and it was not at all clear just what it could and could not be expected to accomplish. During the century innovators sought to apply it to belt work and plowing, to use it for illumination, and use it as a substitute for fertilizer to stimulate plant growth. By the 1870s and 1880s electric plowing was finally accomplished in England and on the European continent; by the end of World War II there were an estimated 1,600 electric plows in Germany alone. In 1890 an electric traction engine was displayed at the California State Fair, but nothing came of it. Electric plows never became common in the United States.

Electricity had greater success in belt work, general stationary power supply, and illumination than it had in field work. In 1892 it was first used for belt work at the Agricultural Experiment Station at Alabama Polytechnic Institute, where a 10-horsepower motor was used to operate a thresher, feed cutter, cotton press, cotton gin, and cotton-seed crusher. In that same year, the Crystal Hill Dairy in Pennsylvania began to use electricity for dairy equipment. . . .

Such technological advances as steam plowing and electric milkers were relatively exotic in American agriculture before the twentieth century. Rather, the technological aid received by the average farmer came in the form of better hand tools and a wider range of horse-powered equipment, both manufactured more cheaply and in greater abundance by the adoption of the American system of manufactures [i.e., the use of interchangeable parts]. . . .

In all regions of the country, but especially in the Northeast and South, there was a lingering tendency to rely on hand tools down to the twentieth century. Whole areas of farming—such as dairying, poultry raising, horticulture, local transport, and housework—received little mechanical aid. The greatest single factor in this retardation of mechanization was the lack of any cheap and flexible power. What progress was made in the nineteenth century was largely the result of harnessing the horse to perform what had previously been done by hand. It was not until the appearance of the small rubber-tired, gasoline-powered tractor and the Rural Electrification Agency of the 1930s that adequate power was finally available to the nation's farmers.

The most important results were that farming remained a hand operation to a large extent, and the relatively simple technology remained fairly inexpensive to acquire. Patents for farm devices had been among the most numerous during the nineteenth century, and a wide range of small hand-operated machines were available. Small horsepowers, which used an animal on a treadmill to produce mechanical power, were widely available. In 1862 it cost only $968 to equip a medium-size general farm. The increasing application of something like mass production to simple hand and horse-drawn equipment brought prices down, and by 1907 one could equip that same farm for only $785.

The breaking of the power bottleneck on the vast majority of farms came only in the early twentieth century, with the wide availability of electricity and tractors: these technologies, and the kind of capital-intensive agriculture they represented, brought to a close more than 300 years of small family-owned farms in America. The days when the yeoman farmer was the backbone of the nation had only been made possible by a solicitous political system, an abundance of cheap land, and the relatively slow development of farm technology.

The Effect of Labor-Saving Devices on Housework

Ruth Schwartz Cowan

In the following article, Ruth Schwartz Cowan writes that the Industrial Revolution directly impacted the average home through new technologies, such as central heating, indoor plumbing, and electric lights, that vastly improved living conditions. Furthermore, the nature of housework was significantly altered by the invention of labor-saving appliances, including washing machines, electric irons, and gas stoves. Nevertheless, Cowan maintains, these labor-saving devices did not lead to a reduction in the amount of work performed by homemakers: Instead, housewives decreased their reliance on hired help, adopted higher standards of cleanliness, and added new chores to their responsibilities. A professor of history at the State University of New York at Stony Brook, Cowan is the author of *A Social History of American Technology* and *More Work for Mother: The Ironies of Household Technology from the Open Hearth to the Microwave*.

When we think about the interaction between technology and society, we tend to think in fairly grandiose terms: massive computers invading the workplace, railroad tracks cutting through vast wildernesses, armies of women and children toiling in the mills. These grand visions have blinded us to an important and rather peculiar technological revolution which has been going on right under our noses: the technological revolution in the home. This revolution has transformed the conduct of our daily lives, but in somewhat unexpected ways. The industrialization of the home was a process very differ-

Excerpted from "The 'Industrial Revolution' in the Home: Household Technology and Social Change in the 20th Century," by Ruth Schwartz Cowan, *Technology and Culture*, January 1976. Copyright © 1976 by *Technology and Culture*. Reprinted with permission.

ent from the industrialization of other means of production, and the impact of that process was neither what we have been led to believe it was nor what students of the other industrial revolutions would have been led to predict. . . .

Changes in Everyday Household Work

I have, for the purposes of this study, deliberately limited myself to one kind of technological change affecting one aspect of family life in only one of the many social classes of families that might have been considered. What happened, I asked, to middle-class American women when the implements with which they did their everyday household work changed? Did the technological change in household appliances have any effect upon the structure of American households, or upon the ideologies that governed the behavior of American women, or upon the functions that families needed to perform? Middle-class American women were defined as actual or potential readers of the better-quality women's magazines, such as the *Ladies' Home Journal, American Home, Parents' Magazine, Good Housekeeping,* and *McCall's.* Nonfictional material (articles and advertisements) in those magazines was used as a partial indicator of some of the technological and social changes that were occurring.

The *Ladies' Home Journal* has been in continuous publication since 1886. A casual survey of the nonfiction in the *Journal* yields the immediate impression that that decade between the end of World War I and the beginning of the depression witnessed the most drastic changes in patterns of household work. Statistical data bear out this impression. Before 1918, for example, illustrations of homes lit by gaslight could still be found in the *Journal;* by 1928 gaslight had disappeared. In 1917 only one-quarter (24.3 percent) of the dwellings in the United States had been electrified, but by 1920 this figure had doubled (47.4 percent—for rural nonfarm and urban dwellings), and by 1930 it had risen to four-fifths percent). If electrification had meant simply the change from gas or oil lamps to electric lights, the changes in the housewife's routines might not have been very great (except for eliminating the chore of cleaning and filling oil lamps); but changes in lighting were the least of the changes that electrification implied. Small electric appliances followed quickly on the heels of the electric light, and some of those augured much more profound changes in the housewife's routine.

Ironing, for example, had traditionally been one of the most dreadful household chores, especially in warm weather when the kitchen stove had to be kept hot for the better part of the day; irons were heavy and they had to be returned to the stove frequently to be reheated. Electric irons eased a good part of this burden. They were relatively inexpensive and very quickly replaced their predecessors; advertisements for electric irons first began to appear in the ladies' magazines after the war, and by the end of the decade the old flat-iron had disappeared; by 1929 a survey of 100 Ford employees revealed that ninety-eight of them had the new electric irons in their homes.

Data on the diffusion of electric washing machines are somewhat harder to come by; but it is clear from the advertisements in the magazines, particularly advertisements for laundry soap, that by the middle of the 1920s those machines could be found in a significant number of homes. The washing machine is depicted just about as frequently as the laundry tub by the middle of the 1920s; in 1929, forty-nine out of those 100 Ford workers had the machines in their homes. The washing machines did not drastically reduce the time that had to be spent on household laundry, as they did not go through their cycles automatically and did not spin dry; the housewife had to stand guard, stopping and starting the machine at appropriate times, adding soap, sometimes attaching the drain pipes, and putting the clothes through the wringer manually. The machines did, however, reduce a good part of the drudgery that once had been associated with washday, and this was a matter of no small consequence. Soap powders appeared on the market in the early 1920s, thus eliminating the need to scrape and boil bars of laundry soap. By the end of the 1920s Blue Monday must have been considerably less blue for some housewives—and probably considerably less "Monday," for with an electric iron, a washing machine, and a hot water heater, there was no reason to limit the washing to just one day of the week.

Modernized Houses

Like the routines of washing the laundry, the routines of personal hygiene must have been transformed for many households during the 1920s—the years of the bathroom mania. More and more bathrooms were built in older homes, and new homes began to include them as a matter of course. Before the war most bathroom fixtures (tubs, sinks, and toilets) were made out of porcelain by hand; each bathroom was custom-made for the house in which it was installed. After the war industrialization descended upon the bathroom industry; cast iron enamelware went into mass production and fittings were standardized. In 1921 the dollar value of the production of enameled sanitary fixtures was $2.4 million, the same as it had been in 1915. By 1923, just two years later, that figure had doubled to $4.8 million; it rose again, to $5.1 million, in 1925. The first recessed, double-shell cast iron enameled bathtub was put on the market in the early 1920s. A decade later the standard American bathroom had achieved its standard American form: the recessed tub, plus tiled floors and walls, brass plumbing, a single-unit toilet, an enameled sink, and a medicine chest, all set into a small room which was very often 5 feet square. The bathroom evolved more quickly than any other room of the house; its standardized form was accomplished in just over a decade.

Along with bathrooms came modernized systems for heating hot water: 61 percent of the homes in Zanesville, Ohio, had indoor plumbing with centrally heated water by 1926, and 83 percent of the homes valued over $2,000 in Muncie, Indiana, had hot and cold running water by 1935. These figures may not be typical of small American cities (or even large American cities) at those times, but they do jibe with the impression that one gets from the magazines: after 1918 references to hot water heated on the kitchen range, either for laundering or for bathing, become increasingly difficult to find.

Similarly, during the 1920s many homes were outfitted with central heating; in Muncie most of the homes of the business class had basement heating in 1924; by 1935 Federal

Emergency Relief Administration data for the city indicated that only 22.4 percent of the dwellings valued over $2,000 were still heated by a kitchen stove. What all these changes meant in terms of new habits for the average housewife is somewhat hard to calculate; changes there must have been, but it is difficult to know whether those changes produced an overall saving of labor and/or time. Some chores were eliminated—hauling water, heating water on the stove, maintaining the kitchen fire—but other chores were added—most notably the chore of keeping yet another room scrupulously clean.

It is not, however, difficult to be certain about the changing habits that were associated with the new American kitchen—a kitchen from which the coal stove had disappeared. In Muncie in 1924, cooking with gas was done in two out of three homes; in 1935 only 5 percent of the homes valued over $2,000 still had coal or wood stoves for cooking. After 1918 advertisements for coal and wood stoves disappeared from the *Ladies' Home Journal;* stove manufacturers purveyed only their gas, oil, or electric models. Articles giving advice to homemakers on how to deal with the trials and tribulations of starting, stoking, and maintaining a coal or a wood fire also disappeared. Thus it seems a safe assumption that most middle-class homes had switched to the new method of cooking by the time the depression began. The change in routine that was predicated on the change from coal or wood to gas or oil was profound; aside from the elimination of such chores as loading the fuel and removing the ashes, the new stoves were much easier to light, maintain, and regulate (even when they did not have thermostats, as the earliest models did not). Kitchens were, in addition, much easier to clean when they did not have coal dust regularly tracked through them; one writer in the *Ladies' Home Journal* estimated that kitchen cleaning was reduced by one-half when coal stoves were eliminated. . . .

The Impact of New Household Technologies

Many of the changes just described—from hand power to electric power, from coal and wood to gas and oil as fuels for cooking, from one-room heating to central heating, from pumping water to running water—are enormous technological changes. Changes of a similar dimension, either in the fundamental technology of an industry, in the diffusion of that technology, or in the routines of workers, would have long since been labeled an "industrial revolution." The change from the laundry tub to the washing machine is no less profound than the change from the hand loom to the power loom; the change from pumping water to turning on a water faucet is no less destructive of traditional habits than the change from manual to electric calculating. It seems odd to speak of an "industrial revolution" connected with housework, odd because we are talking about the technology of such homely things, and odd because we are not accustomed to thinking of housewives as a labor force or of housework as an economic commodity—but despite this oddity, I think the term is altogether appropriate.

In this case other questions come immediately to mind, questions that we do not hesitate to ask, say, about textile workers in Britain in the early 19th century, but we have never thought to ask about housewives in America in the 20th century. What happened to this particular work force when the technology of its work was revolutionized? Did structural changes occur? Were new jobs created for which new skills were required? Can we discern new ideologies that influenced the behavior of the workers?

The answer to all of these questions, surprisingly enough, seems to be yes. There were marked structural changes in the work force, changes that increased the work load and the job description of the workers that remained. New jobs were created for which new skills were required; these jobs were not physically burdensome, but they may have taken up as much time as the jobs they had replaced. New ideologies were also created, ideologies which reinforced new behavioral patterns, patterns that we might not expect. Middle-class housewives, the women who must have first felt the impact of the new household technology, were not flocking into the divorce courts or the labor market or the forums of political protest in the years immediately after the revolution in their work. What they were doing was sterilizing baby bottles, shepherding their children to dancing classes and music lessons, planning nutritious meals, shopping for new clothes, studying child psychology, and hand stitching color-coordinated curtains. The significant change in the structure of the household labor force was the disappearance of paid and unpaid servants (unmarried daughters, maiden aunts, and grandparents fall in the latter category) as household workers—and the imposition of the entire job on the housewife herself. Leaving aside for a moment the question of which was cause and which effect (did the disappearance of the servant create a demand for the new technology, or did the new technology make the servant obsolete?), the phenomenon itself is relatively easy to document. Before World War I, when illustrators in the women's magazines depicted women doing housework, the women were very often servants. When the lady of the house was drawn, she was often the person being served, or she was supervising the serving, or she was adding an elegant finishing touch to the work. Nursemaids diapered babies, seamstresses pinned up hems, waitresses served meals, laundresses did the wash, and cooks did the cooking. By the end of the 1920s the servants had disappeared from those illustrations; all those jobs were being done by housewives—elegantly manicured and coiffed, to be sure, but housewives nonetheless.

If we are tempted to suppose that illustrations in advertisements are not a reliable indicator of structural changes of this sort, we can corroborate the changes in other ways. Apparently, the illustrators really did know whereof they drew. Statistically the number of persons throughout the country employed in household service dropped from 1,851,000 in 1910 to 1,411,000 in 1920, while the number of households enumerated in the census rose from 20.3 million to 24.4 million. In Indiana the ratio of households to servants increased from 13.5/1 in 1890 to 30.5/1 in 1920, and in the country as a whole the number of paid domestic servants per 1,000 population dropped from 98.9 in 1900 to 58.0 in 1920. . . .

An Increase in Housework

As the number of household assistants declined, the number of household tasks increased. The middle-class housewife was expected to demonstrate competence at several tasks that previously had not been in her purview or had not existed at all. Child care is the most obvious example. The average housewife had fewer children than her mother had had, but she was expected to do things for her children that her mother would never have dreamed of doing: to prepare their special infant formulas, sterilize their bottles, weigh them every day, see to it that they ate nutritionally balanced meals, keep them isolated and confined when they had even the slightest illness, consult with their teachers frequently, and chauffeur them to dancing lessons, music lessons, and evening parties. There was very little Freudianism in this new attitude toward child care: mothers were not spending more time and effort on their children because they feared the psychological trauma of separation, but because competent nursemaids could not be found, and the new theories of child care required constant attention from well-informed persons—persons who were willing and able to read about the latest discoveries in nutrition, in the control of contagious diseases, or in the techniques of behavioral psychology. These persons simply had to be their mothers. . . .

Several contemporary observers also believed that standards of household care changed during the decade of the 1920s. The discovery of the "household germ" led to almost fetishistic concern about the cleanliness of the home. The amount and frequency of laundering probably increased, as bed linen and underwear were changed more often, children's clothes were made increasingly out of washable fabrics, and men's shirts no longer had replaceable collars and cuffs. Unfortunately all these changes in standards are difficult to document, being changes in the things that people regard as so insignificant as to be unworthy of comment; the improvement in standards seems a likely possibility, but not something that can be proved.

In any event we do have various time studies which demonstrate somewhat surprisingly that housewives with conveniences were spending just as much time on household duties as were housewives without them—or, to put it another way, housework, like so many other types of work, expands to fill the time available. A study comparing the time spent per week in housework by 288 farm families and 154 town families in Oregon in 1928 revealed 61 hours spent by farm wives and 63.4 hours by town wives; in 1929 a U.S. Department of Agriculture study of families in various states produced almost identical results. [If the new conveniences had led to a reduction of housework, surely] housewives in towns, where presumably the benefits of specialization and electrification were most likely to be available, should have been spending far less time at their work than their rural sisters. However, just after World War II economists at Bryn Mawr College reported the same phenomenon: 60.55 hours spent by farm housewives, 78.35 hours by women in small cities, 80.57 hours by women in large ones—precisely the reverse of the results that were expected. A 1973 survey of time studies conducted between 1920 and 1970 concludes that the time spent on housework by nonemployed housewives has remained remarkably constant throughout the period. All these results point in the same direction: mechanization of the household meant that time expended on some jobs decreased, but also that new jobs were substituted, and in some cases—notably laundering—time expenditures for old jobs increased because of higher standards. The advantages of mechanization may be somewhat more dubious than they seem at first glance.

The Industrial Revolution's Effect on Education

Edward C. Kirkland

Edward C. Kirkland was a professor of history at Bowdoin College in Brunswick, Maine, for more than twenty years. Among his numerous books are *A History of American Economic Life* and *Men, Cities, and Transportation: A Study in New England History, 1820–1900*. In the following selection, excerpted from *Industry Comes of Age: Business, Labor, and Public Policy, 1860–1897*, Kirkland traces the influence of the Industrial Revolution on the U.S. public education system. Before industrialization, he explains, workers typically served a long apprenticeship in which they thoroughly learned the intricacies of their chosen trade. However, he writes, the apprentice system did not work within the new industrial factories, which emphasized speed and specialization. Industry's need for trained workers sparked the growth of vocational education within the public schools, Kirkland concludes.

One result of the [industrial revolution] was a new form of education for industrial pursuits. Formerly a beginner had customarily learned his handicraft by indenturing himself for a period of years to a master. Nearly all the states had legislation regulating the conditions of apprenticeship; [by the era of 1860–1897] they were anachronisms. One uncertainty was how much skill the new way of industry required. Some occupations, such as the building trade, depended, in spite of the woodworking factory, upon skilled workers to assemble and finish a building. In the coal mines, fathers continued to take their sons down to learn the trade at the

Excerpted from *Industry Comes of Age: Business, Labor, and Public Policy, 1860–1897*, by Edward C. Kirkland (New York: Holt, Rinehart and Winston, 1961). Copyright © 1961 by Holt, Rinehart and Winston, renewed 1989 by Edward C. Kirkland. Reprinted by permission of the publisher. This material may not be reproduced in any form or by any means without the prior written permission of the publisher.

seam's face. In industry in general, however, there was, as economist Francis Amasa Walker explained, "automatic machinery . . . operated by a rough boy called in from the streets or farm." He learned his specialized task soon. But the automatic machines required machinists to design and construct them, to make adjustments, to detect "mysterious faults," and to repair or replace broken parts. There had not been enough skill in 1870 to keep automatic machines running if they had been available.

Apprenticeship collapsed. There was no one in the factory to give the instruction. The foreman couldn't spare the time; the employer couldn't afford to pay wages to a skilled worker and lose his productivity while he instructed someone else, nor could he pay standard wages to a beginner. The regular employees were alarmed at the presence of a worker paid on a sub-standard basis, and, since they believed in the law of supply and demand as a determinant of wages, were as unwilling to enlarge the labor force with apprentices as they were to have the employer import workers from abroad. The evidence suggests that apprentices had a hard, dull time in the factory. Whether they suffered more from the indifference of the employer or the callousness of fellow employees is difficult to ascertain. In any case, once a novice jumped the high hurdle of admission limitations that workers were always striving to erect, he was put on trivial tasks like "sweeping out" or did errands, and if he learned how to handle a simple machine he was kept at it, because he was thus more immediately useful than if he had been moved around the shop until he had learned many processes. Although the breakdown in apprenticeship was probably bearable in most instances and nostalgia over its passing was excessive, the old-fashioned ways did develop all-round talents and the habit of meeting production emergencies, qualities invaluable in foreman or superintendent.

Industrial Education

The whole period was alive with experiment in new forms of industrial education. Since professional instruction [in engineering and similar fields] was confined to higher education, the vital questions were the provision of preparatory work for such institutions, or of final training for those who were to remain privates in the industrial ranks rather than become "captains of industry." Little could be done with the instruction in the elementary public school, which had to concern itself with the inculcation of reading, writing, spelling and arithmetic. Those bent on reform, therefore, had to be content with tinkering with those subjects to make them "more practical" or with introducing supplementary subjects such as manual training and drawing to acquaint pupils with perception of form and space and to educate them through training the hand and the eye as well as the head. Since such innovations could be denominated "general education," every student could be compelled to take them.

More vulnerable to change was the high school. In this era the public education movement was rapidly providing institutions for secondary schools and enacting compulsory attendance laws. Some thought these new schools should train students for entrance to the academic colleges, where they could be trained for the professions, for a life of scholarship, or the life of a gentleman. To many it seemed wiser in an industrial commercial culture, clearly on the march and clearly competing with rivals in Europe, especially Germany, for the high school to give instruction in the scientific principles applicable to industry. This meant more chemistry, physics, and mathematics perhaps through calculus, and also instruction in the trades. How specialized the latter instruction should be depended upon the size and wealth of the community, its distinctive industries, and the willingness of the laboring community to tolerate a method of educating workers which it did not control.

Trade or industrial schools had to have a shop. Whether it should inculcate the skill of plumbers, carpenters or machinists in particular or just general mechanical aptitude was a matter of dispute. Many of the tangles inherent in establishing industrial schools at public expense were avoided if private philanthropy could be induced to finance them. So it happened that from Worcester, Massachusetts, where a group of enlightened industrialists founded and supported the Worcester County Free Institute of Industrial Science, to Terre Haute, Indiana, where Chauncey Rose, a man with a fortune derived from railroads and commerce, founded the Terre Haute School of Industrial Science, private persons with means were pioneers in the new education.

Whether under private or public ownership, these schools were plagued with persistent dilemmas. In a fluid, individualistic society such as that of the United States it was impossible, for one thing, to single out those with mechanical aptitudes and compel or induce them to follow a course of training appropriate to their abilities. For another thing, it was impossible to eradicate the notion of "general education." Even engineers were pointing out that man is more than a producer; he is a social and political being. Education must, therefore, set the character and habits for these functions. Sometimes an even broader context was employed. For example, in 1900 George I. Rockwood stated, "The end and aim of life is not simply to equip professional men; it is not simply to equip people with the power to 'do business'; it is not *simply* to enable people to earn a living." Admittedly it was hard to correlate general education with American industrial supremacy. But British observers ascribed the latter achievement to our great common school education. Employers, also, were generally talking about the value for manufacturing of general intelligence and knowledge. A narrowly vocational educational system would in a period of rapid technological change produce only outmoded or useless skills.

Appendix of Documents

Document 1: God's Chosen People

Many of the early leaders of the United States felt that the nation should refrain from industrializing, especially since they believed the factory system had caused significant societal problems in England. In the following excerpt from his 1785 book Notes on the State of Virginia, *Thomas Jefferson, one of the most prominent founding fathers, argues that agriculture is morally superior to manufacturing.*

The political oeconomists of Europe have established it as a principle that every state should endeavour to manufacture for itself: and this principle, like many others, we transfer to America, without calculating the difference of circumstance which should often produce a difference of result. In Europe the lands are either cultivated, or locked up against the cultivator. Manufacture must therefore be resorted to of necessity not of choice, to support the surplus of their people. But we have an immensity of land courting the industry of the husbandman. Is it best then that all our citizens should be employed in its improvement, or that one half should be called off from that to exercise manufactures and handicraft arts for the other? Those who labour in the earth are the chosen people of God, if ever he had a chosen people, whose breasts he has made his peculiar deposit for substantial and genuine virtue. . . . Generally speaking, the proportion which the aggregate of the other classes of citizens bears in any state to that of its husbandmen, is the proportion of its unsound to its healthy parts, and is a good-enough barometer whereby to measure its degree of corruption. While we have land to labour then, let us never wish to see our citizens occupied at a work-bench, or twirling a distaff. Carpenters, masons, smiths, are wanting in husbandry: but, for the general operations of manufacture, let our work-shops remain in Europe. It is better to carry provisions and materials to workmen there, than bring them to the provisions and materials, and with them their manners and principles. The loss by the transportation of commodities across the Atlantic will be made up in happiness.

Thomas Jefferson, *Notes on the State of Virginia*. Ed. Frank Shuffelton. New York: Penguin Books, 1999.

Document 2: An Economic Necessity

Alexander Hamilton, the first U.S. secretary of the treasury, actively encouraged the adoption of manufacturing. One of his main arguments, as presented in the following excerpt from his 1791 Report on the Subject of Manufactures, *was that the United States needed a class of industrial workers to create a demand for its agricultural surplus.*

The expediency of encouraging manufactures in the United States, which was not long since deemed very questionable, appears at this time to be pretty generally admitted. The embarrassments, which have obstructed the progress of our external trade, have led to serious reflections on the necessity of enlarging the sphere of our domestic commerce: the restrictive regulations, which in foreign markets abrige the vent of the increasing surplus of our Agricultural produce, serve to beget an earnest desire, that a more extensive demand for that surplus may be created at home: And the complete success, which has rewarded manufacturing enterprise, in some valuable branches, conspiring with the promising symptoms, which attend some less mature essays, in others, justify a hope, that the obstacles to the growth of this species of industry are less formidable than they were apprehended to be. . . .

The United States are to a certain extent in the situation of a country precluded from foreign Commerce. They can indeed, without difficulty obtain from abroad the manufactured supplies, of which they are in want; but they experience numerous and very injurious impediments to the emission and vent of their own commodities. Nor is this the case in reference to a single foreign nation only. The regulations of several countries, with which we have the most extensive intercourse, throw serious obstructions in the way of the principal staples of the United States.

In such a position of things, the United States cannot exchange with Europe on equal terms; and the want of reciprocity would render them the victim of a system, which should induce them to confine their views to Agriculture and refrain from Manufactures. A constant and encreasing necessity, on their part, for the commodities of Europe, and only a partial and occasional demand for their own, in return, could not but expose them to a state of impoverishment.

Harold C. Syrett et al., eds., *The Papers of Alexander Hamilton.* Vol. 10, *December 1791–January 1792.* New York: Columbia University Press, 1966.

Document 3: Destroying the Machines

The introduction of new machinery often led to the elimination of jobs or demands for drastic increases in production. In the early stages of the Industrial Revolution, workers in England and Europe sometimes protested these changes by breaking the machines. The following account describes an 1819 riot in France.

We, king's attorney in the court of first instance at Vienne, department of the Isère, acting on the information which we have just received this day February 26, 1819, that the new cloth-shearing machine belonging to Messrs. Gentin and Odoard had just reached the bank of the Gère river near the building intended to house it when a numerous band of workers hastened toward the spot crying *"Down with the shearing machine"*; that some rifle shots were heard, and in general everything about this meeting of workers announced the will and the intent to pillage by force a piece of property, we immediately went to the place where the mayor and the police commissioner agreed to authorize us to use armed force. . . .

Having arrived near the shop of Messrs. Odoard and Gentin, on the right bank of the river, we saw in the stream, at a distance of about fifteen feet, a carriage without horses, its shafts in the air, loaded with four or five crates, one of which was obviously broken, and at three or four paces off in the water, an instrument of iron or some other metal of the same size as the crate, in terms of its length. . . .

M. Desprémenil, lieutenant-colonel of the dragoons, the commander on the spot, declared to us that some minutes before our arrival, when the armed force had not yet managed to disperse the gathering on the right bank, many individuals in short vests whom he did not know but whom he presumed to be workers, hurled themselves into the water and rushed the carriage, armed with wooden clubs and an iron instrument called a cloth-shearer, that they broke the first crate which fell to their hands and threw into the water one of the instruments which it contained, that they were going to continue when . . . the soldiers, dragoons and police . . . put the assailants to flight, in spite of a hail of stones from the windows and the two banks of the Gère.

Peter N. Stearns, ed., *The Impact of the Industrial Revolution: Protest and Alienation*. Englewood Cliffs, NJ: Prentice-Hall, 1972.

Document 4: American Innovations

The manufacturers of the United States originally borrowed industrial inventions from England, but they soon began to improve on these designs. Writing in 1821, American author William Tudor praised his fellow citizens' creativity.

There are no people more ingenious in the use and invention of machinery, no country more prolific in patents, than the one under consideration. Good mechanics are to be found in every one of the mechanic arts, and the improvements they have made in some old, and the invention of many new instruments, are strong proofs of their skill and enterprise. These are not shown merely in the common tools in use in various trades, but in the most complicated and useful machines. Such, for instance, are the card and nail machines, which are so extensively used in the United States. These are entirely of their own invention. They have also improved the machines used in Europe, in the process of spinning and weaving;—though the machinery was considered almost perfect there, they have made many ameliorations. In this department, also, we have an advantage over the European manufacturer;—no resistance is made here to the introduction of any machinery; every kind of labour-saving machine is eagerly sought after, and new ones are constantly coming into use. In Europe, the manufacturer is often limited in this respect; he is often afraid to make use of machinery that would be of essential service to him. Machinery that is used in one country, sometimes cannot be brought into another, without producing a riot among the workmen. Within a few years the most serious mischief, alarming and long continued disturbances, have arisen from this source. Our manufacturers have no fears of this kind to encounter.

William Tudor, *Letters on Eastern States*. Boston: Wells & Lilly, 1821.

Document 5: The Transformation of Rural Life in Britain

William Radcliffe's parents, who ran a small cottage industry, taught him to weave at a young age. As an adult, he became a cloth manufacturer, operating several factories. In the following passage, he provides a firsthand account of the benefits that machinery brought to his small English community during the 1780s.

To show the immediate effects produced when all hands went to work on machine yarns, I shall confine myself to the families in my own neighborhood. These families, . . . whether as cottagers or small farmers, had supported themselves by different occupations

. . . in spinning and manufacturing, as their progenitors from the earliest institutions of society had done before them. But the mule-twist now coming into vogue, for the warp, as well as weft, added to the water-twist and common jenny yarns, with an increasing demand for every fabric the loom could produce, put all hands in request of every age and description. The fabrics made from wool or linen vanished, while the old loom-shops being insufficient, every lumber-room, even old barns, cart-houses, and outbuildings of any description were repaired, windows broke through the old blank walls, and fitted up for loom-shops. This source of making room being at length exhausted, new weavers' cottages with loom-shops rose up in every direction; all immediately filled, and when in full work the weekly circulation as the price of labor only, rose to five times the amount ever experienced before in this sub-division, every family bringing home weekly 40, 60, 80, 100, or even 120 shillings per week!!! It may be easily conceived that this sudden increase of the circulating medium would in a few years not only show itself in affording all the necessaries and comforts of life these families might require, but also be felt by those who, abstractedly speaking, might be considered disinterested spectators; but, in reality, they were not so, for all felt it, and that in the most agreeable way, too; for this money in its peregrinations left something in the pockets of every stone-mason, carpenter, slater, plasterer, glazier, joiner, &c. as well as the corn dealer, cheese-monger, butcher, and shopkeepers of every description. The farmers participated as much as any class by the prices they obtained for their corn, butter, eggs, fowls, with every other article the soil or farm-yard could produce, all of which advanced at length to nearly three times the former price.

William Radcliffe, *Origin of the New System of Manufacture Commonly Called Power-Loom Weaving.* Stockport, England, 1828.

Document 6: Child's Play

The practice of employing children in the factories was controversial almost from the start. Reports of severe overwork and physical abuse led officials to investigate the factories. In 1835, English physician Andrew Ure reported favorably on the conditions that he found, as described below.

I have visited many factories, both in Manchester and in the surrounding districts, during a period of several months, entering the spinning rooms, unexpectedly, and often alone, at different times of the day, and I never saw a single instance of corporal chastisement inflicted on a child, nor indeed did I ever see children in ill-humour. They seemed to be always cheerful and alert, taking pleasure in the light play of their muscles,—enjoying the mobility natural to their age. The scene of industry, so far from exciting sad emotions in my mind, was always exhilarating. . . . The work of these lively elves seemed to resemble a sport, in which habit gave them a pleasing dexterity. Conscious of their skill, they were delighted to show it off to any stranger.

As to exhaustion by the day's work, they evinced no trace of it on emerging from the mill in the evening; for they immediately began to skip about any neighbouring play-ground, and to commence their little amusements with the same alacrity as boys issuing from a school.

Andrew Ure, *The Philosophy of Manufactures; or, An Exposition of the Scientific, Moral, and Commercial Economy of the Factory System of Great Britain*. London: C. Knight, 1835.

Document 7: Worked to the Utmost

John Fielden was born in England in 1784, the son of a cloth manufacturer. He went to work in his father's mill at the age of ten and took over the business as an adult. Fielden supported the 1830s campaign to prohibit factory owners from requiring children to work more than ten hours a day, citing his own experience as a young millhand.

As I have been personally and from an early age engaged in the operations connected with factory labour; that is to say, for about forty years, a short account of my own experience may not be useless in this place, as it is this experience which teaches me to scoff at the representations of those who speak of the labour of factories as "very light," and "so easy, as to require no muscular exertion." I well remember being set to work in my father's mill when I was little more than ten years old. . . . For several years after I began to work in the mill, the hours of labour at our works did not exceed *ten* in the day, winter and summer, and even with the labour of those hours, I shall never forget the fatigue I often felt before the day ended, and the anxiety of us all to be relieved from the unvarying and irksome toil we had gone through before we could obtain relief by such play and amusements as we resorted to when liberated from our work. I allude to this fact, because it is not uncommon for persons to infer, that, because the children who work in factories are seen to play like other children when they have time to do so, the labour is, therefore, light, and does not fatigue them. The reverse of this conclusion I know to be the truth. I know the effect which ten hours' labour had upon myself; I who had the attention of parents better able than those of my companions to allow me extraordinary occasional indulgence. And he knows very little of human nature who does not know, that, to a child, diversion is so essential, that it will undergo even exhaustion in its amusements. I protest, therefore, against the reasoning, that, because a child is not brought so low in spirit as to be incapable of enjoying the diversions of a child, it is not worked to the utmost that its feeble frame and constitution will bear.

John Fielden, *The Curse of the Factory System*. London: A. Cobbett, 1836.

Document 8: No Cheerful Home

English surgeon Peter Gaskell is best known for his book Artisans and Machinery, *in which he examined the lifestyle of impoverished factory workers. In the following excerpt, Gaskell describes the effect of the long workday on the operatives' domestic life.*

The mode of life which the system of labour pursued in manufactories forces upon the operative, is one singularly unfavourable to domesticity. Rising at or before day-break, between four and five o'clock the year round, he swallows a hasty meal, or hurries to the mill without taking any food whatever. At eight o'clock half an hour, and in some instances forty minutes, are allowed for breakfast. In many cases, the engine continues at work during mealtime, obliging the labourer to eat and still overlook his work. . . .

At twelve o'clock the engine stops, and an hour is given for dinner. The hands leave the mill, and seek their homes, where this meal is usually taken. It consists of potatoes boiled, very often eaten alone; sometimes with a little bacon, and sometimes with a portion of animal food. This latter is, however, only found at the tables of the more provident and reputable workmen. If, as it often happens, the majority of the labourers reside at some distance, a great portion of the allotted time is necessarily taken up by the walk, or rather run, backwards and forwards. No time is allowed for the observances of ceremony. The meal has been imperfectly cooked, by some one left for that purpose, not unusually a mere child, or superannuated man or woman. The entire family surround the table, if they possess one, each striving which can most rapidly devour the fare before them, which is sufficient, by its quantity, to satisfy the cravings of hunger, but possesses little nutritive quality. It is not half masticated, is hastily swallowed in crude morsels, and thrust into the stomach in a state unfavourable to the progress of those subsequent changes which it ought to undergo. As soon as this is effected, the family is again scattered. No rest has been taken; and even the exercise, such as it is, is useless, from its excess, and even harmful, being taken at a time when repose is necessary for the digestive operations.

Again they are engaged from one o'clock till eight or nine, with the exception of twenty minutes, this being allowed for tea, or baggin-time, as it is called. This imperfect meal is almost universally taken in the mill: it consists of tea and wheaten bread, with very few exceptions.

It must be remembered, that father, mother, son, and daughter, are alike engaged; no one capable of working is spared to make home comfortable and desirable. No clean and tidy wife appears to welcome her husband—no smiling and affectionate mother to receive her children—no home, cheerful and inviting, to make it regarded. On the contrary, it is badly furnished—dirty and squalid in its appearance. Another meal sometimes of a better quality, is now taken, and they either seek repose, or leave home in the pursuit of pleasure or amusements.

P. Gaskell, *Artisans and Machinery: The Moral and Physical Condition of the Manufacturing Population*. London: John W. Parker, 1836.

Document 9: Blacklisting Union Members

Early in the Industrial Revolution, factory operatives began to form trade unions—often called combinations—in order to provide a united front when seeking pay raises or improvements in the workplace. This practice garnered much criticism, with many observers arguing that the unions' strategy of striking was unduly harmful to the economy. As Peter Gaskell relates, the factory owners responded by creating their own combinations in which they agreed not to employ workers who were known to belong to unions.

The repeated evils brought upon the masters by the combinations of their hands, made it imperatively necessary that they should be met in a similar way. No master could cope single-handed with a combination of his own men, who were leagued together to prevent any sufficient supply of new hands, and were liberally supported by their co-mates. The interests of the masters having become more generally understood, and that of one identified with the rest, they in turn refused to employ any operative who made himself conspicuous in the combinations, and gradually feeling their own strength, dismissed all those who could be detected as belonging to the obnoxious unions. Not satisfied with this, however, they refused to engage a workman who had been dismissed or had voluntarily withdrawn himself from the service of another master, provided he did not bring with him a certificate as to character. This point gained, the masters had the destiny of each operative in their keeping. If he disbehaved himself he was straightway dismissed, and found himself, unless under very peculiar circumstances, utterly excluded from all chance of getting occupation in that town or district, and had no little difficulty in procuring it even if he removed. . . .

So long as masters confine themselves to the legitimate objects which should govern their unions, viz. protection against the unfounded and unreasonable demands of their workmen—the cultivation of their own undoubted authority, with the interior regulation of their mills—their efforts will be hailed and cordially seconded by every man who has a knowledge of the miseries incident to the want of these, and who looks forward to a regeneration in the moral and social condition of the operatives.

P. Gaskell, *Artisans and Machinery: The Moral and Physical Condition of the Manufacturing Population*. London: John W. Parker, 1836.

Document 10: Benefits for Women

The Industrial Revolution marked the first time that large numbers of women and girls could find paid employment outside the home. In his 1840 report to the British Parliament on the condition of hand-loom weavers, W.E. Hickson praised this development as being highly beneficial for young women.

One of the greatest advantages resulting from the progress of manufacturing industry, and from severe manual labour being superseded by machinery, is its tendency to raise the condition of women. Education only is wanting to place the women of Lancashire higher in the social scale than in any other part of the world.

The great drawback to female happiness, among the middle and working classes is, their complete dependence and almost helplessness in securing the means of subsistence. The want of other employment than the needle cheapens their labour, in ordinary cases, until it is almost valueless. In Lancashire profitable employment for females is abundant. Domestic servants are in consequence so scarce, that they can only be obtained from the neighbouring counties.

A young woman, prudent and careful, and living with her parents, from the age of 16 to 25, may, in that time, by factory employment, save £100 as a wedding portion. I believe it to be the interest of the community that every young woman should have this in her power. She is not then driven into an early marriage by the necessity of seeking a home; and the consciousness of independence, in being able to earn her own living, is favourable to the development of her best moral energies.

E. Royston Pike, *Human Documents of the Industrial Revolution in Britain*. London: George Allen & Unwin, 1966.

Document 11: The Factory Girls of Lowell

Lowell, Massachusetts, emerged as a center of textile manufacturing in the early 1800s. The workers in Lowell's factories were primarily girls and young women from nearby farms; they resided in boardinghouses and enjoyed educational opportunities provided by their employers. In 1842, English novelist Charles Dickens toured the Lowell mills and recorded his impressions as follows.

These girls . . . were all well dressed: and that phrase necessarily includes extreme cleanliness. They had serviceable bonnets, good warm cloaks, and shawls; and were not above clogs and pattens. Moreover, there were places in the mill in which they could deposit these things without injury; and there were conveniences for washing. They were healthy in appearance, many of them remarkably so, and had the manners and deportment of young women: not of degraded brutes of burden. . . .

The rooms in which they worked, were as well ordered as themselves. In the windows of some, there were green plants, which were trained to shade the glass; in all, there was as much fresh air, cleanliness, and comfort, as the nature of the occupation would possibly admit of. . . .

They reside in various boarding-houses near at hand. The owners of the mills are particularly careful to allow no persons to enter upon the possession of these houses, whose characters have not undergone the most searching and thorough inquiry. . . . There are a few children employed in these factories, but not many. The laws of the State forbid their working more than nine months in the year, and require that they be educated during the other three. For this purpose there are schools in Lowell; and there are churches and chapels of various persuasions, in which the young women may observe that form of worship in which they have been educated. . . .

I am now going to state three facts, which will startle a large class of readers on this side of the Atlantic, very much.

Firstly, there is a joint-stock piano in a great many of the boarding-houses. Secondly, nearly all these young ladies subscribe to circulating libraries. Thirdly, they have got up among themselves a periodical called THE LOWELL OFFERING, "A repository of original articles, written exclusively by females actively employed in the mills,"—which is duly printed, published, and sold; and whereof I brought away from Lowell four hundred good solid pages, which I have read from beginning to end. . . .

Of the merits of The Lowell Offering as a literary production, I will only observe, putting entirely out of sight the fact of the articles having been written by these girls after the arduous labours of the day, that it will compare advantageously with a great many English Annuals. It is pleasant to find that many of its Tales are of the Mills and of those who work in them; that they inculcate habits of self-denial and contentment, and teach good doctrines of enlarged benevolence.

Charles Dickens, *American Notes*. London: Chapman and Hall, 1842.

Document 12: Hurry, Bustle, and Confusion

Despite the praise of Dickens and other commentators, the workers in Lowell's factories were not uniformly content with their situation. In 1845, the Lowell Female Labor Reform Association published a series of pamphlets that provided a more negative view of life in the mills. The following selection is taken from one of these tracts, "The Evils of Factory Life," written by a Lowell operative identified only as Julianna.

It is a common remark, that by the time a young lady has worked in a factory one year, she will lose all relish for the quiet, fireside comforts of life, and the neatness attendant upon order and precision. The truth is, time is wanting, and opportunity, in order to cultivate the mind and form good habits. All is hurry, bustle and confusion in the street, in the mill, and in the overflowing boarding house. If there chance to be an intelligent mind in that crowd which is striving to lay up treasures of knowledge, how unfavorably it is situated. Crowded into a small room which contains three beds and six females, all possessing the "without end" tongue of woman, what chance is there for *studying?* and much less for sober thinking and reflecting? Some lofty, original minds, we will allow, have surmounted all the obstacles of a factory life and come out, like gold, refined from all the dross of baneful society and pernicious examples, but they are cases of rare occurrence. But few have the moral courage and perseverance to travel on in the rugged paths of science and improvement amid all these and many other discouragements. After thirteen hours unremitting toil, day after day and week after week, how much energy and life would remain to nerve on the once vigorous mind in the path of wisdom? What ambition or pride would such females possess, to enable them to practice good order and neatness! They are confined so long in close, unhealthy rooms that it is a greater wonder that they possess any life or animation, more than the machines which they have watched so unceasingly!

Philip S. Foner, ed., *The Factory Girls*. Urbana: University of Illinois Press, 1977.

Document 13: The Necessity of Child Labor

Irish writer William Cooke Taylor was a prominent opponent of legislation designed to reform the factory system. In the following passage, he maintains that industrial work is not the worst fate that could befall the children of the poor.

It comes within our knowledge that children who were deprived of the easy work of the factories have been sent to toil in the coal-mines, and to other avocations equally injurious to health, and far more ruinous to morals. The parents are compelled by sheer necessity to send their children to work. . . .

Persons enter a mill . . . they see the figures of the little piecers and cleaners employed in their monotonous routine, . . . and they think how much more delightful would have been the gambol of free limbs on the hill-side, the inhaling of the fresh breeze, the sight of the green mead with its spangles of buttercups and daisies, the song of the bird, and the humming of the bee! But they should compare the aspect of the youthful operatives with other sights which they must have met in the course of their experience, as we too often have in ours: we have seen children perishing from sheer hunger in the mud-hovel, or in the ditch by the way-side . . . the juvenile mendicant, and the juvenile vagrant, with famine in their cheeks and despair in their hearts. We have seen the juvenile delinquent, his conscience seared by misery, his moral nature destroyed by suffering, his intellectual powers trained to perversity by the irresistible force of the circumstances that surrounded him. It is a sad confession to make, but owing, perhaps, to some peculiar obliquity of intellect or hardness of heart—we would rather see boys and girls earning the means of support in the mill than starving by the road-side.

W. Cooke Taylor, *Factories and the Factory System*, 1844.

Document 14: The Naturalness of Industry

Thomas Ewbank was a metal manufacturer who served as the U.S. Commissioner of Patents from 1849 to 1852. He believed that God created the earth for humans to improve through technology and that industry was therefore the highest form of labor.

It is only as a Factory, a GENERAL FACTORY, that the whole materials and influences of the earth are to be brought into play; and with this professional character of our globe every feature in creation will be found to harmonize.

For what classes then chiefly was the world of inorganic matter provided? Observe that dwelling; it belongs to a family neither rich nor poor; neat, commodious, and attractive in itself; it has a garden in front, an orchard and corn-field behind. Mark the social enjoyments, intelligence, and contentment of its inmates; the abundance of necessaries, of comforts and conveniences; the ornaments and elegances in dress and furniture, with contributions from almost every productive and decorative art. But, hark! a train of cars is approaching. It stops one moment and starts the next with a shriek for the city, whirling us along level and undulating lands, through tunnelled mountains, over rivers on bridges of granite, and others of iron. In the quick-moving panorama arise before us, and in a moment pass by, brick and lime kilns; potteries; tanneries; grist, saw, paper, and cotton mills; foundries; machine shops; chair, cloth, and carpet factories. We come in sight of a bay, on which ships laden with foreign merchandise are floating in with the tide, and others with home manufactures passing out. Crossing over in a steamer we find an extensive border of leafless forest resolved into masts of vessels crowded into continuous docks, and on landing, feel the air rent and agitated, like rippled water, with the noise of stevedores and draymen. We have business to transact for a friend, and pick our way along the side-walks, among packing-cases of dry-goods, casks of hardware, bundles of sheet and hoop iron, and loads of other goods. Next we stop at a telegraph office, and in five minutes our friend, though two hundred miles distant, receives and answers our note. On leaving the street of merchants for others occupied by watchmakers, jewellers, opticians, philosophical and musical instrument makers, engravers and printers, we call at a newspaper office to insert an advertisement and order the daily sheet for a neighbor. Need we proceed? It was for men who bring such things out of inert matter that this world of matter was made.

Thomas Ewbank, *The World a Workshop: The Physical Relationship of Man to the Earth*. New York: Appleton, 1855.

Document 15: Wild Desires and Wilder Dreams

During the summer of 1877, when the United States was in the midst of an economic depression, labor protests erupted in unprecedented numbers. Over two-thirds of the nation's railroads were paralyzed by strikers. State militias and federal troops were called in to break the strikes, often with deadly results. The following editorial was written after workers in Martinsburg, West Virginia, seized the railway depot and stopped all movement of freight trains.

We have had what appears a widespread rising, not against political oppression or unpopular government, but against society itself. What is most curious about it is that it has probably taken people here nearly as much by surprise as people in Europe. The optimism in which most Americans are carefully trained, and which the experience of life justifies to the industrious, energetic, and provident, combined with the long-settled political habit of considering riotous poor as the products of a monarchy and aristocracy, and impossible in the absence of "down-trodden masses," has concealed from most of the well-to-do and intelligent classes of the population the profound changes which have during the last thirty years been wrought in the composition and character of the population, especially in the great cities. Vast additions have been made to it within that period, to whom American political and social ideals appeal but faintly, if at all. . . .

The kindest thing which can be done for the great multitudes of untaught men who have been received on these shores, and are daily arriving, and who are torn perhaps even more here than in Europe by wild desires and wilder dreams, is to show them promptly that society as here organized, on individual freedom of thought and action, is impregnable, and can be no more shaken than the order of nature. The most cruel thing is to let them suppose, even for one week, that if they had only chosen their time better, or had been better led or better armed, they would have succeeded in forcing it to capitulate. In what way better provision, in the shape of public force, should be made for its defence we have no space left to discuss, but that it will not do to be caught again as the rising at Martinsburg caught us; that it would be fatal to private and public credit and security to allow a state of things to subsist in which 8,000 or 9,000 day-laborers of the lowest class can suspend, even for a whole day, the traffic and industry of a great nation, merely as a means of extorting ten or twenty cents a day more wages from their employers, we presume everybody now sees. Means of prompt and effectual prevention—so plainly effectual that it will never need to be resorted to—must be provided, either by an increase of the standing army or some change in the organization of the militia which will improve its discipline and increase its mobility.

"The Late Riots," *The Nation*, August 2, 1877.

Document 16: The Creation of Monopolies

American social reformer Henry George connects the rise of monopolies to the Industrial Revolution in the following excerpt from his book Social Problems. *He warns that the concentration of wealth in the hands of a few is a dangerous trend that can harm the democratic traditions of the United States.*

The tendency of steam and of machinery is to the division of labor, to the concentration of wealth and power. Workmen are becoming massed by hundreds and thousands in the employ of single individuals and firms; small storekeepers and merchants are becoming the clerks and salesmen of great business houses; we have already corporations whose revenues and pay-rolls belittle those of the greatest States. And with this concentration grows the facility of combination among these great business interests. How readily the railroad companies, the coal operators, the steel producers, even the match manufacturers, combine, either to regulate prices or to use the powers of government! The tendency in all branches of industry is to the formation of rings against which the individual is helpless, and which exert their power upon government whenever their interests may thus be served. . . .

That he who produces should have, that he who saves should enjoy, is consistent with human reason and with the natural order. But existing inequalities of wealth cannot be justified on this ground. As a matter of fact, how many great fortunes can be truthfully said to have been fairly earned? How many of them represent wealth produced by their possessors or those from whom their present possessors derived them? Did there not go to the formation of all of them something more than superior industry and skill? Such qualities may give the first start, but when fortunes begin to roll up into millions there will always be found some element of monopoly, some appropriation of wealth produced by others. Often there is a total absence of superior industry, skill or self-denial, and merely better luck or greater unscrupulousness.

Henry George, *Social Problems*. Garden City, NY: Country Life Press, 1883.

Document 17: Saving and Spending

Joseph Medill served as mayor of Chicago during the 1870s. The following passage is taken from his statements during the 1883 congressional hearings investigating the causes of industrial strikes.

The chief cause of the impecunious condition of millions of the wage classes of this country is due to their own improvidence and misdirected efforts. Too many are trying to live without labor—that is, industrial or productive labor, and too many squander their earnings on intoxicating drinks, cigars, and amusements, who cannot afford it. While they continue to spend their surplus earnings on these things they will not get on in the world and will fail to accumulate property. The possession of property among the masses is really due more to saving than to earning; on small earnings a man may still save something, while no amount of earnings will improve his bank account without economy. The power of waste is vastly greater than the power of production. . . .

I have never known a workman, no matter what might be his wages, who freely indulged his appetite for liquor and nicotine, that ever made much headway. And that observation covers a good many thousand workmen with whom I have come in contact during my life—of all classes. This sort of people always remain poor and dissatisfied—complain of their "bad luck," denounce the tyranny of capital, and allege that they are cheated in the division of the profits produced by capital and labor.

John A. Garraty, ed., *Labor and Capital in the Gilded Age: Testimony Taken by the Senate Committee upon the Relations Between Labor and Capital—1883.* Boston: Little, Brown, 1968.

Document 18: The Haymarket Bombing

On the evening of May 4, 1886, a workers' rally was held in Haymarket Square in Chicago to protest police violence against strikers. Toward the end of the rally, a bomb exploded near a group of policemen, killing one instantly and mortally wounding several others. The police opened fire on the crowd, killing several people. Following the riot, eight union leaders were arrested and tried, but not for actually throwing the bomb: Rather, they were accused of inciting murder on the grounds that the unknown assailant had been influenced by their speeches. One of these prisoners, Albert R. Parsons, told his side of the Haymarket bombing in the following account, published in October 1886. Convicted of murder, Parsons was executed on November 11, 1887.

We . . . went over to the Haymarket in a body, where I was introduced at once and spoke for about an hour to the 3,000 persons present urging them to support the eight-hour movement and stick to their unions. There was little said about the police brutalities of the previous day, other than to complain of the use of the military on every slight occasion. I said it was a shame that the moderate and just claims of the wage-workers should be met with police clubs, pistols, and bayonets, or that the murmurs of discontented laborers, should be drowned in their own blood. When I had finished speaking and Mr. Fielden began, I got down from the wagon we were using as a speaker's stand, and stepping over to another wagon nearby on which sat the ladies (among them my wife and children), and it soon appearing as though it would rain, and the crowd beginning to disperse and the speaker having announced that he would finish in a few moments; I assisted the ladies down from the wagon and accompanied them to Zepf's hall, one block away, where we intended to wait for the adjournment and the company of other friends on our walk home. I had been in this hall about five minutes and was looking towards the meeting, expecting it to close every moment, and standing nearby where the ladies sat, when there appeared a white sheet of light at the place of meeting, followed instantly by a loud roar. This was at once followed by a fusillade of pistol shots (in full view of my sight) which appeared as though fifty or more men had emptied their self-acting revolvers as rapidly as possible. Several shots whizzed by and struck beside the door of the hall, from which I was looking, and soon men came rushing wildly into the building. I escorted the ladies to a place of safety in the rear. . . .

The next day, observing that many innocent people who were not even present at the meeting were being dragooned and imprisoned by the authorities, and not courting such indignities for myself I left the city. . . . I procured the Chicago newspapers every day, and from them I learned that I, with a great many others, had been indicted for murder, conspiracy and unlawful assembly at the Haymarket. From the editorials of the capitalist papers every day for two months during my seclusion, I could see that the ruling class were wild with rage and fear against labor organizations. Ample means were offered me to carry me safely to distant parts of the earth, if I chose to go. . . . Nevertheless, knowing that I was innocent and that my comrades were innocent of the charge against them, I resolved to return and share whatever persecution labor's enemies could impose upon them. . . .

For free speech and the right of assembly, five labor orators and organizers of labor are condemned to die. For free press and free thought three labor editors are sent to the scaffold. "These eight men," said the attorneys of the monopolists, "are picked up by the grand jury because they are the leaders of thousands who are equally guilty with them and we punish them to make examples of them for the others." This much for opinion's sake, for free thought, free speech, free press and public assembly.

Philip S. Foner, ed., *The Autobiographies of the Haymarket Martyrs*. New York: Humanities Press, 1969.

Document 19: The Progress of the Race

Andrew Carnegie, one of the most successful nineteenth-century industrialists in the United States, presents his justification for the creation of concentrations of wealth in the following selection.

The problem of our age is the proper administration of wealth, that the ties of brotherhood may still bind together the rich and poor in harmonious relationship. The conditions of human life have not only been changed, but revolutionized, within the past few hundred years. In former days there was little difference between the dwelling, dress, food, and environment of the chief and those of his retainers. The Indians are today where civilized man then was. When visiting the Sioux, I was led to the wigwam of the chief. It was like the others in external appearance, and even within the difference was trifling between it and those of the poorest of his braves. The contrast between the palace of the millionaire and the cottage of the laborer with us today measures the change which has come with civilization. This change, however, is not to be deplored, but welcomed as highly beneficial. It is well, nay, essential, for the progress of the race that the houses of some should be homes for all that is highest and best in literature and the arts, and for all the refinements of civilization, rather than that none should be so. . . . The "good old times" were not good old times. Neither master nor servant was as well situated then as today. A relapse to old conditions would be disastrous to both—not the least so to him who serves—and would sweep away civilization with it. But whether the change be for good or ill, it is upon us, beyond our power to alter, and, therefore, to be accepted and made the best of. It is a waste of time to criticize the inevitable.

Andrew Carnegie, "Wealth," *North American Review*, June 1889.

Document 20: Summer in the Slums

The job opportunities created by the Industrial Revolution sparked a surge of immigration to cities such as New York. Most of these newcomers ended up living in densely populated tenements. Social reformer Jacob A. Riis exposed the harsh living conditions in New York's slums through his writings and photographs.

With the first hot nights in June police dispatches, that record the killing of men and women by rolling off roofs and windowsills while asleep, announce that the time of greatest suffering among the poor is at hand. It is in hot weather, when life indoors is well-nigh unbearable with cooking, sleeping, and working, all crowded into the small rooms together, that the tenement expands, reckless of all restraint. Then a strange and picturesque life moves upon the flat roofs. In the day and early evening mothers air their babies there, the boys fly their kites from the housetops, undismayed by police regulations, and the young men and girls court and pass the growler. In the stifling July nights, when the big barracks are like fiery furnaces, their very walls giving out absorbed heat, men and women lie in restless, sweltering rows, panting for air and sleep. Then every truck in the street, every crowded fire escape, becomes a bedroom, infinitely preferable to any the house affords. A cooling shower on such a night is hailed as a heaven-sent blessing in a hundred thousand homes.

Life in the tenements in July and August spells death to an army of little ones whom the doctor's skill is powerless to save. When the white badge of mourning flutters from every second door, sleepless mothers walk the streets in the gray of the early dawn, trying to stir a cooling breeze to fan the brow of the sick baby. There is no sadder sight than this patient devotion striving against fearfully hopeless odds.

Jacob A. Riis, *How the Other Half Lives: Studies Among the Tenements of New York.* New York: Charles Scribner's Sons, 1890.

Document 21: Hazardous Employment

By the beginning of the twentieth century, a fair amount of legislation had been passed to protect child laborers in industrial jobs. But as John Spargo reveals in the following excerpt from his book The Bitter Cry of the Children, *young factory workers still faced considerable hardships.*

It is a sorry but indisputable fact that where children are employed, the most unhealthful work is generally given them. In the spinning and carding rooms of cotton and woollen mills, where large numbers of children are employed, clouds of lint-dust fill the lungs and menace the health. The children have often a distressing cough, caused by the irritation of the throat, and many are hoarse from the same cause. In bottle factories and other branches of glass manufacture, the atmosphere is constantly charged with microscopic particles of glass. In the wood-working industries, such as the manufacture of cheap furniture and wooden boxes, and packing cases, the air is laden with fine sawdust. Children employed in soap and soap-powder factories work, many of them, in clouds of alkaline dust which inflames the eyelids and nostrils. . . .

The children who work in the dye rooms and print-shops of textile factories, and the color rooms of factories where the materials for making artificial flowers are manufactured, are subject to contact with poisonous dyes, and the results are often terrible. Very frequently they are dyed in parts of their bodies as literally as the fabrics are dyed. One little fellow, who was employed in a Pennsylvania carpet factory, opened his shirt one day and showed me his chest and stomach dyed a deep, rich crimson. I mentioned the incident to a local physician, and was told that such cases were common. "They are simply saturated with the dye," he said. "The results are extremely severe, though very often slow and, for a long time, almost imperceptible. If they should cut or scratch themselves where they are so thoroughly dyed, it might mean death.". . .

Children employed as varnishers in cheap furniture factories inhale poisonous fumes all day long and suffer from a variety of intestinal troubles in consequence. . . . The children who are employed in the manufacture of wall papers and poisonous paints suffer from slow poisoning. The naphtha fumes in the manufacture of rubber goods produce paralysis and premature decay. . . . The little boys who make matches, and the little girls who pack them in boxes, suffer from phosphorous necrosis, or "phossy-jaw," a gangrene of the lower jaw due to phosphor poisoning. Boys employed in type foundries and stereotyping establishments are employed on the most dangerous part of the work, namely, rubbing the type and the plates, and lead poisoning is excessively prevalent among them as a result. . . .

These are only a few of the many occupations of children that are inherently unhealthful and should be prohibited entirely for children and all young persons under eighteen years of age.

John Spargo, *The Bitter Cry of the Children*. New York: Macmillan, 1909.

Document 22: The Triangle Shirtwaist Fire

More than one hundred young women perished on March 25, 1911, in a fire at the Triangle Shirtwaist Company in New York City. Subsequent investigations revealed that the company kept the doors to the stairs locked during working hours in order to prevent theft by employees; when the fire broke out, the workers were trapped in the factory with no way to escape. At a meeting held two months later on the subject of better safety regulations, labor organizer Rose Schneiderman made an angry speech, which was reported in the New York Times *as follows.*

Rose Schneiderman, who led the workers out of the Triangle factory in their strike two years ago and bailed them out after being arrested, found words difficult when she tried to speak. She stood silently for a moment and then began to speak hardly above a whisper. But the silence was such that everywhere they carried clearly.

"I would be a traitor to these poor burned bodies," began Miss Schneiderman after she had gained possession of her voice, "If I came here to talk good fellowship. We have tried you good people of the public and we have found you wanting. The old Inquisition had its rack and its thumbscrews and its instruments of torture with iron teeth. We know what these things are today: the iron teeth are our necessities, the thumbscrews the high-powered and swift machinery close to which we must work, and the rack is here in the fire-proof structures that will destroy us the minute they catch on fire.

"This is not the first time girls have been burned alive in the city. Every week I must learn of the untimely death of one of my sister workers. Every year thousands of us are maimed. The life of men and women is so cheap and property is so sacred. There are so many of us for one job it matters little if 143 of us are burned to death.

"We have tried you, citizens; we are trying you now, and you have a couple of dollars for the sorrowing mothers and daughters and sisters by way of a charity gift. But every time the workers come out in the only way they know to protest against conditions which are unbearable, the strong hand of the law is allowed to press down heavily upon us. . . .

"I can't talk fellowship to you who are gathered here. Too much blood has been spilled. I know from my experience it is up to the working people to save themselves. The only way they can save themselves is by a strong working-class movement."

Rose Schneiderman with Lucy Goldthwaite, *All for One.* New York: Paul S. Eriksson, 1967.

Document 23: What We Have Lost

In the following essay, college professor and editor Joseph K. Hart considers the impact of the Industrial Revolution on society. He stresses the growing alienation from the natural world and the destruction of old standards of craftsmanship.

Some are not wholly convinced by [the] reputed virtues of the machine age. . . . The sense of loss is too great:

We have lost contact with nature—the contact that gave to man his first challenges, his first joy of battle, his first sense of victory.

We have lost that neighborliness which was characteristic of the older community, when men lived in homes and worked with their hands. The steam engine first undermined that community, and the automobile has completed its destruction.

We have lost practically all of the integrity of our old craftsmanship. The machine is not interested in integrity: only in form. Both the artist and the artisan have suffered spiritual dislocation. The artisan now works, dispiritedly, for the machine; and the artist, competing with the machine, too often sells his soul to feed his body.

We have lost practically all control of our destinies. We work when the machine works; we do what the machine commands; we use the products the machine turns out. We are educated to work with the machine and to use machine-made products.

Joseph K. Hart, "Power and Culture," *The Survey*, March 1, 1924.

Document 24: Modern Conveniences in the Home

Robert S. Lynd and Helen Merrell Lynd's famous 1929 sociological study focused on Muncie, Indiana, which they called "Middletown" for anonymity's sake. In the following passage, they note the transformations in housework brought about by mechanization.

Smaller houses, easier to "keep up," labor-saving devices, canned goods, baker's bread, less heavy meals, and ready-made clothing are among the places where the lack of servants is being compensated for and time saved today. . . .

Most important among these various factors affecting women's work is the increased use of labor-saving devices. Just as the advent of the Owens machine in one of Middletown's largest plants has unseated a glass-blowing process that had come down largely unchanged from the days of the early Egyptians, so in the homes of Middletown certain primitive hand skills have been shifted overnight to modern machines. The oil lamp, the gas flare, the broom, the pump, the water bucket, the washboard, the flatiron, the cook stove, all only slightly modified forms of some of man's most primitive tools, dominated Middletown housework in the nineties. In 1924, all but 1 per cent. of Middletown's houses were wired for electricity. Between March, 1920, and February, 1924, there was an average increase of 25 per cent. in the K.W.H. of current used by each local family. How this additional current is being used may be inferred from the following record of sales of electrical appliances by five local electrical shops, a prominent drug store, and the local electric power company for the only items it sells, irons and toasters, over the six-month period from May first to October thirty-first, 1923: curlers sold, 1,173; irons, 1,114; vacuum cleaners, 709; toasters, 463; washing machines, 371; heaters, 114; heating pads, 18; electric refrigerators, 11; electric ranges, 3; electric ironers, 1. The manager of the local electric power company estimates that nearly 90 per cent. of Middletown homes have electric irons.

Robert S. Lynd and Helen Merrell Lynd, *Middletown: A Study in Contemporary American Culture*. New York: Harcourt, Brace, 1929.

Discussion Questions

Chapter 1: The Start of the Industrial Revolution

1. The causes of the Industrial Revolution can be grouped into three broad and interrelated categories, according to Eric Pawson. Name these categories and describe their basic characteristics. In what ways did these three causes interact, in Pawson's opinion?

2. W.O. Henderson examines the various ways in which British industrial knowledge was transferred to the European continent. According to the author, what factors prevented the European continent from creating its own Industrial Revolution?

3. In his essay, George Soule explores the divergent views of Thomas Jefferson and Alexander Hamilton concerning the wisdom of industrializing the United States. Briefly summarize the arguments of Jefferson and Hamilton. According to Soule, which argument ultimately proved to be more accurate? Do you agree with Soule's assessment? Why or why not?

4. Carroll Pursell explains how British industrial knowledge was brought to the United States. According to the author, how did the different wars of the time affect America's adoption of British industrial technology?

5. According to Gary Cross and Rick Szostak, in what ways did improvements in transportation affect the development of factories in the United States? What similarities and differences can be found between early British and American factories?

6. Daniel Nelson describes the factors leading to the creation of the company town in the United States. How did company towns with largely immigrant populations differ from those with mostly native workers, in Nelson's opinion?

Chapter 2: The Great Innovators of the Industrial Revolution

1. According to Dennis Karwatka, where did Eli Whitney get his idea for the cotton gin? How did this invention affect the production of cotton?

2. In his essay, Franklin M. Reck writes that Robert Fulton was not the first inventor of the steamboat. Who were Fulton's prede-

cessors, according to Reck, and how did Fulton build upon their work to create the first commercially successful steamboat?

3. Cyrus McCormick's mechanical reaper allowed agriculture to become industrialized, as H.W. Brands states in his essay. What long-term effect did the industrialization of agriculture have on the growth of urban industry, in the author's view?

4. Although Samuel Morse is best remembered for his invention of the telegraph, Brooke Hindle explains that Morse primarily worked as an artist. What scientific experience did Morse have, according to Hindle, and what were his shortcomings? In what ways did Morse's artistic abilities contribute to his work in conceptualizing and inventing the telegraph?

5. Thomas Parke Hughes describes Thomas Edison's work in inventing the electrical lightbulb and the power stations that enabled its use. What technical problems did Edison need to overcome to make his invention a commercial success?

6. According to Thomas V. DiBacco, what measures did Henry Ford take to make the automobile accessible to the average consumer? How did the consumer mindset change during the 1920s, and how did this affect the public's attitude toward the Model T?

Chapter 3: Laborers and Robber Barons

1. What aspects of the Industrial Revolution do J.L. Hammond and Barbara Hammond blame for the decrease in workers' overall standard of living? In what ways did the laborers' work conditions change for the worse?

2. Ludwig von Mises maintains that industrialization improved the standard of living for most lower-class workers. What was the outstanding fact about the Industrial Revolution, in the author's opinion, and how did it benefit the laboring class?

3. In his essay, Carl N. Degler describes the differences between Utopian unionism and bread-and-butter unionism. Explain these two theories. In what ways are their structures and goals similar or dissimilar? According to Degler, which theory eventually became predominant in the United States? Why?

4. According to Howard Zinn, how did the U.S. government aid the robber barons in their quest for wealth? In what ways did the government fail to protect the workers and farmers of America? Why did most members of the government favor big business, in Zinn's view?

5. Burton W. Folsom Jr. contends that many historians have misconceptions about the industrial entrepreneurs known as robber barons. List the misconceptions that Folsom describes. What historical evidence does he cite to counter these negative beliefs? Do you find this evidence compelling? Why or why not?

Chapter 4: The Impact of the Industrial Revolution

1. In his essay, Harold U. Faulkner discusses the reasons behind the movement of African Americans and European immigrants to the urban centers of the United States. List the reasons. Which reasons apply to both groups, and which are specific to only one group? What factors might account for these similarities and differences?

2. Martin V. Melosi describes the environmental impact of the Industrial Revolution, especially in the cities. In Melosi's opinion, how did the pollution created by the factories affect the workers and the local residents?

3. According to Carroll Pursell, what was "bonanza farming"? How did the Industrial Revolution make it possible?

4. Ruth Schwartz Cowan maintains that the washing machine and other new household tools made possible by the Industrial Revolution did not decrease the overall time spent on housework, as might be expected. From what sources does Cowan gather her data concerning the changes that occurred in homemaking techniques and standards? In your opinion, are these sources reliable? Why or why not?

5. How did the Industrial Revolution affect the traditional ways of training new workers, according to Edward C. Kirkland? As the system of apprenticeship collapsed, what took its place?

Chronology

1712
Thomas Newcomen invents the first practical steam engine.

1733
John Kay invents the flying shuttle.

1750
England's Parliament bans the exportation of silk- or wool-making machinery or the emigration of workers in those trades.

1764
James Hargreaves invents the spinning jenny; James Watt improves on Newcomen's steam engine.

1769
Watt patents the design for his steam engine; Richard Arkwright invents the water frame.

1774
Parliament prohibits the export of technology used in the production of cotton and linen textiles.

1776
Matthew Boulton invents a steam engine suitable for industry; the American colonies declare their independence from England.

1779
Samuel Crompton invents the spinning mule.

1785
Edmund Cartwright patents his power loom.

1789
Samuel Slater leaves England, bringing the knowledge of how to mass-produce thread to the United States.

1790
Slater designs and constructs a water-powered cotton mill in Rhode Island.

1791
Alexander Hamilton issues his *Report on the Subject of Manufactures*.

1793
Eli Whitney invents the cotton gin.

1794
The first major turnpike road in America begins operation.

1798
Whitney wins a government contract to produce muskets with interchangeable parts; he institutes the first assembly line.

1799–1800
The English Combination Acts prohibit unions and strikes.

1799–1815
The Napoleonic Wars.

1802
The first English Factory Act limits children to twelve hours of work a day.

1807
Robert Fulton introduces the *Clermont*, the first commercially successful steamboat.

early 1810s
England experiences an outbreak of Luddite riots.

1812–1814
The War of 1812 between England and the United States.

1813
The first fully mechanized textile mill in America opens in Massachusetts.

1815
Construction begins on the National Road, which eventually runs from Maryland to Ohio and Illinois.

1818
Construction begins on the Erie Canal in New York.

1819
Parliament prohibits employers from hiring children under the age of nine.

1825
England lifts the ban on the emigration of skilled artisans; the Erie Canal is completed.

1826
The town of Lowell, Massachusetts, is founded; six textile firms are established there.

1827
Children employed at a mill in Paterson, New Jersey, instigate the first recorded strike of factory workers in U.S. history.

1830
The first locomotive built in America begins service out of Baltimore, Maryland.

1842
England lifts the ban on the export of industrial machinery; the Springfield Armory in the United States begins to produce interchangeable parts for rifles.

1844
Samuel Morse sends the first telegraph message between cities.

1846
Elias Howe patents the first sewing machine.

1848
Cyrus McCormick establishes a factory to build his mechanical reapers.

1849
The first portable steam engine is produced.

1856
Henry Bessemer invents the Bessemer converter, which improves the manufacturing of steel.

1859
The first American oil well is drilled in Pennsylvania.

1861–1865
The American Civil War.

1866
The National Labor Union is organized; a transatlantic telegraph cable is laid.

1867
Christopher Sholes introduces the first commercially successful typewriter.

1869

The first U.S. transcontinental railroad is completed; the Knights of Labor forms.

1870

John D. Rockefeller incorporates the Standard Oil Company.

1871

England legalizes workers' unions.

1873

Andrew Carnegie opens the world's largest steelworks in Pittsburgh, Pennsylvania.

1876

Alexander Graham Bell patents the telephone.

1877

During the summer, the Great Railroad Strike paralyzes America's railroads.

1879

Thomas Edison invents the incandescent lightbulb.

1881

The first coal-fired electrical power station is established in England.

1882

The first self-steering, self-propelled traction engine is produced.

1885

The combine harvester is invented.

1886

Gottlieb Wilhelm Daimler invents the internal combustion engine; the American Federation of Labor is formed; the Haymarket bombing occurs in May.

1887

The U.S. Congress passes the Interstate Commerce Act.

1890

Congress passes the Sherman Anti-Trust Act.

1892

Steelworkers strike in Homestead, Pennsylvania.

1895

The National Association of Manufactures is organized.

1897

Rudolf Diesel perfects an efficient internal combustion engine.

1900

The International Ladies Garment Workers Union is established.

1903

Henry Ford founds the Ford Motor Company; the U.S. Department of Commerce and Labor is formed.

1905

The Industrial Workers of the World, a radical labor organization, is founded.

1908

Ford introduces the Model T, the first widely popular automobile in America.

1911

The tragic fire at the Triangle Shirtwaist Company occurs on March 25.

1913

The Ford Motor Company fully incorporates the moving assembly line in its manufacture of cars.

1914–1918

The First World War.

1915

The first transcontinental telephone line opens.

1916

The U.S. Congress passes the Federal Child Labor Act.

1920

The U.S. census reveals that for the first time in the nation's history, more Americans live in cities than on farms.

For Further Research

Original Documents Concerning the Industrial Revolution

Mary H. Blewett, *We Will Rise in Our Might: Workingwomen's Voices from Nineteenth-Century New England*. Ithaca, NY: Cornell University Press, 1991.

Witt Bowden, *The Industrial Revolution*. New York: F.S. Crofts, 1928.

Alfred D. Chandler Jr., ed., *The Railroads: The Nation's First Big Business: Sources and Readings*. New York: Harcourt, Brace, and World, 1965.

Thomas C. Cochran, *Basic History of American Business*. Princeton, NJ: D. Van Nostrand, 1959.

Benita Eisler, ed., *The Lowell Offering: Writings by New England Mill Women (1840–1845)*. Philadelphia, PA: J.B. Lippincott, 1977.

Henry Nash Smith, *Popular Culture and Industrialism, 1865–1890*. New York: New York University Press, 1967.

Richard L. Tames, ed., *Documents of the Industrial Revolution, 1750–1850*. London: Hutchinson Educational, 1971.

Frederick Winslow Taylor, *The Principles of Scientific Management*. Norwood, MA: The Plimpton Press, 1911.

J.T. Ward, *The Factory System*, 2 vols. Devon, UK: David & Charles, 1970.

Charles Wing, *Evils of the Factory System, Demonstrated by Parliamentary Evidence*. New York: A.M. Kelley, 1967.

Histories of the Industrial Revolution

T.S. Ashton, *The Industrial Revolution, 1760–1830*. New York: Oxford University Press, 1997.

S.G. Checkland, *The Rise of Industrial Society in England, 1815–1885*. London: Longmans, Green, 1964.

Thomas C. Cochran and William Miller, *The Age of Enterprise: A Social History of Industrial America*. New York: Harper & Brothers, 1961.

Phyllis Deane, *The First Industrial Revolution*. New York: Cambridge University Press, 1965.

C. Stewart Doty, ed., *The Industrial Revolution*. Huntington, NY: Robert E. Krieger, 1976.

Thomas Dublin, *Transforming Women's Work: New England Lives in the Industrial Revolution*. Ithaca, NY: Cornell University Press, 1994.

Robert Gray, *The Factory Question and Industrial England, 1830–1860*. New York: Cambridge University Press, 1995.

R.M. Hartwell, *The Industrial Revolution and Economic Growth*. London: Methuen, 1971.

Samuel P. Hays, *The Response to Industrialism, 1885–1914*. Chicago: University of Chicago Press, 1995.

W.O. Henderson, *The Industrialization of Europe: 1780–1914*. London: Thames and Hudson, 1969.

Brooke Hindle and Steven Lubar, *Engines of Change: The American Industrial Revolution, 1790–1860*. Washington, DC: Smithsonian Institution Press, 1986.

Eric Hobsbawm, *Industry and Empire: The Birth of the Industrial Revolution*. New York: The New Press, 1999.

Pat Hudson, *The Industrial Revolution*. New York: Oxford University Press, 1992.

Brian Inglis, *Poverty and the Industrial Revolution*. London: Hodder & Stoughton, 1971.

Steven King and Geoffrey Timmins, *Making Sense of the Industrial Revolution*. Manchester, UK: Manchester University Press, 2001.

Peter Lane, *The Industrial Revolution: The Birth of the Modern Age*. New York: Harper & Row, 1978.

Sima Lieberman, ed., *Europe and the Industrial Revolution*. Cambridge, MA: Schenkman, 1972.

Paul Mantoux, *The Industrial Revolution in the Eighteenth Century: An Outline of the Beginnings of the Modern Factory System in England*. Chicago: University of Chicago Press, 1983.

Otto Mayr and Robert C. Post, eds., *Yankee Enterprise: The Rise of the American System of Manufactures*. Washington, DC: Smithsonian Institution Press, 1981.

Charles More, *Understanding the Industrial Revolution*. New York: Routledge, 2000.

Page Smith, *The Rise of Industrial America*. New York: McGraw-Hill, 1984.

Peter N. Stearns and John H. Hinshaw, *The ABC-CLIO World History Companion to the Industrial Revolution*. Santa Barbara, CA: ABC-CLIO, 1996.

Philip A.M. Taylor, ed., *The Industrial Revolution in Britain: Triumph or Disaster?* Lexington, MA: D.C. Heath, 1970.

Peter Temin, ed., *Engines of Enterprise: An Economic History of New England*. Cambridge, MA: Harvard University Press, 2000.

Innovations, Inventors, and Entrepreneurs

John Brooks, *Telephone: The First Hundred Years*. New York: Harper & Row, 1976.

Ira G. Clark, *Then Came the Railroads: The Century from Steam to Diesel in the Southwest*. Norman: University of Oklahoma Press, 1958.

François Crouzet, *The First Industrialists: The Problem of Origins*. New York: Cambridge University Press, 1985.

Robert Friedel and Paul Israel, *Edison's Electric Light: Biography of an Invention*. New Brunswick, NJ: Rutgers University Press, 1986.

Joseph and Frances Gies, *The Ingenious Yankees*. New York: Thomas Y. Crowell, 1976.

Constance McLaughlin Green, *Eli Whitney and the Birth of American Technology*. Boston: Little, Brown, 1956.

Matthew Josephson, *The Robber Barons*. New York: Harcourt Brace, 1962.

E.A. Marland, *Early Electrical Communication*. New York: Abelard-Schuman, 1964.

Elting E. Morison, *From Know-How to Nowhere: The Development of American Technology*. New York: BasicBooks, 1974.

A.E. Musson and Eric Robinson, *Science and Technology in the Industrial Revolution*. New York: Gordon and Breach, 1989.

W. Paul Strassmann, *Risk and Technological Innovation: American Manufacturing Methods During the Nineteenth Century*. Ithaca,

NY: Cornell University Press, 1959.

George Rogers Taylor, *The Transportation Revolution, 1815–1860*. New York: Holt, Rinehart, and Winston, 1951.

Barbara M. Tucker, *Samuel Slater and the Origins of the American Textile Industry, 1790–1860*. Ithaca, NY: Cornell University Press, 1984.

Industrial Workers and the Labor Movement

Paul Avrich, *The Haymarket Tragedy*. Princeton, NJ: Princeton University Press, 1984.

David Brody, *In Labor's Cause: Main Themes on the History of the American Worker*. New York: Oxford University Press, 1993.

Paul Buhle and Alan Dawley, eds., *Working for Democracy: American Workers from the Revolution to the Present*. Urbana: University of Illinois Press, 1985.

Dan Clawson, *Bureaucracy and the Labor Process: The Transformation of U.S. Industry, 1860–1920*. New York: Monthly Review Press, 1980.

Philip S. Foner, *History of the Labor Movement in the United States*, 3 vols. New York: International Publishers, 1947–1964.

Herbert G. Gutman, *Work, Culture, and Society in Industrializing America: Essays in American Working-Class and Social History*. New York: Alfred A. Knopf, 1976.

Ruth Milkman, *Women, Work, and Protest: A Century of Women's Labor History*. Boston: Routledge & Kegan Paul, 1985.

Clark Nardinelli, *Child Labor and the Industrial Revolution*. Bloomington: Indiana University Press, 1990.

Daniel T. Rodgers, *The Work Ethic in Industrial America, 1850–1920*. Chicago: University of Chicago Press, 1978.

Malcolm I. Thomis, *The Luddites: Machine-Breaking in Regency England*. Hamden, CT: Archon Books, 1970.

Carolyn Tuttle, *Hard at Work in Factories and Mines: The Economics of Child Labor During the British Industrial Revolution*. Boulder, CO: Westview Press, 1999.

Index

DATE DUE

Demco, Inc. 38-293